The Confederate General

Volume 2

✳ *The Confederate General* ✳

Volume 2

Cobb, Thomas to Goggin, James

William C. Davis, Editor

Julie Hoffman, Assistant Editor

A Publication of the
National Historical Society

Library of Congress Cataloging-in-Publication Data
The Confederate General / William C. Davis,
   editor; Julie Hoffman, assistant editor.
      p. cm.
   ISBN 0-918678-64-1 (v. 2) : $29.95
   Contents: v. 1. Adams, Daniel W. to Cobb, Howell—v. 2. Cobb, Thomas to Goggin, James.
      1. United States—History—Civil War, 1861-1865—Biography. 2. Confederate States of America. Army.—Biography. 3. Generals—Confederate States of America—Biography. 4. Generals—Southern States—Biography. 5. Generals—United States —Biography.
I. Davis, William C., 1946-   II. Hoffman, Julie.
   E467.C75   1991
   973.7'42'0922 [B]   91-8508
(B)   CIP

Editorial Assistant, Eleanor Mauck
Designed by Art Unlimited
Printed in the United States of America

✷ Contents ✷

Cobb, Thomas Reade Rootes 2	Elzey, Arnold 98
Cocke, Philip St. George 4	Evans, Clement Anselm 104
Cockrell, Francis Marion 6	Evans, Nathan George 106
Colquitt, Alfred Holt 8	Ewell, Richard Stoddert 110
Colston, Raleigh Edward 12	Fagan, James Fleming 114
Conner, James 16	Featherston, Winfield Scott 118
Cook, Philip 20	Ferguson, Samuel Wragg 122
Cooke, John Rogers 24	Field, Charles William 124
Cooper, Douglas Hancock 26	Finegan, Joseph 126
Cooper, Samuel 28	Finley, Jesse Johnson 128
Corse, Montgomery Dent 30	Floyd, John Buchanan 132
Cosby, George Blake 34	Forney, John Horace 134
Cox, William Ruffin 38	Forney, William Henry 136
Crittenden, George Bibb 42	Forrest, Nathan Bedford 138
Cumming, Alfred 44	Frazer, John Wesley 146
Daniel, Junius 46	French, Samuel Gibbs 148
Davidson, Henry Brevard 48	Frost, Daniel Marsh 150
Davis, Joseph Robert 50	Fry, Birkett Davenport 152
Davis, William George Mackey 52	Gano, Richard Montgomery 154
Dearing, James 54	Gardner, Franklin 156
Deas, Zachariah Cantey 60	Gardner, William Montgomery 162
de Lagnel, Julius Adolph 64	Garland, Samuel Jr. 164
Deshler, James 66	Garnett, Richard Brooke 168
Dibrell, George Gibbs 68	Garnett, Robert Selden 170
Dockery, Thomas Pleasant 70	Garrott, Isham Warren 172
Doles, George Pierce 72	Gartrell, Lucius Jeremiah 174
Donelson, Daniel Smith 74	Gary, Martin Witherspoon 176
Drayton, Thomas Fenwick 76	Gatlin, Richard Caswell 180
DuBose, Dudley McIver 78	Gholson, Samuel Jameson 182
Duke, Basil Wilson 80	Gibson, Randall Lee 184
Duncan, Johnson Kelly 84	Gilmer, Jeremy Francis 190
Dunovant, John 86	Girardey, Victor Jean Baptiste 192
Early, Jubal Anderson 88	Gist, States Rights 194
Echols, John 92	Gladden, Adley Hogan 198
Ector, Matthew Duncan 94	Godwin, Archibald Campbell 200
Elliott, Stephen Jr. 96	Goggin, James Monroe 202

✷ *Thomas Reade Rootes Cobb* ✷

Thomas Reade Rootes Cobb was born at "Cherry Hill" in Jefferson County, Georgia, on April 10, 1823. His incredible birth weight of twenty-one and one-half pounds gave an early indication that Cobb would be an unusual man. His three given names came from his maternal grandfather, who lived in Fredericksburg, Virginia.

Young Cobb matriculated at Franklin College, which later became the University of Georgia, in 1837. Finishing first in the class of 1841, Cobb's college career displayed a brilliance that was evident in all of his prewar endeavors. After reading law in Athens for a few months, Cobb won admittance to the bar in 1842 before his nineteenth birthday. He launched his legal career at a time of economic difficulty in Georgia. The depression also impaired his father's fortune, which placed extra burdens on his son. The elder Cobb had, at one time, owned six thousand acres worked by 150 slaves at "Cherry Hill" alone, but by the mid-1840s he was partially dependent upon his children. Thomas R. R. Cobb built his own estate through the years before the war. His worth as shown in the 1860 census was $120,000 and at that time he owned twenty-three slaves.

There is ample evidence that Cobb possessed a volatile temperament that provided him with the energy to achieve great things but at the same time made him impulsive and mercurial. This energy found a productive outlet in Cobb's combined literary and legal work, and produced seminal treatises and groundbreaking digests of Georgia statutes. The most famous of Cobb's published works was *An Inquiry into the Law of Negro Slavery in the United States of America* to which is prefixed *An Historical Sketch of Slavery* (Philadelphia, 1858). That book combined three of Cobb's primary

interests: the law, the defense of the institution of slavery, and a fervent religious endeavor, including justification of slavery on biblical grounds.

Cobb also exerted himself on behalf of education. He was the moving force behind a female high school begun in Athens just before the war named the Lucy Cobb Institute in memory of his much-beloved deceased daughter. In politics Cobb played a prominent role as an ardent and uncompromising secessionist, though he was not nearly so active or distinguished as his brother Howell. Tom Cobb's only political posts of importance came during the Confederate era when he was a delegate to Georgia's secession convention and a member of the Provisional Congress of the Confederate States.

During the summer of 1861, Cobb moved from the political realm into military affairs when he undertook the raising of a legion of Georgia troops. The legion concept, popular politically but entirely useless militarily, combined in one organization all three major arms—infantry, cavalry, and artillery. Cobb used his political power to override the opposition of professional soldiers and received permission to raise such a unit. On August 28 he was commissioned colonel of the Cobb Legion and took the field, apparently not in the least intimidated by the fact that he had no experience or training to prepare him for the awesome responsibilities of mortal combat.

Colonel Cobb's military career was marked by an endless succession of bitter and even paranoid

Thomas R.R. Cobb posed for this striking portrait in 1862 when he was colonel of the unit he raised, the Cobb Legion. His death six weeks after being promoted brigadier probably means that no photo was taken of him as a general. (Museum of the Confederacy, Richmond, Va.)

complaints about virtually all of his superiors, including Jefferson Davis, and nearly as many of his subordinates. His letters to his wife and other intimates, which survive in large volume, reveal a querulous spirit always at odds with almost everything in its sphere. They also reflect the same impulsive swings of temperament that marked Cobb's prewar life.

Predictably the enlisted men and subordinate officers in the legion, and in the brigade that Cobb later commanded, viewed their brilliant and difficult leader with mixed feelings. Elijah H. Sutton of the 24th Georgia of Cobb's brigade declared that both Howell and Tom, who commanded the brigade in succession, earned the thorough loathing of their men; Sutton supplied examples to substantiate his position. Another member of the brigade later claimed that one of his comrades purposefully inflicted the mortal wound that killed Tom Cobb. Although that story cannot be substantiated and in fact is clearly inaccurate, its calm assertion lends credence to the other negative declarations about Cobb.

Other men who served under Cobb or observed him admired his achievements. W. R. Montgomery of Cobb's brigade called his commander "brave and beloved" and "brave and gallant" in the same letter. Major Henry D. McDaniel, a literate and thoughtful man not directly affiliated with Cobb, declared in a war letter: "I admired him more, perhaps, than any other son of my state."

One of the prime irritants to Cobb throughout his restless military career was the steady separation of the components of his legion by his superiors. The colonel and his fragmented command spent the months from September 1861 to early May 1862 engaged in the tedious, quiet war on the Virginia Peninsula and its environs. By mid-May, Cobb was insisting unconvincingly that he would resign rather than suffer further insults from generals who sent his cavalry away to spots where it was needed, rather than leaving it immobilized with his infantry detachments. The irate colonel summarized the root of his difficulty well when he wrote that the separation of his legion pieces "is most mortifying to my pride...I chafe under this injustice and long for an opportunity to expose the malignant persecution with which Davis and his minions have followed me." There seemed no hope that the new army commander, R. E. Lee, could soothe Cobb, since the colonel professed to know somehow that "Lee hates me...and sneers whenever my name is mentioned with approbation." After contact with Lee during the Seven Days, Cobb was sure of his diagnosis: "Lee...is haughty and boorish and supercilious in his bearing and is particularly so to me."

Colonel Cobb led his cavalry contingent in some desultory skirmishing under Stuart during the Seven Days, but still had seen no sustained combat during more than one year in service by late August 1862. A furlough took him back to Georgia just in time to miss the heavy fighting of the Maryland Campaign, in which his brother Howell performed extremely poorly at Crampton's Gap. When he returned to Virginia that fall, Tom Cobb continued to request transfer to another theater—almost anywhere else, for a change of scenery. On November 1, 1862, he was promoted to the rank of brigadier general and given command of the brigade that had been his brother's. Perhaps because the promotion (which he had noisily insisted that he would refuse to accept) assuaged him, Cobb ameliorated his hatred of Lee somewhat during the last weeks of his life.

Thomas R. R. Cobb's first battle experience as a general officer—indeed his first intense battle experience of any sort—also proved to be his last. On December 13, 1862, his brigade held the famous Sunken Road and Stone Wall at Fredericksburg. At the first Federal onset, Cobb "pulled off his hat & waving it over his head exclaimed, 'Get ready Boys here they come.'" After the repulse of a Federal assault early that long afternoon, a random artillery round sent a piece of metal into the general's left thigh, severing the femoral artery. Cobb lapsed quickly into unconsciousness and died a little after 2:00 P.M. at a field hospital behind Marye's Heights. A widely disseminated tradition, which is not provable but by no means improbable, asserts the ironic fact that the cannon that hit Tom Cobb was fired from the yard of his mother's childhood home, Thomas Reade Rootes' "Federal Hill," which stood on the edge of Fredericksburg opposite the Sunken Road. General Cobb is buried in Oconee Hill Cemetery in Athens.

Robert K. Krick

McCash, William B., *Thomas R. R. Cobb* (Memphis, 1983).
Porter, Rufus K., "Sketch of General T. R. R. Cobb," *Land We Love*, III.

⋆ *Philip St. George Cocke* ⋆

No genuine photograph of Philip Cocke has emerged thus far, much less any that shows him during the two brief months he was a general. This likeness comes from an ante-bellum painting. (Library of Congress, Washington, D.C.)

Of the many tragic stories to be found among the generals of the Confederacy, few are more poignant than that of this genteel Virginian, born April 17, 1809, at the family home, "Bremo Bluff," in Fluvanna County. Like his friend R. E. Lee, he won an appointment to the United States Military Academy, and graduated with nearly as high a standing, finishing sixth out of forty-five graduates in the class of 1832. He went immediately into the artillery but served only two years of garrison duty at Charleston, rising to adjutant of the 2d Artillery before he resigned on April 1, 1834 to return to Virginia. There the wealthy young Cocke owned several plantations, as well as some in Mississippi, and he would devote the next twenty-seven years to their management. Like another Virginian, Edmund Ruffin, he also achieved notoriety as a progressive farmer, championing new agricultural techniques, and writing widely on the subject. He became president of the Virginia Agricultural Society, and at the same time served on the board of visitors of Lexington's Virginia Military Institute.

It was inevitable that the prominent planter would receive a summons to command when Virginia seceded. Governor Letcher made him a brigadier general of state forces and assigned him command of the territory along the Potomac bordering Maryland. When Virginia forces were amalgamated into the Confederacy, Cocke became a colonel in the Provisional Army. Among his first acts was a proclamation delivered from his headquarters at Culpeper Court House on May 5, calling all able-bodied young men of the region to come forward to take arms in the defense of the Old Dominion. That same day, however, his small command at Alexandria evacuated in the face of a Federal advance; and though Cocke at first ordered them to reoccupy the place, when that appeared to be impractical, he directed that they fall back on Manassas Junction.

Cocke, in his early weeks on command of the so-called "Potomac Line," studied the countryside carefully, and conferred frequently and fully with Lee, now commanding all Virginia state forces. It appears to have been Cocke who first conceived not only the importance of Manassas Junction and the line of Bull Run for defense, but also the possibility of using the Manassas Gap Railroad, connecting the junction with the Shenandoah, as a means of shifting troops from one side of the Blue Ridge to the other for a concentration against any enemy advance.

Cocke was upset when his state rank of brigadier was demoted to colonel in the Confederate service, but Lee soothed his feelings, apparently successfully, for the colonel continued to show considerable energy in raising regiments, erecting defenses, and preparing for the inevitable Yankee advance. Lee expressed himself as well pleased with Cocke's efforts, and when Beauregard was sent out in June 1861 to assume overall command, he gave Cocke command of his Fifth Brigade, consisting of the 18th, 19th, 28th, and 49th Virginia infantries, some of them units Cocke had raised.

When McDowell's Federal army finally approached Manassas in July, Cocke and his brigade were stationed at the left of the line, covering the Stone Bridge and Lewis Ford and Ball's Ford. Added to his command were Wheat's Louisiana "Tigers," Nathan Evans' miniature brigade, and a few other isolated units, and it was these troops under Cocke's command, especially Evans and Wheat, who set the stage for the crushing victory on July 21.

Following the battle, Cocke remained on the Manassas line with the army, advancing to Centreville in August. Finally, in recognition of his able efforts, President Davis appointed him a brigadier general on October 21, 1861, apparently to rank immediately—the records have disappeared—for by November 16 he was being referred to as "General Cocke." When Johnston reorganized his army into divisions, Cocke took command of what became the Fourth Brigade of the Second Division.

He did not hold his new rank or command for very long. Cocke had spent eight months in the field, under almost constant strain. Apparently his health was not good at the outset, and these strains, along with a probable nervous or emotional susceptibility, left him badly worn down physically and mentally. Sometime during December he went back to his home plantation for rest, and perhaps for the holidays. Even the usual joys of Christmas did not revive him. Indeed, maybe the depression that the holiday visits upon some only made him worse. The next day, December 26, perhaps on an impulse growing out of desperation, he committed suicide. Buried at first on his plantation, his body was reinterred in Richmond's cemetery of the generals, Hollywood, in 1904.

Cocke's loss was undoubtedly a great one. He had shown energy, skill, daring, and an ability to command at least as good as that of most of the other virtual amateur generals in the first months of the war. Had he lived, and had his system allowed him to serve, he should have been a great asset to the Confederacy.

William C. Davis

Hotchkiss, Jedediah, *Virginia*, Vol. III in Evans, *Confederate Military History.*

✶ *Francis Marion Cockrell* ✶

Francis M. Cockrell as a brigadier, probably taken sometime after 1863.
(Alabama Department of Archives and History, Montgomery)

Francis Marion Cockrell was born October 1, 1834, near Warrensburg, Missouri. He attended college at Chapel Hill in Lafayette County, graduating in 1853, and became a lawyer in 1855. When the war began, he raised a company of militia for the Missouri State Guard and fought at Carthage and Wilson's Creek. Early in 1862 he was transferred to the Confederate service, and participated in the Battle at Pea Ridge. After crossing the Mississippi River with Earl Van Dorn as colonel of the 2d Missouri Infantry, Cockrell took part in the fighting around Corinth, the 2d Missouri being used as a final support to drive the enemy from the field at Hatchie Bridge.

In the Vicksburg Campaign he fought at the head of the First Missouri Brigade, Bowen's Division, Department of Mississippi and East Louisiana. As Grant's army moved through Louisiana down the west bank of the Mississippi River, Cockrell led a force opposing the Federal advance. Unable to obstruct Grant's movement, Cockrell recrossed the river at Hard Times on April 17, then led the brigade in the fighting at Grand Gulf, Port Gibson, Big Black, and Champion's Hill. Cockrell was wounded in the hand during the siege of Vicksburg, and captured when Pemberton surrendered. Cockrell reported that his men had not wanted to capitulate, and were "desirous of holding out and fighting as long as there was a cartridge or a ration or mule or horse, and when the garrison capitulated they felt, and were, distressed, but in no wise whipped, conquered, or subjugated."

On July 23, 1863, he was promoted to brigadier general, to date from July 18, and exchanged on September 12, 1863. Cockrell formed another brigade of Missourians at Demopolis, Alabama, and on September 18, 1863, reported that it was fully armed. In November his brigade comprised part of the Army of the Department of Mississippi and East Louisiana, numbering 3,377 with 1,790 present. In February 1864 he belonged to W. W. Loring's Division in Leonidas Polk's army, and went with Polk to reinforce Joseph E. Johnston's army in the Atlanta Campaign. At Kennesaw Mountain an officer said: "Whatever credit is due for the complete repulse of this [Federal] assaulting column, therefore, belongs exclusively to the brigade of General Cockrell and the left of General [Claudius W.] Sears', then commanded by Colonel W. S. Barry."

When Hood assumed command of the army in mid-July, Cockrell was absent because of a wound that caused the loss of several fingers; he did not command his brigade until August 8. He fought with the army throughout the rest of the campaign, and at Franklin was seriously wounded. After he recovered, he returned to Alabama, where he was second in command at Fort Blakely on the Apalachee River—on the garrison that guarded the back door to Mobile. When the fort fell on April 9, 1865, Cockrell was captured along with thirteen hundred Confederates.

After the war ended, he returned to Missouri and practiced law with his partner T. T. Crittenden. In 1874 he was elected to succeed Carl Schurz in the United States Senate, where he served for the next thirty years. In 1905, President Theodore Roosevelt appointed Cockrell to the Interstate Commerce Commission, and he held this position for the next five years. Cockrell was a large man, standing over six feet tall and weighing over two hundred pounds. He died in Washington on December 13, 1915, and is buried at Warrensburg.

Anne Bailey

Moore, John C., *Missouri*, Vol. X in Evans, *Confederate Military History*.

Alfred H. Colquitt was colonel of the 6th Georgia when he posed in Charleston for this portrait by George S. Cook in 1861. (Courtesy of Mark Katz)

⋆ Alfred Holt Colquitt ⋆

A native of Monroe, Georgia, Colquitt was born April 20, 1824, the son of a former United States senator. Like his father, Colquitt soon developed what would be twin life-long interests, politics and the military. He attended the College of New Jersey at Princeton, graduating in 1844, then read law and passed the Georgia bar just prior to the Mexican War. When the conflict came, however, he volunteered for staff service, and did duty throughout the war, only entering his law practice afterwards. But then in 1852, when only twenty-eight, he won a campaign for a congressional seat, served one term, and took an increasingly active part in the deliberations of Georgia's Southern rights men. He served in the state legislature in 1859, and in 1860 campaigned for the election of John C. Breckinridge. With the coming of the crisis after Lincoln's election, he sat in Georgia's secession convention in January 1861.

Colquitt was almost immediately elected colonel of the 6th Georgia Infantry when it organized in May, and led it to Virginia during the concentration of Confederate units prior to First Manassas. Colquitt was not present for that battle, however, and had to wait until the following spring on the Peninsula to see his first action with D. H. Hill's Division. He saw combat at Seven Pines, and shortly afterward Hill reorganized his command and assigned Colquitt to replace General Gabriel Rains in command of his brigade. Throughout the Seven Days, Colquitt performed well enough to attract Hill's attention and that of Lee and the War Department. His reputation for sobriety and his much-vaunted piety added to his political prominence, and no doubt helped in securing him a promotion to brigadier general sometime in early September 1862, to rank from September 2.

Colquitt's Brigade were almost all fellow Georgians of the 6th, 23d, 27th, and 28th Infantries, along with the 13th

Alabama, and with them he fought through the Antietam Campaign. First at Turner's Gap, where he and his men stood almost alone during most of the day of hot fighting, and then at Antietam itself, Colquitt gave an excellent account of himself. He held the line at the Cornfield until half of his command and all of his field officers went down, while his old 6th Georgia lost ninety percent of its strength. Still, he rallied the fragments of his command and helped to hold out on Bloody Lane.

Colquitt went on to command his rebuilt brigade at Fredericksburg, though not seriously engaged in the battle, and then at Chancellorsville through the following May. Here his brigade now became a part of Robert Rodes' Division, following Hill's reassignment to North Carolina. As a unit in Jackson's Corps, Colquitt and his brigade took the lead in the great flank march that surprised and routed half of Hooker's army. Very shortly after the battle, however, Lee transferred the depleted brigade to Hill in North Carolina, and then subsequently Colquitt was sent to Florida, chiefly because his brigade was so understrength that service in an inactive theater of the war seemed the best use for it. Nevertheless, while there the Georgian commanded the small "army" that won the Battle of Olustee on February 20, 1864, and then in the concentration of troops preparatory to the opening of the spring campaign in Virginia, Colquitt was once more ordered back to Lee.

Colquitt spent the balance of the campaign with Lee, serving through the Siege of Petersburg until he was once more ordered back to North Carolina. There, in January 1865, he was ordered to take command of Fort Fisher, though he did not find an immediately

A portrait believed to be of Colonel Colquitt in 1862. (Museum of the Confederacy, Richmond, Va.)

Colquitt's promotion to brigadier dates this portrait to sometime after September 1862. (Museum of the Confederacy, Richmond, Va.)

warm welcome from his subordinates, who regarded him as a "Georgia militia general." When he arrived, it was only to find that the fort had already fallen to attacking Federals, and Colquitt himself seems simply to have turned on his heel and left just a few yards ahead of the onrushing foe.

Colquitt remained in North Carolina for the balance of the war, giving his parole on May 1. He went home to Georgia and resumed the practice of law and the cultivation of his fields, but he could not stay out of politics for long. He became a leader, along with former Governor Joseph Brown and General John B. Gordon, of the progressive Bourbon faction of the Democratic Party, and was its successful candidate for governor in 1876, winning reelection four years later. In 1882 he took a seat in the Senate and held it for the next twelve years, dying in office on March 26, 1894, a champion of the so-called New South. He was buried at Rose Hill Cemetery in Macon, much honored for his competent, if not inspired, leadership in war, and his progressive leadership in the peace that followed.

William C. Davis

Derry, Joseph, *Georgia*, Vol. VI in Evans, *Confederate Military History*.

Gragg, Rod, *Confederate Goliath* (New York, 1990).

Colquitt's finest wartime portrait is this one, possibly made in Richmond by Cook, and likely dating from late 1864 or early 1865. (Cook Collection, Valentine Museum, Richmond, Va.)

☆ *Raleigh Edward Colston* ☆

A handsome, previously unpublished carte-de-visite of Raleigh Colston as a brigadier. (Museum of the Confederacy, Richmond, Va.)

Raleigh Edward Colston was born in Paris, France, on October 31, 1825, the adopted son of a Virginia man and a French woman, the divorced wife of Napoleon's Marshal Kellerman. He came to America at the age of sixteen to enter the Virginia Military Institute in its class of 1846, from which he graduated fourth in academic rank. During his term at the institute, young Colston learned of his mother's deathbed confession that she had deceived both her son and her husband by adopting Raleigh near the end of an extended absence by her husband, pretending the baby was their natural child. One of Raleigh's contemporaries at V.M.I. noted that the news astonished and very much depressed the young immigrant cadet.

Colston remained at Lexington and spent the fifteen years between his graduation and the onset of the Civil War filling staff and faculty roles at V.M.I. During that whole period he took advantage of his native tongue by teaching French. The cadets called him "Old Polly" (as in "parlez vous") but respected him enough to honor his calming example during riotous times that accompanied the sectional upheaval 1860–61. Colston also served for shorter periods as professor of military history and strategy, and of modern history and political economy. From 1849 to 1858 he was treasurer of the institute, and during the spring of 1861 held the important post of commandant.

Raleigh Colston carried the prewar Virginia rank of major for his V.M.I. duties but quickly received promotion during the military crisis that faced his adopted state. After a brief stint with the V.M.I. Corps of Cadets at the war's outset, Colston became colonel of the 16th Virginia Infantry to rank from May 17, 1861. He also assumed command of the camp of instruction at Norfolk. Colston and his regiment spent a very quiet 1861. On Christmas Eve of that year Colston received promotion to the rank of brigadier general. The promotion was announced, ranked, and accepted the same day, but not confirmed until February 17, 1864, under the cumbersome Confederate system.

Through 1862 Colston occupied billets that gave him little opportunity for either difficulty or distinction. For months he commanded in the Blackwater district of southeastern Virginia. During the fall of 1862 he was absent on sick furlough for an extended period, and during December he commanded a brigade serving in the Richmond defenses that was made up of Virginia regiments that had seen little serious fighting.

General Colston's most prominent Civil War assignment began in the spring of 1863 and lasted for just seven weeks. On April 4, 1863, at the insistence of his old V.M.I. colleague "Stonewall" Jackson, Colston was transferred to the Army of Northern Virginia to take command of the brigade in Jackson's old division that had long been commanded by William B. Taliaferro. Because of Colston's early date of rank as brigadier, and because of the absence of nominal division commander Isaac R. Trimble, the newly arrived officer assumed not only brigade command, but also acting command of the division. With active spring campaigning not many days ahead, many of the bypassed officers in Jackson's command must have wondered what in Colston's background and experience prepared him for such substantial responsibilities. In fact, the appointment was another example of Jackson's penchant for appointing ill-suited acquaintances to positions beyond their grasp.

On May 3, 1863, less than a month after arriving in the army, Colston disappointed R. E. Lee so thoroughly by his behavior at Chancellorsville that the army commander transferred him away with uncharacteristic speed and finality. The particulars cannot be established directly, but apparently Colston lost control of the division on that chaotic morning—or perhaps he never had control from the start. A British journalist wrote at the time, probably reflecting talk in the army, that Colston "inefficiently handled" his division and "failed to advance." The London article suggested that "disaster might have resulted" had not R. E. Rodes intervened. An officer in the division thought that his commander was disoriented and apparently needed guidance, and was brave but inept. By contrast, a postmortem tribute to Colston by a United Confederate Veterans camp (normally the most adulatory forum imaginable) remarked gently that at Chancellorsville Colston was "possibly a little impetuous." A surviving dispatch dated May 7 suggests that acting corps commander J. E. B. Stuart mistrusted Colston's ability. It reiterates a relatively simple order in detail far more minute than customary.

Lee relieved Colston from duty with his army on May 28, 1863, masking his displeasure by declaring that Colston's mixed brigade of Virginia and North Carolina troops needed a professional officer native to neither state. When Colston later applied for a succession of open brigade commands that had all Virginia units, first with Lee's army, then elsewhere in

Virginia, he was rejected without further explanation.

In June 1863 Colston returned to V.M.I. with orders to observe the final examinations there on behalf of the government—hardly standard duty for general officers (the feckless General Roger A. Pryor received similar orders). After a summer-long quest for brigade command, Colston finally received orders on September 21 to report to Charleston. From there he went to Savannah to command a brigade that eventually was transferred away from him, and he was relieved on April 16, 1864.

During the crises of May and June around Petersburg, Colston attached himself to General Henry A. Wise as a volunteer. On July 6, 1864, Colston assumed duties as the commandant of the Post and District of Lynchburg. In that relative backwater the general served out the rest of the war. A member of General L. L. Lomax's staff described Colston's behavior at Lynchburg on the night after Appomattox in bitterly hostile words: "Colston…beat his retreat with a considerable body guard at the silent hour and midst the dark stillness of the night, before the dawn of day could bring a foe to molest or the shrill blast of some fancied avenging bugle to fright his feeble soul or make him afraid."

For eight years after the war Colston occupied himself by lecturing on Stonewall Jackson and by operating two military academies. From 1873 to 1878 he held the rank of colonel in the Egyptian Army—one of a number of American officers in that service. Colston's experiences in the Middle East included some fascinating adventures, more exploratory than military in tenor, in which his French-speaking ability and congenial nature served him well. On his return to North America, Colston lived in increasing poverty and under the constraints of a weakening constitution. On September 25, 1894, he entered the Soldiers' Home in Richmond, suffering from paralysis. The European-born veteran of military service in both North America and Africa died in the home on July 29, 1896, and was buried in Hollywood Cemetery.

Robert K. Krick

Hesseltine, William B., and Hazel C. Wolf, *The Blue and the Gray on the Nile* (Chicago, 1961).

Raleigh Colston Papers, Southern Historical Collection, University of North Carolina, Chapel Hill.

At the same sitting, Colston had this slight variant shot. (Cook Collection, Valentine Museum, Richmond, Va.)

An excellent portrait of James Conner as colonel of the 22d North Carolina, made probably in 1863. (Library of Congress, Washington, D.C.)

✳ *James Conner* ✳

A number of future generals came out of that unusual South Carolina unit, the Hampton Legion, and Conner was to be one of them. Born September 1, 1829, in Charleston, he attended South Carolina College, graduating in 1849, and then read law at the side of the distinguished South Carolina jurist and unionist, James L. Pettigru. Entering his own practice in 1852, Conner quickly rose to prominence, and within four years had won an appointment as a U.S. Attorney, one of his prosecutions being a celebrated case against a ship practicing the illegal slave trade.

Conner took an early lead in the secession activities of 1860, showing obviously that his mentor Pettigru's sympathies had not influenced him overmuch. He served on a committee that called on the state legislature to urge calling a secession convention, and immediately after South Carolina passed its ordinance of secession, he volunteered, gaining a captaincy in the legion being raised by the wealthy Wade Hampton, after serving briefly as captain of the Montgomery Guards.

Conner took command of Company A of the Hampton Legion and went with it north to Virginia to participate in the First Battle of Manassas. When Hampton fell and other field officers were wounded or dispersed, Conner took charge of the remnant of the legion after the day's bitter fighting on the Henry Hill line. His performance won him promotion to major, and the following spring, when the 22d North Carolina needed a colonel, Conner was promoted and given his own regiment.

He did not command it in the field for long at first, for in the fighting at Gaines' Mill in the Seven Days' Campaign, he took a terrible wound in his leg that broke the bone and put him out of action for several months. He was not with his regiment at Antietam, but appears to have resumed command shortly after Fredericksburg, though the absence of any mention of him in reports or correspondence relating to the battle suggests that he was not present. Indeed, he does not

figure in any reports of active service for almost two years following his Gaines' Mill wound, and seems to have spent most of the time serving on military courts in the II Corps.

On June 1, 1864, the president appointed Conner a brigadier, effective immediately, and three days later Lee assigned him to the temporary command of Samuel McGowan's brigade in Hill's III Corps. Thus Conner was at last sufficiently recovered, and he accepted his promotion on June 6. During the summer that followed, Lee assigned him to command the defenses at Chaffin's Bluff, perhaps because Conner was still not up to more arduous field service. He also temporarily commanded James Lane's brigade, as a temporary division commander, and in the end was assigned to command of Joseph B. Kershaw's old brigade on a permanent basis, Kershaw himself commanding the division.

Under him Conner had six South Carolina regiments, the 2d, 3d, 7th, 8th, 15th, and 20th, and the 3d Battalion, and led them out to the Valley when Kershaw accompanied Jubal Early west of the Blue Ridge. Conner participated in all of the Shenandoah campaigning almost up to Cedar Creek. A few days before that climactic battle, during a skirmish on October 13, his unlucky leg took another bullet near Fisher's Hill, and this time the limb had to be amputated.

Conner was still recovering in December, when Governor Magrath of South Carolina asked that Richmond reassign him to his native state. "The presence of General Conner with his brigade would greatly tend to inspire confidence and excite hope," Magrath suggested. By January 1865 Conner had been so reassigned, and on the 4th the South Carolinians were on their way. Conner's leg may not have healed sufficiently for him to take active duty, however, for when the brigade subsequently joined Joseph E. Johnston's army in the Carolinas for the final campaign, the general was not in command.

Following the war, Conner returned to Charleston and resumed his law practice, attaining once more the same reputation he enjoyed before the conflict. Two railroads used him as their counsel and receiver, as did the Bank of Charleston, and in political affairs he excelled, becoming attorney general in 1876, his most noteworthy endeavor being the legal validation of the contested election of Hampton as governor. The 1876 campaign was a tumultuous one, hotly contested, and with violence lurking constantly beneath the surface, and Conner, legless as he was, commanded the so-called "rifle clubs" of men determined not to allow disorder to disrupt the election—or Hampton's chances.

Conner died in Richmond on June 26, 1883, well regarded to the end, and the frequent confidant of Lee and Beauregard and others. Though his wartime service was cruelly restricted by his unlucky leg, he had proven himself an able battlefield commander, and one much admired by his soldiers and his people.

William C. Davis

Capers, Ellison, *South Carolina*, Vol. V in Evans, *Confederate Military History*.

Now, General Conner sat for this portrait almost certainly in the latter half of 1864. (Duke University, Durham, N.C.)

An excellent vignette portrait of General Cook taken in the
fall or winter of 1864, probably in Richmond. (U.S. Army
Military History Institute, Carlisle, Pa.)

⋆ *Philip Cook* ⋆

The so-called "old field schools" of the South pro-duced many a Confederate, among them Jefferson Davis. Another who attended these rude country academies was Philip Cook, born July 31, 1817, in Twiggs County, Georgia. Education appealed to the young Georgian, and he soon afterward enrolled in the Milton Wilder academy at age fifteen, then studied at Forsythe until the Seminole War in 1836 lured the adventurous nineteen-year-old to leave school and enlist in a company that later marched to Florida and participated in the relief of General Gaines. His brief war service done, young Cook returned to school, first at Oglethorpe University, and three years later at the University of Virginia, where he studied law. His studies were interrupted by the death of his father in 1841. Cook returned home before graduation but read law privately, passed the state bar, and set up a prac-tice in Forsythe, and later in Oglethorpe, where he remained until the crisis of 1861.

His old military leanings emerged again at the out-break of war when he went with the Macon County Volunteers in April 1861 to Augusta, where the fol-lowing month they mustered in as the 4th Georgia. First a private, Cook was soon appointed adjutant, and he served on staff duty for nearly a year, chiefly on the Peninsula. At the conclusion of the Seven Days' battles, however, when the men of the regiment reelected new officers upon reenlisting for the war, they chose Cook as their lieutenant colonel, partly in recognition of his activities on the battlefields, includ-ing a severe wound taken at Malvern Hill. There fol-lowed the Second Battle of Manassas, at which he may not have been present due to his wound, but by the time of the Antietam Campaign he was firmly in place and at South Mountain and Antietam won D. H. Hill's applause for his "gallant and meritorious conduct."

Cook was promoted to full colonel and command of the 4th Georgia on November 1, 1862, in recognition of his performance, and he led his regiment that December at Fredericksburg. The following spring, at Chancellorsville, he was wounded yet again, this time

with a bullet in the leg, early on May 3. Still, he was mentioned prominently in his superiors' reports for his charge against an enemy position, and in true Victorian style, when he fell, he did it near his colors.

The wound ensured that Cook would miss Gettysburg, and he returned home to Georgia for sev-eral months, even finding time to serve more than a month of a term in the state senate before he recov-ered. He was intermittently with the army through the spring of 1864, and when his brigade commander, George Doles, was killed in action on June 2 at Bethesda Church, Cook rose to permanent command of the brigade. On August 8, the was appointed brigadier general, effective from August 5. Cook him-self formally accepted the commission on August 16, and the Senate confirmed it the following February.

Cook now served in Rodes' Division of Early's II Corps, commanding the 4th, 12th, 21st, and 44th Georgia infantries. However, by the time Cook went to the Shenandoah with Lieutenant General Jubal A. Early, his brigade was such in little more than name alone, mustering barely four hundred effectives pre-sent for duty. Having served through the Shenandoah Valley Campaign of 1864, Cook and his brigade returned to Lee in the lines around Petersburg in time to participate in the abortive attack on Fort Stedman on March 25, 1865, and once again Cook sustained a wound, this one in the arm. Two weeks later when his brigade surrendered at Appomattox, the unit num-bered only 350, Cook not among them. When the Federals had overrun Petersburg on April 2, they had captured the general in the hospital where he was recovering from his wound.

He finally left service on July 30 when paroled, and went home to Oglethorpe, Georgia, to recommence his law practice. A few years later he moved to Americus and continued in the law, meanwhile win-ning the election to Congress in 1873 and serving five consecutive terms. Afterward he acted as secretary of state for Georgia, helped oversee the building of the new state capitol, then finally ended his days as a farmer. General Cook died May 21, 1894, in Atlanta, and was buried at Rose Hill Cemetery in Macon.

He had been a competent, though unlucky, commander, though not in any way a standout. Superiors sometimes called attention to his bravery, but his many wounds prevented him from realizing any more of the potential that may have lain within.

William C. Davis

Derry, Joseph T., *Georgia*, Vol. VI in Evans, *Confederate Military History.*

Probably at the same sitting, Cook posed for this alternative view which, though it may betray faint traces of retouching by an artist, still definitely depicts him in a genuine uniform. (Cook Collection, Valentine Museum, Richmond, Va.)

⋆ *John Rogers Cooke* ⋆

John R. Cooke had already been wounded some seven times by the time of his promotion to brigadier, as he is shown in this, his only war portrait known to date. (Cook Collection, Valentine Museum, Richmond, Va.)

The old theme of brother-against-brother and families torn apart by the war is almost a cliche by now, but it happened to an astonishing degree, as John Rogers Cooke amply demonstrates. He was born into the Old Army at Jefferson Barracks, St. Louis, Missouri, on June 9, 1833. His father was Philip St. George Cooke, a lieutenant in the old 1st Dragoons and a native Virginian. The younger Cooke chose not to attend the Military Academy, but instead went to Massachusetts and Harvard University, where he studied civil engineering. Then in 1855, when barely out of college, he changed his mind about the military, and perhaps with some influence from his father, obtained a direct commission as 2d lieutenant in the 8th Infantry.

Cooke spent the balance of the prewar years in the Southwest, serving at posts in New Mexico and Arizona territories, and in Texas. His military family included others in uniform, such as Lieutenant J. E. B. Stuart, who had married Cooke's sister, Flora, in 1855. But the coming of secession literally tore the family apart. The father had spent more than twenty years in the uniform of his country, and despite being a native Virginian, he chose to stand by his old uniform. His son, John, and his son-in-law Stuart, on the other hand, could not reconcile their Southern heritage with their oaths to the Union and both resigned their commissions.

John R. Cooke thus broke a bond with his father, leaving a wound that did not close again until many years after the war. He went east immediately and took a commission as a 1st lieutenant in the Confederate service, being assigned first to Colonel Theophilus H. Holmes' command at Fredericksburg. Cooke was with Holmes during the First Manassas fighting but was not engaged. Soon afterward he raised his own company of light artillery, but served with it only briefly before being promoted to major and posted to North Carolina as chief of artillery to the department commander in February 1862. It was to be a brief assignment. When the first twelve-months' regiments were reorganized for longer terms of service, the officers of the 27th North Carolina Infantry chose him to be their colonel; he almost immediately led them back to Virginia in time to join in the fighting at Seven Pines. Serving in A. P. Hill's division, Cooke and his regiment fought through the balance of the Seven Days' battles, then went on to Second Manassas and Cedar Mountain. Cooke attracted real attention for his conduct at Antietam that September, where he received probably the first of seven wounds he would suffer during the war.

In recognition of his performance, Cooke was given an appointment as brigadier general on November 1, 1862, to take effect immediately, though the Senate did not get around to confirming it until April 22, 1863. He recovered in time to be present in Fredericksburg, then commanding a brigade containing the 15th, 27th, 46th, 48th, and 59th North Carolina infantries. It fell to Cooke's Brigade to stand with Thomas Cobb's Georgians behind the stone wall at the foot of Marye's Heights, and there they turned back assault after assault in one of the most gallant actions of Confederate arms. He took another wound there on December 13, but was back in action again by the following spring, first at Chancellorsville, and then on the march into Pennsylvania. Cooke was one of the few not wounded at Gettysburg, but later that year at Bristoe Station he felt the enemy's lead once again.

Thereafter Cooke was never away from the Army of Northern Virginia or his brigade, except when recuperating from even more wounds. He was hit again at the Wilderness, but back in command for the defense of Richmond and the final campaigns for Petersburg. An admitted admirer, the son of General D. H. Hill, later declared that "no officer bore a more enviable reputation than General Cooke for prompt obedience to orders, skill in handling his men, splendid dash in the charge, or heroic, patient, stubborn courage in the defense."

When the end came, General Cooke remained in Richmond and entered upon mercantile pursuits, and later took a prominent role in civic government, serving on the city Democratic committee, the chamber of commerce, and then as a director of the Virginia State Penitentiary. He also founded and acted as manager of the Confederate Soldiers' Home in Richmond, and acted as the first commander of the Robert E. Lee Camp No. 1, United Confederate Veterans. In these, and most other veterans' affairs, he took a prominent part.

The old theme of brother-against-brother remained a large one in Cooke's life. Besides the sister who married Stuart, another married a Confederate surgeon, and yet another married Federal Colonel Jacob Sharpe. Cooke's own wife, Nannie, was the daughter of Dr. William Patton, a surgeon in the Union navy. Happily, the passage of years gradually healed old wounds, and what remained of the family was reunited, Cooke himself doing his part to strengthen the family by siring eight children.

General Cooke died when he was only fifty-seven, on April 10, 1891, and went to his final rest in the graveyard of the generals, Richmond's Hollywood Cemetery, where his brother-in-law Stuart already lay. By the testimony of all observers, he had been an outstanding battlefield leader, whose services to the Confederacy would only have been greater had he managed not to step in front of so many bullets.

William C. Davis

Hill, D. H., Jr., *North Carolina*, Vol. IV in Evans, *Confederate Military History*.

☆ *Douglas Hancock Cooper* ☆

To date no genuine uniformed portrait of Douglas Cooper has emerged. This one is probably of early postwar vintage. (Museum of the Confederacy, Richmond, Va.)

Born November 1, 1815, in Mississippi, Cooper attended the University of Virginia from 1832 until 1834 but failed to graduate so he returned to Mississippi to become a planter. When the war with Mexico began, Cooper served as captain in Jefferson Davis' First Mississippi Rifles, and remained a close friend of the future president of the Confederacy. In 1853 President Franklin Pierce appointed Cooper the United States agent to the Choctaw Nation in the Indian Territory.

He was a strong proslavery advocate, and when the Civil War began, the Confederate government asked him to secure an alliance with the five civilized tribes, Choctaw, Chickasaw, Cherokee, Creek, and Seminole. Cooper successfully persuaded members of all five tribes to join the Confederate Army. As a result, Cooper was commissioned colonel of the 1st Choctaw and Chickasaw Mounted Rifles, making him the only commander of a Confederate Indian unit from the Indian Nation who was not an Indian. Moreover, he was adopted as a member of the Chickasaw Nation on May 25, 1861.

In November 1861, with the Indians and some Texas cavalry, Cooper tracked an unfriendly force that consisted of Creeks, Seminoles, and former slaves. He was determined to break up the Indians under Opothleyahola (known to the Confederates as Hopoeithleyohola) and capture the fugitive slaves. He fought in the Battle of Chusto-Talasah on December 9, and forced Opothleyahola's party to retreat toward Kansas. On December 26 the Battle of Chustenahlah in the Cherokee Nation took place, but Cooper was unable to offer much assistance to Colonel James McIntosh of the 2d Arkansas Mounted Rifles because his teamsters had deserted. At the Battle of Pea Ridge, Cooper, along with Colonel Daniel McIntosh, joined the retreating Confederate train under Albert Pike.

In May 1862 Pike offered to resign from his position as commander of the Department of the Indian Territory because of arguments with other Confederate officers. Cooper, who wanted to replace him, asked for command of the Indian Brigade and for the post of Superintendent of Indian Affairs. But Pike withdrew his resignation, and instead accused the other Confederate generals of stealing supplies from him. In the confused state of affairs in the Indian Territory, on June 23, 1862, Cooper was given command of almost all of the Confederate troops north of the Canadian River, but was permitted to act independently of Pike. Cooper was instructed not to raid into Union-held regions for booty or revenge.

Problems between Pike and the other Confederate generals continued to plague the department, and in August 1862 Cooper ordered Pike's arrest. Cooper believed Pike was "partly deranged, and a dangerous person to be at liberty among the Indians." Moreover, Cooper told his friend Jefferson Davis that Pike was mad. As accusations passed back and forth, the Confederate War Department decided to accept Pike's original resignation. With the position vacant, Cooper was nominated to command the Indian Territory and to the office of superintendent. But his political enemies pointed out his problems with alcohol and the Senate refused to confirm the joint position. In September, however, Cooper was assigned to duty as superintendent, and led the Indians in the Battle at Newtonia of September 20. As an attempt by his enemies to keep Cooper from gaining too much authority in the Indian Territory, Brigadier General William Steele was made commander of the district in January 1863.

Cooper had powerful friends in Richmond, however, and was appointed a brigadier general on June 23 to rank from May 2, 1863, in time to fight in the engagement at Elk Creek, near Honey Springs, on July 17, 1863. Cooper was extremely popular with most of the Indians, and representatives of the various Confederate Indian tribes had petitioned for him to replace Brigadier General William Steele, whose Northern birth made him unpopular among the Indians as well as many Confederates. Steele was convinced that Cooper was part of a conspiracy that wanted to disgrace him. Although Steele was replaced, unfortunately for Cooper, his political enemies were again successful at denying him the command of the district. On January 9, 1864, Cooper was made commander of the Indian troops, but he was placed under Brigadier General Samuel Bell Maxey, who succeeded Steele as commander of the Indian Territory. Cooper held an unusual intermediate position between the Indians and Maxey. In July 1864 the Confederate War Department finally issued an order that would give Cooper command of the Indian Territory—Cooper was supposed to replace Maxey. When General E. Kirby Smith heard of this change, he wrote to Richmond asking that the War Department revoke Maxey's removal

order. Smith believed that Maxey "has with skill, judgment, and success administered his duties" and "serious injury would result to the service were this order enforced." Furthermore, Smith pointed out: "Brigadier General D. H. Cooper cannot perform properly the duties of a general officer and superintendent of Indian affairs." But Adjutant and Inspector General Samuel Cooper said the order was "deemed imperative and must be carried into effect."

In Richmond the Indian council pushed for Cooper's selection, and Territorial Delegate Elias Boudinot personally met with Confederate congressmen. Cooper even traveled to Richmond to further his own promotion. When Samuel Cooper finally informed Smith that the order must be carried out, Smith delayed it for several weeks. On February 21, 1865, however, Maxey was relieved and Cooper assigned to command the District of the Indian Territory, and Stand Watie replaced Cooper as commander of the division of Indian Affairs. At about the same time, February 14, 1865, Cooper was also assigned to duty as Superintendent of Indian Affairs. On March 1, in spite of Smith's objections, Cooper assumed command of the District of Indian Territory and superintendency of Indian Affairs. Smith wrote, "I shall give Cooper my full support," but "the change has not the concurrence of my judgment, and I believe will not result beneficially."

When the war ended, no one notified Cooper, and he did not learn of the surrender until late June. When he found out, Cooper wrote the Union commandant at Shreveport and offered his "services…in restoring order among the Indians." His offer was "cheerfully accepted." Following the war, Cooper continued to live in the Indian Territory, where he helped the Choctaw and Chickasaw sue the United States government for failed promises that dated as far back as the Indian removal in the 1830s. Cooper died at Old Fort Washita in the Chickasaw Nation, Indian Territory, on April 29, 1879. He is buried in the cemetery there in an unmarked grave.

Anne Bailey

Duncan, Robert Lipscomb, *Reluctant General: The Life and Times of General Albert Pike* (New York, 1961).

Gaines, W. Craig, *The Confederate Cherokees: John Drew's Regiment of Mounted Rifles* (Baton Rouge, 1989).

Rampp, Larry C., and Donald L. Rampp, *The Civil War in the Indian Territory* (Austin, 1975).

⋆ *Samuel Cooper* ⋆

One of the oldest officers in the Confederate Army, and its senior ranking general, Samuel Cooper was a native of New Jersey, born in Hackensack on June 12, 1798. His father, Samuel Cooper, had been one of the Minute Men who fired the first shots of the Revolution at Lexington in 1775, afterward serving with distinction through the war. Thus a strong military tradition was passed on to his two sons, both of whom attended the United States Military Academy. Samuel, the younger son, entered the academy in 1813 at the age of fifteen, and two years later finished thirty-sixth in a class of forty, just missing a chance to serve in the War of 1812.

Commissioned a brevet 2d lieutenant in the light artillery on December 11, 1815, Cooper commenced a career in uniform that lasted almost fifty years. He spent thirteen of those years moving from the 1st to the 2d, and finally to the 4th Artillery, where he received a first lieutenancy on July 6, 1821. In 1828 his career took an important, and permanent, new direction, when General-in-Chief Alexander Macomb made him an aide-de-camp. On June 11, 1836, Cooper received promotion to captain, and two years later a brevet to major on July 7, the same day that he was assigned to the War Department as an assistant adjutant general. Thereafter he never left staff service.

As chief of staff to Colonel William Worth during the Seminole War, Cooper saw his one and only action on April 19, 1842, at Pila-Kil-Kaha, Florida. When the war with Mexico came, Cooper was given a promotion to lieutenant colonel in the adjutant general's office, and the next year won a brevet to full colonel for meritorious service during the late war. His actual promotion to confirmed grade of colonel came on July 15, 1852, the same day that General-in-Chief Winfield Scott appointed Cooper adjutant general of the United States Army.

Cooper ran his office for nearly nine years, and apparently to the satisfaction of everyone. Just eight months after his appointment, Jefferson Davis took office as Franklin Pierce's secretary of war, and for the next four years the two men worked closely and harmoniously together, forming a close personal and professional bond. Furthermore, despite his Northern birth, Cooper had developed increasingly pro-Southern political feelings. His marriage into the prominent Virginia family of George Mason no doubt helped, but Davis, who knew him as well as anyone, believed that the shift owed more to the influence of Joel R. Poinsett of South Carolina, secretary of war from 1837 to 1841. Cooper was also a great favorite with President Pierce, whose conservative beliefs endeared him to Southerners despite his Yankee birth.

As a result, when the secession crisis arrived, Cooper believed that any use of force by the Union to keep states from leaving amounted to a violation of Constitutional rights. This, his Southern family ties, and his close association with Davis and many of the

No uniformed photographs of General Cooper are known from the war years. This previously unpublished image dates from the late 1850s, when he was adjutant general of the U.S. Army. (Lawrence T. Jones Collection)

ranking officers who were leaving to "go South" decided his course. On March 7, 1861, he handed in his own resignation and returned to his home in Fairfax County, Virginia, near Alexandria. Five days later he left for the new Confederate capital at Montgomery, arriving on March 14. Now-president Davis was waiting for him, hoping that Cooper "would consent, while his juniors led armies in the field, to devote himself to the little attractive labors of the Adjutant-General's office." Cooper did consent, and on March 16 Davis appointed him a brigadier general in the Confederate Regular Army—at that time the highest rank mandated by Congress. The Senate confirmed Cooper the same day, to take rank immediately, and the next day Cooper formally accepted his new commission. "I entered, at once, upon the duties of the office," said Cooper, "and so continued until termination of the war." When Congress subsequently authorized the higher grade of full general, Davis nominated him to head the list of five such generals on August 31, to rank from May 16, the date of the enabling legislation. Thus Cooper, by seniority, stood above all other general officers of the Confederacy.

His responsibilities as adjutant and inspector general were entirely administrative, and Cooper almost never left the capital. All orders to field commands and departments had to emanate from or pass through his office. Further, he was ultimately responsible for army records, the assignment of officers, leaves, disabilities, resignations, muster and pay rolls, inspection reports, prison camp rolls, and much more. Cooper did not, of course, do all this himself, but supervised a series of subordinate offices within his department, each charged with specific tasks. Cooper himself, however, was involved to varying degrees in transmitting the more important orders for assignment of high-ranking generals and the movements of significant bodies of troops.

His role became controversial from the first, largely because of his close relationship with Davis, a man who repeatedly demonstrated that he did not like strong subordinates. Speaking of Cooper as an example, Bureau of War Chief Robert Kean lamented Davis' peculiarity of "preferring accommodating, civil-spoken persons of small capacity about him." Kean found Cooper "uniformly courteous and uniformly noncommittal. He never decides anything, rarely ever *reports* upon a question, and when he does the report is very thin." Kean complained that thirty months into the war Cooper still had not managed to produce a complete return of Confederate forces in the field and could not give "even a tolerably close *guess*."

Many others agreed with Kean's conclusion about "the incompetency of the Adjutant and Inspector General," and most of Richmond regarded him as merely Davis' tool, a charge that troubled Cooper throughout the war. Many officers treated him as a cipher, acting as if he were no more than a clerk, and Cooper occasionally complained of this to Davis in strong terms, leading the president to scold more than one general. Yet by its nature, Cooper's portfolio was from the outset largely a powerless one, especially when Davis hoarded most important decision-making to himself. Worse, Cooper more than once helped Davis in circumventing secretaries of war who showed too much independence, and it is clear that the working relationship begun in the 1850s continued unchanged into the 1860s. Davis, who always praised men who never troubled him, later declared that those who were "in a position to *know* what he did, what he prevented, what he directed, will not fail to place him among those who contributed most to whatever was achieved."

Surely Cooper's most lasting contribution to the Confederacy was overseeing the removal of War Department records from Richmond in April 1865, and protecting them until they could be turned over to Federal authorities in North Carolina after Johnston's surrender. Unmolested at the end of the war, he returned to find his home near Alexandria replaced by a Federal fort. Nevertheless, he moved into what had been an overseer's house, and there took up small farming until his death on December 3, 1876, being laid to rest in Alexandria's Christ Church Cemetery.

William C. Davis

Beers, Henry P., *Guide to the Archives of the Government of the Confederate States of America* (Washington, 1968).

Cooper, Samuel, to Charles C. Jones, May 27, 1871, copy in possession of the author.

Kean, Robert G. H., *Inside the Confederate Government* (New York, 1957).

Lee, Fitzhugh, "Sketch of the Late General S. Cooper," *Southern Historical Society Papers*, III (May-June, 1877).

Montgomery Corse's finest wartime portrait, made in 1863 or later. (Museum of the Confederacy, Richmond, Va.)

✳ *Montgomery Dent Corse* ✳

Born on March 14, 1816, in Alexandria, Virginia, Corse worked in his father's business before volunteering for the Mexican War, serving as captain of Company B, 1st Virginia Volunteers, in that conflict. In 1849 he settled in California, panned for gold, and held the captaincy of the Sutter Rifles, a militia company. Returning to his hometown in 1856, he joined his brother in the banking business and enrolled in a local militia command.

When the Civil War began in 1861, Corse commanded a battalion of militia companies, including the Old Dominion Rifles, which he had organized. He initially served as assistant adjutant general in Alexandria until Virginia forces evacuated the community in May. Appointed colonel of the 17th Virginia, Corse led his regiment in action at Blackburn's Ford on July 18, in a preliminary engagement to the First Battle of Manassas.

During the spring and summer of 1862, the 17th Virginia, serving in the brigade of James Kemper, fought at Yorktown, Williamsburg, Seven Pines, and in the Seven Days Campaign. Corse earned the praise of his superiors for his performances in these engagements. At the Second Battle of Manassas, Corse temporarily commanded the brigade in the fighting of August 30, suffering a slight wound.

On September 17, at the Battle of Antietam, Kemper's brigade held a position southeast of the village. Corse's regiment had been so badly reduced during the earlier battles and from straggling that he only had fifty-six men in the ranks on this day. When a Federal offensive rolled across the fields late in the afternoon, the 17th Virginia fought bravely, capturing two enemy battle flags. Corse was severely wounded in the foot, and when the brigade retired, he fell into the hands of the 9th New York. A Confederate counterattack, however, regained the ground, and Corse was saved by his own men. That night his regiment numbered only seven, two officers and five privates.

The Virginian's conduct in the fighting of the 17th elicited praise. "Colonel Corse is one of the most gallant and worthy officers in this army," wrote James Longstreet. "He and his regiment have been distinguished in at least ten of the severest battles of the war," Robert E. Lee stated. "This regiment and its gallant colonel challenge the respect and admiration of their countrymen."

Corse's performance at Antietam secured his promotion. Appointed brigadier general on November 1, to take rank immediately, he assumed command of George Pickett's former brigade despite the protests of the unit's colonels, who wanted Colonel Eppa Hunton of the 8th Virginia. Corse's brigade consisted of the 15th, 17th, 30th, and 32d Virginia, with the 29th Virginia added at a later date.

Pickett's Division operated in southeastern Virginia and North Carolina during the winter and spring of 1863 and missed the Battle of Chancellorsville in May. While Lee's army advanced into Pennsylvania in the Gettysburg Campaign, Corse's brigade was detached from Pickett and remained in Virginia, guarding the Richmond area. The brigade rejoined the army in mid-July, engaging in combat along the Blue Ridge Mountains at Chester and Manassas gaps.

In September, Confederate authorities assigned Corse's brigade to the division of Robert Ransom in the Department of Western Virginia and East Tennessee. The brigade stayed during the winter until transferred to the division of Robert Hoke in North Carolina. In May 1864, Hoke's Division was sent to the defenses of Petersburg, Virginia. On May 16, the Confederates engaged the Union forces of Benjamin Butler at Drewry's Bluff. In the action, Corse's Virginians attacked the Union left flank but were repulsed along with other Confederate units.

Corse and his brigade spent the conflict's final year in the Richmond-Petersburg trenches. On April 1, 1865, at the Battle of Five Forks, the command rendered valiant service. It held the right of the main Confederate line, and when the numerically superior Federals finally overwhelmed the Rebel force, Corse's men maintained their composure while most of their comrades fled the battlefield in a panic. Five days later, as Lee's army retreated from Petersburg, Federal units captured thousands of Confederates, including Corse, at Sayler's Creek. He was imprisoned in Fort Warren in Boston until August.

Corse returned to Alexandria upon his release and resumed his banking business. Years later, while visiting Richmond, he was injured when part of the ceiling of the Virginia state capitol building collapsed on him and others in a crowd. The injury resulted in his near-total blindness. Corse, an accomplished and valiant Confederate general who had demonstrated his prowess at Antietam and Five Forks, died on February 11, 1895, and was buried in St. Paul's Cemetery in Alexandria.

Jeffry D. Wert

Freeman, Douglas Southall, *Lee's Lieutenants: A Study in Command* (New York, 1942–44).

Robertson, William Glenn, *Back Door to Richmond: The Bermuda Hundred Campaign, April–June 1864* (Dayton, 1987).

Quite probably an earlier view, for Corse wears a brigadier's collar insignia but has not yet changed the arrangement of the buttons on his tunic from that of a colonel. (Museum of the Confederacy, Richmond, Va.)

✯ *George Blake Cosby* ✯

General Cosby poses for an 1863 or later image. (U.S. Army Military History Institute, Carlisle, Pa.)

Born in Louisville, Kentucky, on January 19, 1830, Cosby came of a distinguished Kentucky lineage. His father was Fortunatus Cosby, Jr., his grandfather of the same name was a renowned judge, and his brother was Rear Admiral Frank C. Cosby of the U.S. Navy. George Cosby received his early education in private schools and entered the U.S. Military Academy on September 1, 1848. He graduated seventeenth in the class of 1852.

Commissioned a brevet 2d lieutenant in the cavalry, he spent the next year at the Carlisle Barracks cavalry school. Promoted to 2d lieutenant on September 16, 1853, he joined "his regiment—the Mounted Rifles" on the Texas frontier, pulling duty at Forts Ewell and Merritt and at Edinburgh. On May 9, 1854, he was severely wounded in a running fight with Comanche Indians near Lake Trinidad. Garrison assignments at Fort Clark, Texas, and at Jefferson Barracks, Missouri, followed. Cosby returned to West Point as an assistant instructor in cavalry in 1855. Promoted 1st lieutenant on May 1, 1856, he joined the elite 2d U.S. Cavalry in Texas in 1857, and on May 13, 1859, again saw combat, against the Comanches in the Nescatunga Valley.

On May 10, 1861, one day after his promotion to captain in the "Old Army," he resigned his commission, having already tendered his services to the Confederacy in mid-March. His offer was accepted on April 20, and he was appointed a captain of cavalry and ordered to Tennessee. Promoted to major, Cosby entered Kentucky with Brigadier General Simon B. Buckner's command in mid-September and was given the task of guarding the crossing of Green River on the Russellville-Rochester road. On October 2, he became Buckner's assistant adjutant-general, a position he held when Buckner's Division was sent to Fort Donelson in the second week of February 1862. After the decision to surrender Fort Donelson was made and command of the more than thirteen thousand troops holding the perimeter had passed to General Buckner, Cosby was summoned. At daybreak on the 16th, he carried for his general a flag of truce, a communication that proposed an armistice and called for the "appointment of commissioners to agree upon terms of capitulation." He returned with Grant's immortal "Unconditional Surrender" note. Buckner in his report of the campaign wrote, "Major George B. Cosby...deserves the highest commendation for the gallant and intelligent discharge of his duties."

Cosby was initially paroled, saw his parole revoked, and after a brief stay at the Camp Chase, Ohio, prisoner-of-war stockade was sent to Fort Warren in Boston Harbor and finally to Fort Delaware. He was exchanged on August 27, 1862, and promoted to lieutenant colonel. Ordered to Mobile, he rejoined General Buckner, and on December 23, 1862, was named chief of staff for the Department of the Gulf. On January 17, 1863, General Joseph E. Johnston wrote President Jefferson Davis: "Do give me by telegraph [Frank] Armstrong, Cosby and R. A. Howard for brigadier generals. They are strongly recommended by Major Generals [Earl] Van Dorn and Buckner and are, I am confident, fully competent."

Davis, acting on this recommendation, had Cosby promoted to brigadier general on April 23, to rank from January 20. Reporting to Van Dorn, Cosby assumed command of a cavalry brigade and accompanied Van Dorn's Corps from Mississippi to Middle Tennessee. Cosby's brigade was in frequent contact with enemy pickets during the next three months and participated in the Thompson's Station fight on March 5, where the Confederates captured thirteen hundred Yankees, and Cosby was commended for his activity and gallantry.

Following General Van Dorn's death, and confronted by the crisis in Mississippi from the investment of Vicksburg by Union troops, Cosby and his brigade, as a unit in Brigadier General William H. "Red" Jackson's Division, returned to Mississippi, reporting to General Johnston at Canton on June 3. Until the 30th, Cosby picketed the Mechanicsville corridor approach to Yazoo City and Canton and then in rapid succession helped screen Johnston's July 1–4 advance to the Big Black and his retrograde to Jackson and beyond.

On July 19, Cosby and his men skirmished with a Union column that crossed Pearl River and occupied Brandon. The Federals evacuated Jackson on the 23rd and returned to the Vicksburg area. They were trailed by Cosby to beyond Clinton. From headquarters at Clinton, Cosby watched the crossings of the Big Black and guarded against a Union dash towards Jackson or Canton. In mid-October Cosby helped blunt and then turn back Major General James E. McPherson's ten-thousand-man column that had lashed out toward Canton. McPherson lamented that Cosby's and Whitfield's cavalry was "far superior to ours."

As the months passed, Cosby's Mississippians lost respect for him. On December 17, 1863, Major General S. D. Lee, after an investigation, informed Cosby that "there are but few officers or men in your command who have confidence in your judgment and ability in the field and there is an aversion on their part to go into battle under you." Cosby was accordingly replaced by Peter B. Stark and instructed to report to Leonidas Polk and await reassignment.

Orders to command troops were eight months in coming. Finally, on August 10, 1864, Cosby was told to report to John H. Morgan in East Tennessee and assume command of the brigade formerly led by Brigadier General George B. Hodge. By early September he had joined his command, which numbered only three hundred. Morgan was dead by this time, and Cosby and his command were assigned to Major General John C. Breckinridge's Department of Western Virginia and East Tennessee. On October 17, Cosby left Wytheville, Virginia, with two brigades—seven hundred strong—en route to reinforce Jubal A. Early's army in the Lower Shenandoah Valley. He reached Staunton on the 26th, seven days after Early's decisive Cedar Creek defeat. Cosby and his small division remained with Early until late November, when they returned to southwest Virginia.

Some two weeks later, George Stoneman, with a powerful mounted force, rode out of Knoxville en route for southwestern Virginia with the mission of beating up Breckinridge's Confederates and destroying salt works and supply depots. On December 17 and 18, Cosby engaged these Yankees at Marion and after two days of fighting, broke off the engagement and withdrew toward Mt. Airy. Stoneman, having achieved his objective, returned to Knoxville. Cosby and his brigade wintered near Liberty Hill in Tazewell County. Between March 21 and April 25, 1865, Union forces led by Stoneman again carried the war into southwestern Virginia on a raid that took them through Knoxville, and on into North Carolina. Outmaneuvered by the Federals, Cosby found himself isolated. He retreated into southeastern Kentucky, where he surrendered his command and was paroled in May.

Soon after the war Cosby relocated to the West, settling in Butte County, California, where he farmed. Later he held a number of state and federal positions of trust, including secretary of the California State Board of Engineers, and served as a member of the Board of Visitors of the U. S. Military Academy. To combat excruciating pains caused by infirmities, Cosby became increasingly dependent upon drugs. As the years passed, the drugs lost their effect, and Cosby decided that suicide was "preferable to the helplessness that had accrued from a paralytic stroke." Employing gas, he killed himself on June 29, 1909, in his Oakland, California, home. His body was cremated, the ashes placed in an urn, and buried in the Sacramento City Cemetery.

Edwin C. Bearss

Johnston, J. Stoddard, *Kentucky*, Vol. XI in Evans, *Confederate Military History.*

A previously unpublished portrait of General Cosby,
possibly taken late in the war. (William Turner
Collection)

An outstanding portrait of William R. Cox, probably taken in 1864, and showing him with a major general's buttons, though he never rose above brigadier. (Alabama Department of Archives and History, Montgomery)

✶ *William Ruffin Cox* ✶

Cox was born on March 11, 1832, at Scotland Neck, Halifax County, North Carolina. At the age of four, Cox and his widowed mother moved to Tennessee, where he received an education and graduated from Franklin College in 1853. Two years later Cox graduated from Lebanon Law School, passed the bar, and began his legal practice in Nashville. He returned to his native state, however, in 1857, bought a plantation in Edgecomb County, and eventually ran for the state legislature, losing the election by thirteen votes.

A militant secessionist, Cox embraced the Confederate cause upon the secession of North Carolina and was appointed major of the 2d North Carolina. The regiment reported to Virginia after the First Battle of Manassas, spending the next several months with the army along the Potomac River. In March 1862, the 2d North Carolina was transferred back to its native state, forming part of the garrison at Fort Fisher, near Wilmington. The regiment stayed but a few weeks when, upon the request of its officers, Confederate authorities returned the unit to Virginia.

During June, the 2d, 4th, 14th, and 30th North Carolina were organized into a brigade under the command of George B. Anderson, a fellow North Carolinian. Anderson's command fought at Gaines' Mill and suffered so heavily in an attack at Malvern Hill that a member of the 2d North Carolina stated the attack was conducted "in the face of such volleys of grape and shrapnel as we had never met before."

As a part of D. H. Hill's Division, Anderson's brigade missed the Second Battle of Manassas but rejoined the army for the invasion of Maryland. On September 14 at South Mountain, Hill's troops fought valiantly throughout the day at heavy odds. Three days later at Sharpsburg, Anderson's brigade manned the "Bloody Lane," suffering fearful casualties, including a mortally wounded Anderson and Colonel Charles C. Tew of the 2d North Carolina, who was killed by a bullet in the head.

Cox assumed command of the regiment later that fall when Lieutenant Colonel William Bynum resigned. Promotion to colonel followed for Cox months later. The regiment saw limited action at the Battle of Fredericksburg on December 13.

Cox's first real test as regimental commander came at the Battle of Chancellorsville in May 1863. On May 3, the brigade, now under the command of Stephen Dodson Ramseur, launched a spirited assault on the Federal lines. Cox suffered five wounds in the combat. Ramseur later praised him, writing:

"The manly and chivalrous Cox of the 2d North Carolina, the accomplished gentleman, splendid soldier and warm friend, who, though wounded three [sic] times, remained with his regiment until exhausted. In common with the entire command, I regret his absence from the field, where he loves to be."

Cox convalesced for months, missing the Gettysburg Campaign and much of the operations of the fall. He returned to the regiment for the 1864 campaigns. On May 12, at Spotsylvania, Ramseur's brigade hurled itself into the maelstrom of the "Bloody Angle," in what a member called "the crowning glory" of the brigade. After the fearful carnage, Robert E. Lee and Richard S. Ewell thanked Cox on the field for his performance. Cox was promoted to brigadier general on June 2, to rank from May 31, and assumed command of the brigade when Ramseur was elevated to major general and divisional command.

Assigned to Ramseur's Division of the II Corps, Cox's brigade, which now also included the 1st and 3d North Carolina, participated in Jubal Early's raid on Washington, D.C., in July, and in the Shenandoah Valley Campaign of August through October. In the latter operations, Cox led his brigade skillfully at the Third Battle of Winchester on September 19. Three days later, at Fisher's Hill, however, Cox made a critical mistake, becoming confused in the wooded terrain, leading his command away from the action as the Federals rolled up Early's left flank and routed the Southerners. At Cedar Creek, on October 19, Cox once again distinguished himself as the Confederates suffered their third major defeat within a month.

Cox had a reputation in the army as always "dressed up to date." But he was not vain and diligently cared for his men, earning their respect and devotion, helped by the fact that before the war ended, he had suffered at least eleven combat wounds.

Cox's brigade spent the war's final months in the Petersburg trenches. On March 25, 1865, it participated in the doomed Confederate assault on Fort Stedman. The brigade's final action came on the army's final day, April 9, when it fired the last Confederate volley of Lee's army at Appomattox. The capable brigadier was paroled with his men.

Cox returned to North Carolina and enjoyed a varied and successful postwar career. He was district solicitor, president of the Chatham Railroad, superior court judge, and served three terms in the United States House of Representatives during the 1880s. In 1893, Cox was appointed Secretary of the Senate, a post he retained until 1900. Cox died on December 26, 1919, in Richmond, Virginia, and was buried in Oakwood Cemetery in Raleigh.

Jeffry D. Wert

Gallagher, Gary W., *Stephen Dodson Ramseur: Lee's Gallant General* (Chapel Hill, 1985).

Hill, D. H., *North Carolina*, Vol. IV in Evans, *Confederate Military History*.

Wert, Jeffry D., *From Winchester to Cedar Creek: The Shenandoah Campaign of 1864* (Carlisle, 1987).

A variant view of Cox made at the same sitting. (William Turner Collection)

✳ *George Bibb Crittenden* ✳

No photo of Crittenden in what is undoubtedly a Confederate uniform has been found. This is definitely a genuine image, and the uniform appears genuine, though the collar insignia is the same as that artificially added to many early war portraits of Southern generals, and may be the work of an artist. (Louisiana State University, Baton Rouge, La.)

Born on March 20, 1812, in Russellville, Kentucky, Crittenden was the eldest son of future U.S. Senator John J. Crittenden. He entered the U.S. Military Academy in 1832. Graduating twenty-sixth out of forty-five cadets four years later, Brevet 2d Lieutenant Crittenden drew assignment to the 4th Infantry. He served in the Black Hawk War and performed garrison duty in Georgia and Alabama before resigning to pursue a career away from the dreariness of garrison duty. Crittenden began to study law, first under his father and later at Lexington's Transylvania University.

Crittenden's interest in the law dwindled as tempers flared in the Southwest. He moved to the Republic of Texas, in 1842 joining Colonel William Fisher's ill-fated Texas command. Fisher rashly led his troops across the Rio Grande and attacked Mier, a small village. The Mexicans soon overwhelmed Fisher's small force, and after the Texans failed to successfully extricate themselves, Crittenden found himself a prisoner of war.

The Mexicans forced Crittenden and his comrades to draw lots to determine which men out of every ten would be executed. Crittenden drew a white bean, which signified life, gave it to a friend, and was fortunate enough to draw a second white bean for himself. Incarcerated in Mexico City for a year, Crittenden was eventually released, thanks to Andrew Jackson, Daniel Webster, and American Minister to Mexico Waddy Thompson, at the request of George's father. When freed, George returned to Kentucky and resumed practicing law. A renewal in the conflict between Texas, now a state, and Mexico, however, brought a permanent end to Crittenden's law career.

The Mexican War compelled Crittenden to rejoin the army on May 27, 1846, as a captain of the Kentucky mounted riflemen. On August 20, 1847, he was brevetted major for heroism at the Battles of Contreras and Churubusco. Promoted to major on March 15, 1848, he was cashiered on August 19. Reinstated on March 15, 1849, Crittenden remained in the army and was promoted to lieutenant colonel on December 30, 1856. He remained in the army until June 10, 1861, when he resigned and departed New Mexico Territory for Kentucky.

Against the wishes of his father, he cast his lot with the South. Entering Confederate service as a colonel of infantry, he commanded the Trans-Allegheny Department. President Jefferson Davis commissioned him a brigadier general on August 15, to rank immediately, and major general on November 9, effective that same day. Given command of the District of East Tennessee, Crittenden received instructions from Davis to invade eastern Kentucky.

Crittenden's district comprised the eastern portion of General Albert Sidney Johnston's Department No. 2, which stretched westward from the Appalachian Mountains through the Indian Territory. Before Crittenden established his headquarters at Knoxville on November 24, one of his two brigade commanders, Brigadier General Felix Zollicoffer, had disobeyed Johnston's orders and moved his army to Beech Grove, Kentucky, on the north side of the Cumberland River. Zollicoffer acknowledged to Johnston that he had disobeyed orders and informed him that he could not recross the river at present due to a lack of boats.

When Crittenden notified Johnston of his arrival, Johnston called Crittenden's attention to Zollicoffer's precarious position, with the enemy in front and the Cumberland River to his rear. Johnston did not, however, order Crittenden to withdraw Zollicoffer to the south bank, and Crittenden did not take it upon himself to do so because he did not fully comprehend the danger until he joined Zollicoffer in early January. Crittenden promptly ordered the construction of boats, but it was too late. Two Union armies were advancing toward his isolated position.

Unable to extricate his troops without boats because of the rain-swollen Cumberland, Crittenden advanced to assault one of the Union armies before the second arrived to reinforce it. On the morning of January 19, 1862, the Confederates encountered Union pickets near Mill Springs. Before noon, Crittenden had been captured and his defeated army had been outflanked by Union Brigadier General George H. Thomas. Crittenden gathered his routed army at Beech Grove

and managed to ferry his troops across the Cumberland. His wagon train and most of his artillery, however, had to be abandoned. The near-sighted Zollicoffer got himself killed at the outset of the engagement when he mistook a Union officer for a Confederate officer; Crittenden was left to bear the onus of the disaster alone.

Mill Springs proved to be Crittenden's only major engagement. Numerous individuals described Crittenden as a "common drunkard," added that he was "in a beastly state of intoxication" during the engagement, and claimed that he had committed "the greater sins of treason, treachery, and cowardice." The public demanded that the "besotted inebriate" be relieved of his command. Instead, General Albert Sidney Johnston ordered him to Corinth and gave him command of the Reserve Corps in the army being assembled there.

Johnston's effort to help Crittenden salvage his reputation proved fruitless. On April 1, Major General William J. Hardee found Crittenden and Brigadier General William H. Carroll drunk in Iuka, Mississippi, and their commands in a "wretched state of discipline." Hardee arrested Crittenden on the spot. Censored by a court-martial, where General Braxton Bragg declared him unfit to command, the disgraced Crittenden resigned on October 23. He still believed in the Southern cause, however, and served for the remainder of the war without rank on the staff of Brigadier General John S. Williams and other officers in western Virginia.

When the conflict ended, Crittenden returned to Kentucky, where he resided in Frankfort. He soon became a hero among his fellow Kentuckians when they finally converted to the Confederate cause after the war when their slaves were freed. Appointed state librarian in 1867, Crittenden held that office until 1874, when he retired and moved to Danville, Kentucky. He died in Danville on November 27, 1880; he is buried beside his father in the Frankfort State Cemetery. His brother, Thomas Leonidas Crittenden, served as a brigadier general in the Union Army.

Lawrence L. Hewitt

Heitman, Francis B., *Historical Register and Dictionary of the United States Army, From Its Organization, September 29, 1789, to March 2, 1903*, Vol. I (Washington, 1903).

Horn, Stanley F., *The Army of Tennessee: A Military History* (Indianapolis, 1941).

✶ *Alfred Cumming* ✶

Born in Augusta, Georgia, January 30, 1829, Alfred Cumming was appointed to the U.S. Military Academy in 1845, and graduated thirty-fifth in the class of 1849. He was commissioned a brevet 2d lieutenant in the 8th U.S. Infantry and reported to his regiment in Texas. His first months on the frontier found him and a detachment escorting wagon trains into the Trans-Pecos country, followed by successive duty stations at Fort Lincoln, Texas; Jefferson Barracks, Missouri; and Fort Brown, Texas. Promoted 2d lieutenant July 16, 1859, he was transferred to the 7th U.S. Infantry. He was aide-de-camp to Brigadier General David E. Twiggs, the commander of the Western Division, headquartered at New Orleans, from 1851–53. After pulling duty as an escort to the U.S.–Mexico Boundary Commission, Cumming was assigned to the Mormon Expedition of 1857–59 under Colonel Albert Sidney Johnston. Cumming's uncle—of the same name—had been named by President James Buchanan to succeed Brigham Young as governor of the Utah Territory.

While learning of the secession of Georgia, Cumming was on furlough as captain in the 10th U.S. Infantry. On January 19, 1861, he resigned his commission and entered his state's military service. He was elected lieutenant colonel of the Augusta Volunteer Battalion, "a well-equipped and admirably disciplined body of five infantry companies," with attached battery. He soon resigned to become major of the 1st Georgia Infantry and in the absence of Colonel W. H. T. "Shot Pouch" Walker and Lieutenant Colonel E. W. Chastain, played a vital role in the organization and schooling of the regiment and accompanied it to Richmond, Virginia.

On June 17, 1861, Cumming was promoted to lieutenant colonel and detached to the 10th Georgia Infantry, then posted on the Peninsula, covering the approaches to the Yorktown-Warwick line. Colonel Lafayette McLaws was then commanding, and was promoted to brigadier general in September. In October, Cumming became colonel of the regiment, then stationed in the Yorktown area as a unit in John B. Magruder's Department of the Peninsula.

Cumming and his regiment saw action during the Peninsula Campaign. On April 5, 1862, from their positions along the Warwick River downstream from Lee's Mill, they frustrated Union efforts to slip across that formidable water barrier. May 23–24, Cumming's 10th Georgia, now assigned to General Paul J. Semmes' brigade of McLaws' Division, checked McClellan's efforts to cross the Chickahominy at New Bridge. During the Seven Days' battles, Cumming was commended for his conduct at Golding's farm (June 26–28) and at Savage's Station (June 29). Semmes noted that at the latter place Cumming's "regiment being longer and more severely engaged, suffered incomparably more than the two other [brigades and regiments on the field] and inflicted heavier losses on the enemy." At Malvern Hill (July 1), Cumming, while "gallantly leading his regiment, was struck by a shell fragment, stunned, and carried from the field."

He recovered from his injury and accompanied McLaws' Division on its late August march north from the Richmond area. Brigadier General Cadmus M. Wilcox being rendered unfit for duty by sickness, Cumming assumed command of Wilcox's Alabama brigade of Major General Richard Anderson's Division

General Cumming's uniform is quite obviously a clumsy artistic embellishment, like many added to civilian portraits of Confederate generals late in the last century. No genuine uniformed portrait is known. (Museum of the Confederacy, Richmond, Va.)

during the Maryland Campaign. He was wounded at Antietam in the fight for Bloody Lane September 17. Returning to Virginia with the Army of Northern Virginia, he was given convalescent leave to return to Georgia. While at Augusta, on October 19, 1862, he was promoted to brigadier general, to rank immediately. In accordance with orders, he reported for duty to Major General Simon B. Buckner, commanding the Department of the Gulf, at Mobile, and took charge of a second brigade of Alabamans. Late in April, Cumming and his brigade were rushed from Mobile to reinforce General Braxton Bragg's army in Middle Tennessee. Confronted by a recently enacted law mandating that brigades must be commanded by officers from the state from which the majority of the units hailed, Cumming was detached from the Alabama Brigade and ordered to report to Lieutenant General John C. Pemberton in Mississippi.

Cumming reached Vicksburg May 13, 1863, and relieved a Kentuckian, Thomas Taylor, as commander of a brigade in Major General Carter L. Stevenson's Division that included the 34th, 35th, 39th, 56th, and 57th Georgia infantry regiments. At Champion's Hill, three days later, Cumming's brigade was mauled in desperate fighting. Upon retreating into the Vicksburg perimeter, Cumming held the rifle-pits from Square Fort south to the Salient Work. Upon the July 4 surrender of Vicksburg and its defending army, Cumming and his Georgians were paroled. He was declared exchanged on July 13 and resumed command of his Georgians, less the 57th Regiment, at the Decatur, Georgia, camp of instruction following their September 12 exchange.

In mid-October, Cumming's brigade, along with Stevenson's other three brigades, reported to General Bragg's army, which was then besieging Chattanooga. Cumming and his people participated in the Battle of Chattanooga. On November 24, they held rifle-pits between Lookout Mountain and Chattanooga Creek and were lightly engaged. The next day they stood tall alongside Pat Cleburne's men and battered William T. Sherman's divisions at Tunnel Hill. Cleburne credited the Georgians with the capture of two Union stands of colors and Bragg wrote of Cumming being "distinguished for coolness [and] gallantry." The Confederate Army, routed from Missionary Ridge, retreated to Dalton, Georgia, where General Joseph E. Johnston replaced Bragg and the soldiers went into winter quarters.

May 1864 found Cumming and his four-regiment brigade still assigned to Carter Stevenson's command, one of the three divisions constituting John B. Hood's

corps. On the 7th, upon the approach of General Sherman's army group, Cumming posted his Georgians in Crow Valley, confronting John M. Schofield's Army of the Ohio, where they clashed with the enemy on the 9th. At Resaca, May 14–15, Cumming battled the Yankees among the hills and hollows east of the Resaca-Dalton road. At New Hope Church, in late May, Cumming held the rifle-pits southwest of the church. During May, Cumming's brigade had 19 killed, 89 wounded, and 270 missing. At Kolb's Farm, on June 22, General Stevenson, preparing for the attack, placed Cumming in charge of his first line consisting of two brigades. The assault failed and the Confederates suffered heavy casualties, through no fault of Cumming. Meanwhile, Cumming's own brigade had to be reinforced by the 2d Georgia State Troops.

In the weeks following the Confederates' evacuation of the Kennesaw line, the retreat south of the Chattahoochee, and the sacking of General Johnston in favor of General Hood, Cumming and his five Georgia regiments didn't fight but were exposed to the hardship of duties in the Atlanta trenches. At Jonesboro, on August 31, in a futile struggle to keep open the last railroad into Atlanta, General Cumming was seriously wounded as he "nobly" led his Georgians in an attack on soldiers of O. O. Howard's Army of the Tennessee corps, who were posted behind breastworks. This was his last battle action. In late March 1865, General Johnston, recalled to duty, reorganized the battered and demoralized Army of Tennessee in North Carolina and consolidated Cumming's soldiers with two other brigades. Although on crutches from his wounds and unfit for duty, Cumming was named commander. He surrendered at Greensboro on April 25, 1865.

Following the war, he took up farming near Rome, Georgia. In 1888 President Grover Cleveland named him a member of the American Military Commission to Korea. Cumming died in Rome, Georgia, on December 5, 1910, and is buried in Augusta.

Edwin C. Bearss

Cullum, George, *Biographical Register of West Point Graduates*, III (Boston, 1891).

Derry, Joseph, *Georgia*, Vol. IX in Evans, *Confederate Military History*.

✫ *Junius Daniel* ✫

Junius Daniel sat for this image probably during the winter of 1862-63, or 1863-64 prior to his death at Spotsylvania. (Library of Congress, Washington, D.C.)

Just as North Carolina contributed more soldiers to the cause than any other state, so did it also offer more than its share of the men destined to become generals. One of these, Junius Daniel, was the son of a former Congressman and attorney general of North Carolina. He was born June 27, 1828, at Halifax and grew up locally until an appointment at large from President James K. Polk—probably as a favor to his father—sent young Daniel to the U.S. Military Academy, where he entered the class of 1851, finally graduating ranked 33d out of 42. Made a brevet 2d lieutenant in the 3d Infantry and sent to Newport Barracks, Kentucky, he received orders that took him to the far frontier, and several years of garrison duty in New Mexico Territory, at Forts Filmore, Albuquerque, and Stanton. Here he received his only promotion, to 1st lieutenant, and here he saw limited action in occasional skirmishes with the local Indians.

Tiring of the glacial pace of advancement in the Old Army, Daniel resigned after seven years and removed to a Louisiana plantation owned by his father, J.R.J. Daniel. There he tried the life of a farmer until the secession storm forced him to take a side. Apparently there was never a question where Daniel's sympathies and loyalties lay. He returned to North Carolina in the fall of 1860, and was there when the Old North State seceded. Immediately he offered his services to the governor, who assigned him to the 14th North Carolina Infantry, then being organized at Garysburg. Its officers promptly elected him colonel of the regiment on June 3, 1861, and he immediately set about the task of training the unit for active service with the growing army in Virginia.

Other forming regiments also offered Daniel their colonelcies, as it happened, and he had to turn down such tenders from the 43d Infantry and the 2d Cavalry, though he may have put his West Point training and Old Army experience to use in helping them and other state units train.

Daniel did not actually reach the war front until the winter of 1861-62, when he took command, as senior colonel, of a brigade of North Carolina troops including his own regiment, the 43d, 49th, 50th infantries, and a battalion of cavalry. He finally saw his first real action in Joseph E. Johnston's army on the Peninsula, and under Lee after Johnston's wounding. Daniel fought through several of the engagements of the Seven Days' battles, and distinguished himself in the final battle at Malvern Hill, where he came perilously close to losing his life when his horse was killed under him. Daniel's performance attracted the attention of his superiors, especially Lee.

Thereafter Daniel spent the balance of the year on the Peninsula, while the rest of the army took the field for the summer and fall campaigns. Daniel was posted to guard the approaches up the James River, chiefly at Drewry's Bluff. President Davis recognized his ability and the level of responsibility he was exercising when he appointed him brigadier general on September 20, 1862, to rank from the first of the month. The Senate confirmed his promotion immediately. His command now consisted of the 32d, 43d, 45th, and 53d North Carolina, and the 2d Battalion.

Daniel and his brigade were ordered back to North Carolina that winter to meet a threatened Federal incursion, but saw no action. He did not return to the Army of Northern Virginia in time for Chancellorsville, but came up along with Pickett when Lee was beefing up his army for the Pennsylvania invasion. Lee placed Daniel in Rodes' Division of the II Corps, and with him marched to Gettysburg. On July 1, when Ewell's Corps assaulted the town and nearly drove the Federals from the field, Daniel and his brigade distinguished themselves, being foremost in the fight and suffering the greatest casualties of any brigade on the field that day. July 2 he saw more, though less severe, fighting north of Cemetery Hill, but on the last day enjoyed something of a rest as the battle shifted elsewhere.

Following Gettysburg, Daniel commanded his brigade throughout the inconclusive fall campaign, and into winter quarters. When the spring 1864 campaigning commenced, he was engaged again at the Wilderness, and then in the vicious fighting around Spotsylvania. There he saw his last battle. On May 12 Daniel and his brigade joined with the others who were chewed up in assaulting the Federal salient known as the "Bloody Angle." As he cheered his men forward in their charge against the Federal II Corps veterans, Daniel was struck down with a wound that was clearly mortal, just as he was approaching the "mule shoe" that Hancock had taken from the Rebels at dawn.

They carried Daniel from the field, but physicians could do nothing more than ease his pain. Just a few months before the outbreak of war he had married Ellen Long of Northampton County, North Carolina, and on May 13 he sent her "a loving message." That done, he died. Friends sent his body back to Halifax, where it was buried in the old churchyard.

Clearly, on the few fields where he serviced, Daniel had proven himself a competent battle commander at brigade level. There were rumors that Lee had recommended him for promotion to major general just before his mortal wounding, and an associate pronounced him "a thorough soldier, calm, resolute and unpretending." He was just the sort that Lee could ill afford to lose.

William C. Davis

Hill, D.H., Jr., *North Carolina*, Vol. IV in Evans, *Confederate Military History*.

✭ *Henry Brevard Davidson* ✭

In the absence of a wartime uniformed portrait, this image from the 1880s or 1890s is all we have for General Davidson. (Museum of the Confederacy, Richmond, Va.)

Several bits of information about Davidson are uncertain, from his middle name to his birthdate, though it appears that he was probably born January 28, 1831, at Shelbyville, Tennessee. In 1846, when not yet sixteen, he managed to enlist in the 1st Tennessee Volunteers and go to the war with Mexico, where he fought at Monterrey alongside Jefferson Davis' 1st Mississippi. His daring won him promotion to sergeant, and when his regiment returned to Tennessee, he was given an appointment to West Point, where he graduated thirty-second in a class of fifty-two in 1853.

Like most new graduates, he went to the frontier as a lieutenant in the 1st Dragoons, and there he served almost without interruption until 1861, chiefly engaged in operations against the Apache, and the Indians of the Northwest in Washington and Oregon. Davidson was in the East on leave when Tennessee seceded, and at once he resigned his commission as a captain and enlisted with the new cause. He received a commission as a major in the Adjutant and Inspector General's Department and was first assigned to the staff of General John B. Floyd, commanding at Fort Donelson. He soon went over to General Simon B. Buckner as chief of artillery, aiding in the unsuccessful defense of the fort and receiving Buckner's accolades in spite of the final fall of the fort.

Davidson either escaped the surrender or else was immediately released, for two months later he was serving as adjutant on the staff of General William W. Mackall at Island No. 10, and this surrender he did not escape. He was sent to Fort Warren, but in June 1862 the Federals marked him for exchange, in return for a major from Massachusetts, and by August he was serving in the Shenandoah Valley, now promoted to colonel and commanding the post at Staunton.

He remained at this post through the campaigns of Fredericksburg, Chancellorsville, and Gettysburg, until he was appointed a brigadier on August 18, 1863, effective immediately, though the Senate did not confirm his rank until the following February 17. At the same time, Richmond assigned him to command a brigade of cavalry in Forrest's cavalry, though Forrest himself reassigned Davidson to Joseph Wheeler in East Tennessee. Davidson led a brigade of five Tennessee regiments, the 1st, 2d, 4th, 6th, and 11th. He was posted to guard Bragg's rail connections with Atlanta during the Chattanooga Campaign, and was involved in scouting and skirmishing in the days leading up to and during Lookout Mountain and Missionary Ridge in November 1863. Following those disasters, he led his brigade into East Tennessee, protecting rail lines that remained in Confederate hands.

The New Year found Davidson in command at Rome, Georgia, and engaging in some of the preliminary skirmishes leading to the opening of the Atlanta Campaign. When the campaign opened in earnest, he evacuated Rome on May 18, 1864, after making a final spirited attack, though he reportedly had only 150 men with him at the time. Davidson thereafter served on the fringes of the campaign until late summer, when Richmond ordered him to return to the Shenandoah once more, to report to Major General Lunsford Lomax to take command of a cavalry brigade in Jubal Early's army. He took what had been William L. Jackson's brigade, the 1st Maryland, and 19th and 20th Virginia cavalry regiments, and the 46th and 47th Virginia battalions.

Davidson arrived too late for the Third Battle of Winchester, September 19, 1864, and may have missed Fisher's Hill and Cedar Creek as well, though he was certainly present by the end of October. But the Valley fighting was all but over by that time. On January 20, 1865, Jackson resumed command of his brigade, and Davidson was almost immediately assigned command of the 7th, 11th, and 12th Virginia, making a demi-brigade of cavalry that by the end of January constituted the only cavalry remaining with Early in the Shenandoah. Davidson was not with Early for the final rout at Waynesborough on March 2, but was leading his tiny brigade elsewhere. Like other isolated units not immediately encompassed by Lee's surrender

at Appomattox, Davidson's brigade made its way south into North Carolina to join with Johnston, and it was there at last that Davidson surrendered at Greensborough.

After the war Davidson located first in New Orleans, where he served as a sheriff's deputy 1866–1867. Soon thereafter he went west to California, where he applied his engineering training from West Point to public works projects that included an appointment as United States inspector of public works from 1878 to 1886 in and around San Pedro. The following year he became deputy secretary of state for California and held the post for several years before taking an agency with the Southern Pacific Railroad at Danville, near San Francisco. He died March 4, 1899, near Livermore, and is buried in Oakland.

Davidson seems to have given positive service, first on staff duty, and then in his several minor cavalry commands. If his superiors did not praise him especially, neither is there any record of censure. He was a solid, if unspectacular, general who did his job.

William C. Davis

Porter, James D., *Tennessee*, Vol. VIII in Evans, *Confederate Military History*.

✶ *Joseph Robert Davis* ✶

Colonel Joseph R. Davis probably posed for this portrait when he was in Richmond on the personal staff of his uncle, President Davis, and prior to his September 1862 promotion to brigadier. (U.S. Army Military History Institute, Carlisle, Pa.)

Born on January 12, 1825, in Woodville, Mississippi, Davis secured an education in Nashville, Tennessee, and graduated from Miami University in Oxford, Ohio. He was admitted to the bar in his native state, practicing his profession in Madison County, Mississippi. In 1860, he was elected to the state senate and served until the start of the Civil War.

A nephew of Confederate President Jefferson Davis, Davis had held the captaincy of a militia company and accepted the lieutenant colonelcy of the 10th Mississippi. He retained this position until August 31, 1861, when his uncle appointed him colonel and assigned him to the president's staff in Richmond. Davis served in the Confederate capital for over a year until his promotion to brigadier general on October 8, 1862, to rank from September 15. His initial nomination had been rejected by the Senate, which charged Jefferson Davis with nepotism. A pleasant, unpretentious man, the younger Davis nevertheless had no military education or record to warrant his promotion to a brigadiership. As the president's nephew, however, he had the familial connections.

Davis was assigned to a brigade composed of the 2d, 11th, 42d Mississippi, and 55th North Carolina. Both the commander and the troops were inexperienced when they advanced into combat at Gettysburg on July 1, 1863. Davis' troops and the brigade of James Archer spearheaded the assault of Henry Heth's Division during the opening action of the battle. Davis attacked with only three regiments, as the 11th Mississippi was detached with the division's wagon trains.

Coming in north of the Chambersburg Pike, Davis' two thousand men swung toward a railroad cut north of the road. Davis handled his command carelessly and, when a Union brigade counterattacked, the ranks of the 2d and 42d Mississippi were trapped and ravaged in the cut. By the time Davis extricated the regiments, he had lost nearly seven hundred men and all but two of his field officers.

Two days later, the depleted brigade participated in the so-called Pickett-Pettigrew assault. Davis' troops manned the left front of the division's lines. For the Mississippians and North Carolinians, it was redemption for July 1, as they advanced bravely into the cauldron of artillery and musketry fire. They charged the stone wall held by the Federals, nearly as far as any body of Confederate troops had done in the attack. Their losses were staggering, with casualties nearly amounting to three-fourths of the command.

Davis contracted a fever after the campaign and remained out of the army until the spring of 1864. Upon his return, Davis resumed command of his brigade in Heth's Division. He led it through the Overland Campaign in the battles of the Wilderness, Spotsylvania, and Cold Harbor. After Cold Harbor, Ulysses S. Grant's Federals crossed the James River and besieged the railroad center of Petersburg.

Davis' brigade, now augmented by the 1st Confederate Battalion and 26th Mississippi, served in the defensive works throughout the ten-month siege. The unit saw heavy action north of the river during Grant's so-called Fifth Offensive from September 29–October 2, 1864. A member of the brigade described their attack on October 1 as "an awful time...the balls flying, thick and fast in every direction, and men getting killed, and wounded hollering all over the woods." Davis had capably directed his brigade in the assault, but the Confederates were repulsed.

Davis was with the army when it surrendered at Appomattox on April 9, 1865. Returning to his native state, Davis practiced law in Biloxi, Mississippi, until his death there on September 15, 1896. The former, undistinguished Confederate brigadier was buried in the Biloxi Cemetery.

Jeffry D. Wert

Hassler, Jr., Warren W., *Crisis at the Crossroads: The First Day at Gettysburg* (University of Alabama, 1970).

Sommers, Richard J., *Richmond Redeemed: The Siege at Petersburg* (New York, 1981).

Stewart, George, *Pickett's Charge* (New York, 1959).

⭐ *William George Mackey Davis* ⭐

General Davis appears here as colonel of the 1st Florida Cavalry, in an image thus datable to sometime prior to November 1862. (Museum of the Confederacy, Richmond, Va.)

Like most of the generals from Florida, Davis was not a native of the state. Rather, he was born May 9, 1812, in Portsmouth, Virginia, and it was a checkered path that finally led him to the Sunshine State. When just seventeen he left home to go to sea, and in one way or another his fortunes for the rest of his life were tied to shipping. Returning to the land, he read law and finally was admitted to the Florida bar after he settled in Apalachicola, where he soon achieved a reputation as a very able lawyer and a local gentleman of repute. He was also a keen businessman and made a small fortune speculating in cotton before the war came.

In 1861 Davis threw himself wholeheartedly into the cause when he gave $50,000 from his fortune to the Confederacy, and then set about raising, organizing, and equipping the 1st Florida Cavalry between May and July 1861. Davis became its lieutenant colonel, not surprisingly, and soon after the New Year was made colonel, apparently without being elected. At the end of the year he was placed in command of the provisional forces of east Florida, with headquarters at Camp Langford. Davis and his regiment became somewhat controversial when Governor John Milton complained to President Jefferson Davis that cavalry was almost useless in defending terrain like that of Florida, yet every man who could wanted to join Davis' regiment, thus depriving Florida infantry outfits of much-needed manpower. The governor regarded Davis as "a gentleman of fine legal abilities," which may have been a veiled reference to his utter lack of military experience. But the president allowed Davis to go ahead anyhow, despite Milton's continued complaints.

The War Department ordered Davis and his regiment to go west to join Albert Sidney Johnston's army in Tennessee on February 18, 1862, but now the colonel's inexperience at maintaining discipline probably showed itself when an inspector the next month found the regiment "in a state of mutiny" over pay arrearages. Though Davis himself promised to remedy the situation, the regiment was still in Florida on April 7, thus missing the Battle of Shiloh. In fact, Davis did not reach Tennessee until May, and then occupied himself and his regiment in the eastern part of the state in surveillance on Yankee movements. Through the summer and fall he operated in and around Knoxville, at one point assuming command of the city, and with it the temporary command of a brigade of cavalry.

When Bragg launched his invasion of Kentucky, Davis and his command were part of Kirby Smith's forces as they marched into the Bluegrass, and Davis himself got as far as Frankfort by October 2 before being ordered to withdraw. Now in permanent brigade command, he led his own 1st Florida, now dismounted, and the 6th and 7th Florida infantries. This fact, plus the need to ease the pain of the failure of the campaign with promotions, probably induced President Davis to appoint Colonel Davis a brigadier on November 4, 1862, though records of his actual commission have disappeared. Thereafter Davis commanded the Department of East Tennessee, at least temporarily, and it was while he was in command that soldiers under him committed the controversial Shelton Laurel massacre, in which thirteen North Carolina Unionists were shot without trial, though none of the blame for the incident seems to have attached itself to Davis.

Davis remained in command at Knoxville through mid-April 1863 and was then superseded and took over a district within the department. For reasons not clear, Davis submitted his resignation on May 6, 1863, and moved to Richmond, Virginia. Apparently always something of an opportunist, he entered the blockade-running trade, thus returning to his early association with the sea, and once more prospered, later moving to Wilmington, North Carolina, when that became the last usable Confederate port on the Atlantic.

Apparently, his fortunes prospered once more. When the war ceased, he returned to Jacksonville, Florida, but a nomad to the end, he later moved to Washington, D.C., and there practiced law very successfully almost until the time of his death on March 11, 1898, in Alexandria, Virginia. He is buried at nearby Remington.

There was little to distinguish Brigadier General Davis when he was in uniform other than his apparent genuine devotion to the cause. Superiors spoke neither ill nor well of him, and his performance in actual combat was so limited as to make any judgment of his battlefield competence impossible.

William C. Davis

Dickison, J. J., *Florida*, Vol XI in Evans, *Confederate Military History*.

Paludan, Philip, *Victims* (Knoxville, 1981).

✴ *James Dearing* ✴

General James Dearing, photographed by Vannerson and Jones
in Richmond, probably in 1864. (William Turner Collection)

James Dearing was born at the family home, "Otterburne," in Campbell County, Virginia, on April 25, 1840. He attended several preparatory schools in his native state, including the renowned Hanover Academy. Dearing entered the United States Military Academy at West Point in 1858, which began a military career that occupied all of the few remaining years of his life.

The young Virginian displayed a confidence at West Point that won him the same popular acceptance that later marked his Confederate military service. A fellow cadet reported that Dearing introduced the tune "Dixie" to the military academy and was well known for singing and playing the music that would later carry such strong sectional connotations. Dearing's rambunctious behavior at West Point earned him a hefty burden of demerits and prompted a contemporary to call him "a reckless, handsome boy." Recklessness notwithstanding, Dearing achieved solid competence academically; he stood thirteenth among fifty-two cadets who passed his first year, and sixteenth of forty-one his second year.

Cadet Dearing should have finished his third year at West Point in June 1861, but by then he and most other Southerners had gone back to their homes to defend them. He and his friend Thomas L. Rosser both resigned on April 22, 1861, only three days short of Dearing's twenty-first birthday. Rosser became an officer in the Washington Artillery of New Orleans and tried to secure a similar posting for Dearing. When the Louisiana unit rolled through Lynchburg en route to the front June 2–3, 1861, Dearing joined and went off to war, though without any official rank. It was not until July 16 that Dearing was commissioned as 2d lieutenant of infantry, though the commission was delivered to Major J. B. Walton of the Washington Artillery and the new lieutenant remained on artillery duty. Oddly, the commission dated Dearing's rank from March 16, when he had been firmly ensconced in the service of another army, and it was not confirmed until October 4, 1862 (a delay somewhat longer than usual but by no means unique).

Lieutenant Dearing fought with the Washington Artillery through the First Battle of Manassas, riding conspicuously under fire with the battalion's leaders. He remained with the Louisiana artillerists through the long quiet spell that stretched through the remainder of 1861 and into 1862. In February of 1862 Dearing received promotion to the rank of 1st lieutenant and took command of the 3d Company of the Washington Artillery. A few weeks later he jumped another step in rank when a Virginia battery from his hometown of Lynchburg elected him their captain in April during the reorganization of units directed by an act of the Confederate Congress. The new captain led his battery to Virginia's peninsula and quickly found action before the end of April on the Yorktown-Warwick River line. Dearing won plaudits for his performance at the Battle of Williamsburg on May 5, 1862. Again at the end of that month he caught the eyes of superiors while fighting in the Battle of Seven Pines by showing what James Longstreet called "conspicuous courage and energy."

A bout with illness kept Captain Dearing out of the Seven Days' battles. When he returned, Dearing and his battery fought briefly near the climax of Second Manassas, but then left the Army of Northern Virginia and headed for southeastern Virginia on detail during the fall of 1862. Dearing returned to the army and played a minor role at Fredericksburg, then in January 1863 was promoted to major and assigned to artillery duty with Pickett's Division. Commanded by Longstreet, Pickett and Dearing and the rest of the division left on an expedition in the Suffolk region. In keeping with the unsuccessful results of the entire campaign, Dearing lost some guns near Suffolk and missed the Chancellorsville Campaign in the process.

Major Dearing commanded the four-battery artillery battalion assigned to Pickett's Division during the Gettysburg Campaign. On July 1, with his own unit still in reserve, Dearing struggled to the front and found opportunity to serve as a volunteer subordinate to E. P. Alexander during the fighting around the Peach Orchard. The next day Pickett's artillery commander had more than enough to occupy him with his own command, as he supported the division's famous charge. Eppa Hunton, who commanded a regiment in the charge, called Dearing "one of the bravest and best of artillery officers." Dearing told Hunton that after the artillery barrage "he was going with us in the charge...that he had always gone with this Division." As the infantry advanced, though,

An early war view of Dearing, perhaps as a lieutenant. (Evans, *Confederate Military History*)

"Dearing passed with his caissons to the rear at full speed," yelling to Hunton, "For God's sake wait till I get some ammunition!" In the aftermath of Gettysburg, Dearing and Alexander served together on a board that delivered several pointed recommendations for improvement in Southern artillery and ammunition.

Gettysburg proved to be Dearing's last major artillery action. That autumn Pickett detailed his subordinate to cavalry duty; the transplant took hold quickly and permanently. In January 1864 Dearing won promotion to colonel. (A March 14, 1864, promotion to lieutenant colonel of artillery suggests that the January rank ran afoul of some complication.) During that month he also married Roxana Birchett (1844–1926) of Petersburg; the couple had one child, a daughter born August 31, 1864. The newly converted and promoted cavalry commander led mounted troops during the early months of 1864 in operations at New Berne, Plymouth, and Washington in North Carolina. Dearing's success in those affairs, plus the warm endorsements of General R. F. Hoke and others, resulted in promotion for Dearing on April 29 to the rank of brigadier general, though no official record of his promotion survives.

Two weeks after this latest promotion Dearing was back in Virginia, helping Beauregard in the defense of Drewry's Bluff and Petersburg during May and June. The young general played a pivotal part in the June 9 affair at Petersburg, and again during the June 15–18 crisis. As siege operations developed around Petersburg, Dearing led a cavalry brigade in W. H. F. Lee's division. Dearing's brigade also operated independently at times, and sometimes in C. M. Butler's Division, through the long period of the deepening Confederate twilight. The brigade usually consisted of four regiments from North Carolina and Georgia. Dearing frankly admitted the unreliable nature of his command: "I have to stay in the forefront to make these men fight…I'll get myself killed trying to." Even so, Dearing and his men contributed important service during Hampton's highly successful cattle raid in September 1864.

During the Confederacy's waning days, General Dearing took over a command he had long sought—that of the famous Laurel Brigade of Virginia cavalry. He led his new command at Dinwiddie Court House and Five Forks. On April 6, 1865, Dearing and the Laurel Brigade fought one of their country's last

successful cavalry actions. After dramatic hand-to-hand personal combat with two high-ranking Federals, Dearing fell with a severe wound and died in Lynchburg on April 23—two weeks after Appomattox and two days before his twenty-fifth birthday. He had been one of the youngest Confederate generals, and he was the last to die as a direct result of battle wounds.

Robert K. Krick

Halsey, Don P., *Historic and Heroic Lynchburg* (Lynchburg, 1935).
Parker, William L., *General James Dearing* (Lynchburg, 1990).

Young Captain Dearing sat for his portrait while serving with the Washington Artillery, probably in 1862. (Russell W. Hicks, Jr., Collection)

Very probably at the same sitting, this previously unpublished view was made. (Russell W. Hicks, Jr., Collection)

Dearing sat again for the camera after his promotion to major, probably in the spring of 1863, producing this excellent, previously unpublished image. (Russell W. Hicks, Jr., Collection)

Early in 1864, possibly around the time of his April appointment as brigadier, Dearing sat with his new bride for this touching, though faded portrait. A year later he would be dead. (Russell W. Hicks, Jr., Collection)

✶ Zachariah Cantey Deas ✶

Zachariah Deas was born in Camden, South Carolina, on October 25, 1819. He had the benefit of a superior education, first in Columbia, South Carolina, and later at Caudebec in Calvados, France. In 1835 his family moved to Mobile, Alabama, because Zachariah's father could no longer tolerate the presence of his brother-in-law, James Chesnut, Sr., who had defeated him in a South Carolina senate race in 1832.

Mobile's prosperous economy continued to flourish with each improvement in the transportation linking Mobile with the interior, prompting Deas to become a cotton broker. A Democrat and an Episcopalian, by 1860 Deas had amassed a sizeable fortune and had served in the Mexican War. On May 16, 1853, he married Helen Gaines Lyon, the daughter of one of Alabama's most distinguished citizens.

Deas served on the staff of General Joseph E. Johnston during the First Battle of Manassas. In the fall of 1861 he recruited the 22d Alabama Infantry with the assistance of Major Robert B. Armistead. Elected colonel of the regiment, Deas was duly commissioned on October 25, 1861. Unable to secure arms from the government, Deas paid $28,000 in gold to equip his men with the latest Enfield rifles, although the Confederate government did reimburse him with bonds one year later. Mustered into Confederate service at Montgomery in October and ordered to Mobile on November 5, the regiment remained there until ordered to Corinth, Mississippi, on February 26, 1862.

The 22d Alabama received its baptism of fire at Shiloh on April 6. When the fighting ended that

evening, Deas found himself in command of the brigade following the mortal wounding of Brigadier General Adley H. Gladden and the brigade's senior colonel, Daniel W. Adams. Because of the prevailing confusion, daybreak of April 7 found Deas looking for two of his regiments and his divisional commander when the Federals began their attack. Deas reacted to this threat by counterattacking with his troops at hand while attempting to organize a larger force to resist the onslaught. In the process two horses were shot from under him before he sustained a severe wound.

Deas recovered in time to lead his regiment into Kentucky with General Braxton Bragg during the summer of 1862. During that campaign the 22d Alabama fought at Munfordville and Perrysville. Deas' creditable performance at Murfreesboro earned him his brigadier's star. Commissioned on December 20, to rank from December 13, Deas received command of Franklin Gardner's old brigade, Gardner having been promoted and transferred to Port Hudson, Louisiana. Deas' brigade of five Alabama regiments distinguished itself at Chickamauga by routing Major General Philip Sheridan's division, killing Brigadier General William H. Lytle and capturing seventeen cannon. The heroism displayed by the brigade during the latter engagement came at a heavy price. The brigade lost forty percent of its strength, and Deas' old regiment alone

Perhaps the handsomest of General Deas' wartime portraits is this one showing him as a brigadier, and taken in 1863 or later. (Civil War Times Illustrated Collection, Harrisburg, Pa.)

60

sustained eleven percent of its division's casualties—having 203 men killed and wounded of the 371 present, including five color bearers. Deas' division commander, Major General Thomas C. Hindman, reported, "Deas swept like a whirlwind over the breastworks." Deas also led his brigade during the siege of Chattanooga and participated in the Battle of Missionary Ridge.

By the beginning of 1864, Bragg had been replaced by Deas' comrade from First Manassas, Joseph E. Johnston. Hindman now commanded the corps and J. Patton Anderson was promoted to major general, presumably to replace Hindman, but promptly ordered to Florida instead. By January 20, Deas was commanding the division and evidently viewed his new position as permanent and eagerly awaited his major general's commission. Although he was the senior brigadier in the division and despite his performance at Chickamauga, the anticipated promotion did not materialize. He remained in command of the division until he submitted his resignation on March 18, and possibly for some time thereafter as well. Although Johnston notified the War Department of Deas' resignation, it was obviously not accepted, because Deas remained with the army in command of his brigade on April 30.

Deas participated in the opening stages of the Atlanta Campaign but left the army prior to June 30, apparently because of illness. On July 23, Secretary of War James A. Seddon ordered Johnston to have Deas' case, the details of which remain a mystery, brought before an examining board. Johnston notified Seddon on August 10 that he could not comply with the order because of Deas' absence due to illness and Hindman's departure for the Trans-Mississippi. Instead, two days following Deas' return to duty on August 6, Johnston restored him to command of his old brigade despite the fact that George D. Johnston had been promoted to brigadier and given command of it on July 26, only to be seriously wounded two days later. Whatever the details of the case, the matter was apparently forgotten. Deas remained with his brigade, and his performance throughout the remainder of August earned him the praise of J. Patton Anderson, who had resumed command of Deas' division.

After fighting at Jonesborough, where Anderson sustained a serious wound, Deas moved north with General John Bell Hood. His promotion to major general again eluded him, however, the division instead going to the recently exchanged Major General Edward Johnson. Deas' distinguished performance at Franklin, where he sustained a slight wound, gave no indication of animosity on his part, and following the capture of Major General Edward Johnson at Nashville on December 16, Deas once again found himself in command of the division. He led the remnant of the division for the duration of the retreat, but after the army reached Alabama, he was ordered east with his brigade to oppose Major General William T. Sherman's advance through the Carolinas. Deas fought at Kinston and Bentonville, North Carolina, in March 1865, but when the Confederate army reached Raleigh, illness forced Deas to relinquish his command.

After the war Deas moved to New York City, where he again engaged in the cotton trade and became a member of the stock exchange. Despite his continued success in business, Deas lived the life of "a quiet and modest citizen," as he had in Mobile before the war. He died in New York City on March 6, 1882, and is buried there in Woodlawn Cemetery. His first cousin was Confederate Brigadier General James Chesnut, Jr.

Lawrence L. Hewitt

Faust, Patricia L., ed., *Historical Times Illustrated Encyclopedia of the Civil War* (New York, 1986).

Wheeler, Joseph, *Alabama*, Vol. VIII in Evans, *Confederate Military History* .

Deas was colonel of the 22d Alabama when he stood for this 1861 or 1862 portrait which reveals excellent detail in his uniform, and a somewhat bemused expression on his face. (Alabama Department of Archives and History, Montgomery, Ala.)

Probably a late war portrait that shows in Deas' face the authority of a general accustomed to command. (Library of Congress, Washington, D.C.)

⋆ *Julius Adolph de Lagnel* ⋆

The only known wartime portrait of de Lagnel was probably made when he served as a lieutenant colonel in Richmond, though no insignia of rank appears on his collar. (Museum of the Confederacy, Richmond, Va.)

Julius Adolph de Lagnel was descended from a Huguenot family that fled France to start a new life on the island of Hispaniola and then escaped the uprising of the blacks in Haiti by settling in the United States. De Lagnel, whose father was an 1814 graduate of the U.S. Military Academy and an officer in the 2d U.S. Artillery, was born near Newark, New Jersey, on July 24, 1827. He was educated and grew up in Virginia and was commissioned a 2d lieutenant in the 2d U.S. Artillery on March 8, 1847, the unit his father had served in two decades before.

He was promoted 1st lieutenant on January 29, 1849, and in March 1861 posted as the commander of Company D, 2d U.S. Artillery, at the arsenal in Fayetteville, North Carolina. The garrison surrendered and the arsenal was seized by North Carolina state troops on April 11. De Lagnel, in accordance with instructions and as the senior officer present, conducted this company first by train and then by boat to Fort Hamilton, New York, where they disembarked on May 7. After traveling to Washington and turning over the company's papers and funds to the War Department, de Lagnel resigned his commission and volunteered his services to the Confederacy on May 17. Commissioned a captain in the Lee Artillery on June 12, his first assignment was at Richmond as a drill instructor, and in early July he joined the staff of Brigadier General Robert S. Garnett, commanding the Department of Northwestern Virginia, as chief of artillery.

July 11, 1861, found Captain de Lagnel attached to Lieutenant Colonel John Pegram's command on Rich Mountain, guarding Buckhannon Pass. At 11:00 A. M., de Lagnel's force—three companies of the 20th and two companies of the 25th Virginia Infantry Regiment with a brass six-pounder manned by a detachment of the Lee Virginia Artillery—was attacked at Hart's farm by nearly two thousand Federals led by Brigadier General William S. Rosecrans. A savage fire-fight ensued and the artillerists manning the six-pounder were slaughtered. Captain de Lagnel, after his horse was shot from under him, saw that all the cannoneers except a boy had been killed or wounded. Hastening to the gun, he helped load and fire three or four rounds before being shot in the side. The boy dragged de Lagnel behind the gun carriage. The captain, satisfied that his wound was fatal, shouted for his Virginians to save themselves if they could. Some did, while others surrendered, but the boy was shot and bayonetted. De Lagnel, on witnessing this, struggled to his feet and sought to pursue the Yankee responsible, but fainted. When he recovered consciousness, he rolled himself downhill and lay all night in a thicket as the rain beat down.

The next morning, the 12th of July, de Lagnel, using improvised crutches, sought to escape the Rich Mountain debacle. After wandering about for seventy-two hours with little to eat except wild berries and sprouts, he approached a mountaineer's cabin. The woman of the house, upon learning that "I came from Virginia," invited him in and cared for him until he was able to travel.

Disguised as a herder, de Lagnel failed in his attempt to reach the Confederate lines when he encountered a Union patrol. An alert soldier saw that his boots were not the kind worn by locals, and when pulled off, his name was found inside. Careful to avoid being accused a spy, he identified himself and was escorted to the camp of an Ohio infantry regiment. General Rosecrans, desirous of promptly sending de Lagnel to a prisoner-of-war facility, placed him under his bond as an officer and a gentleman to proceed to Fort Hamilton. Upon reaching Governor's Island, de Lagnel was not permitted to enter by the sergeant-of-the-guard. The officer in charge of Fort Hamilton was called, Martin Burke, who had been de Lagnel's commander when they served together in the "Old Army." De Lagnel was initially confined at Fort Lafayette, and on October 30 he was transferred to nearby Fort Columbus. Early in January 1862 he was exchanged for Captain James B. Ricketts, captured at First Manassas on July 21, 1862.

Upon returning to duty Captain de Lagnel reported to John B. Magruder's Army of the Peninsula and was placed in charge of the naval battery positioned on Mulberry Island. Soon thereafter, he was promoted major of the 20th Virginia Artillery Battalion. On April 8, 1862, he was nominated, appointed, and confirmed as a brigadier general to rank from April 15, but for obscure reasons, he declined the commission.

During the Seven Days' battles, de Lagnel, now a lieutenant colonel, served as Isaac Hager's chief of artillery, and on July 17 he was detached from his staff duties and ordered to accompany Major General T. H. Holmes to the Trans-Mississippi. Instead he went on sick leave and on returning to duty on August 22, was ordered to report to the Ordnance Bureau in Richmond.

In September 1862 de Lagnel assumed command of the important Confederate arsenal and armory at Fayetteville, North Carolina, an assignment he held until November 1863, when he returned to Richmond for duty as inspector of arsenals. In May 1864 he filled the billet as officer-in-charge of the Columbus, Georgia, Arsenal, where he remained until September. By October 1, 1864, he had returned to duty in Richmond at the Ordnance Bureau. De Lagnel was paroled at Greensboro, North Carolina, on May 1, 1865.

After the war, he engaged in the Pacific Steamship service for many years. In 1910, at age eighty-two, then living in the nation's capital, the colonel married a widow, Mrs. Josephine Conklin Cowles. He died in the District of Columbia on June 3, 1912, and his remains were buried in St. Paul's Churchyard, Alexandria, Virginia.

Edwin C. Bearss

Hotchkiss, Jedediah, *Virginia*, Vol. III in Evans, *Confederate Military History.*

★ *James Deshler* ★

A uniform has been painted over a civilian portrait of Deshler, perhaps to make up for the fact that his early death at Chickamauga, two months after promotion to brigadier, prevented any uniformed view from being taken. (Museum of the Confederacy, Richmond, Va.)

The son of Pennsylvania natives, Deshler was born on February 18, 1833, in Tuscumbia, Alabama. He graduated from the U. S. Military Academy at West Point in 1854, seventh in a class of forty-six. He stayed in the Regular Army, serving in California, Pennsylvania, in the Sioux campaign, and was with Albert Sidney Johnston in Utah. When the war began, he was a first lieutenant in the 10th Infantry stationed at Fort Wise in Colorado, but was dropped formally from the army rolls on July 15 for not returning after a leave of absence, during which he "went South." Deshler was appointed a captain of artillery and was sent to western Virginia, where his first service was under General Henry R. Jackson. He was next acting brigade adjutant under Colonel Edward Johnson.

In an engagement at Greenbrier River on October 7, 1861, Deshler took command of a battery, and "directed a rapid fire with marked effect." In a skirmish on December 13, Colonel Johnson reported that Deshler, "whilst behaving most gallantly, was shot down in the trenches by a wound through both thighs," but "refused to leave the field, and remained in the trenches until the day was over." Another participant noted that Deshler "utterly refused to be sent from the field until the enemy was repulsed with great loss." After his recovery Deshler was promoted to colonel of artillery. On April 20, 1862, he was assigned to the staff of General Theophilus H. Holmes in North Carolina, and on April 27 Holmes reported that Deshler was the only ordnance officer he had, and could not be assigned elsewhere.

Deshler was Holmes' chief of artillery in the Peninsula Campaign, and fought at Malvern Hill.

When Holmes was appointed commander of the Trans-Mississippi Department in August 1862, Deshler accompanied him to Little Rock, and on September 28 he was relieved from staff duty and ordered to proceed to Thomas C. Hindman for command of a brigade. But Deshler never joined Hindman, for when Brigadier General Allison Nelson died on October 7, Deshler took command of Nelson's brigade of Texans and in November took his brigade to Fort Hindman at Arkansas Post on the lower Arkansas River.

The post, commanded by Thomas J. Churchill, was attacked in January 1863 by the combined Union forces of General John A. McClernand and Admiral David D. Porter. Deshler was taken captive with the surrender of the fort on January 11, exchanged in June, and appointed a brigadier general on July 18, 1863, to rank immediately. Deshler was assigned to Braxton Bragg, and commanded the Army of Tennessee artillery reserve. When Secretary of War James Seddon recommended removing Churchill from command of the Texans because of the bitterness surrounding his actions at Arkansas Post, Deshler replaced him. Deshler had been very popular with the men in Arkansas, while Churchill had to bear the burden of being the man to surrender; this fact alone had made him extremely unpopular with the men, who had spent several months in prison camps. On August 13, Deshler was relieved from command of the artillery reserve and ordered to take command of Churchill's brigade.

On September 20, 1863, while waiting for instructions during the Battle of Chickamauga, Deshler was struck by an artillery projectile and killed instantly. Major General Cleburne wrote that Deshler fell when a shell passed through his chest. "It was the first battle in which this gentleman had the honor of commanding as a general officer. He was a brave and efficient one. He brought always to the discharge of his duty a warm zeal and a high conscientiousness. The army and the country will long remember him." Roger Q. Mills, who succeeded Deshler, reported that he had been coming toward Mills when he was hit by a shell, and "his heart was literally torn from his bosom." Mills reported that Deshler was brave and generous, and kind even to a fault. Ever watchful and careful for the safety of any member of his command, he was ever ready to peril his own. Refusing to permit a staff officer to endanger his life in going to examine the cartridge boxes to see what amount of ammunition his men had, he cheerfully started himself to brave the tempest of death that raged on the crest of the hill. He had gone but little way when he fell—fell as he would wish to fall—in the very center of his brigade, in the midst of the line, between the ranks, and surrounded by the bodies of his fallen comrades.

Moreover, on September 23, Robert E. Lee wrote to Jefferson Davis: "There was no braver soldier in the Confederacy than Deshler. I see he is numbered among the dead." Deshler had done much to improve the fighting quality of the men; the brigade he commanded became Granbury's Texas Brigade, Patrick Cleburne's Division, and one of the finest fighting units in the Army of Tennessee. Deshler is buried in Oakwood Cemetery, Tuscumbia.

Anne Bailey

McCaffrey, James M., *This Band of Heroes: Granbury's Texas Brigade, C.S.A.* (Austin, 1985).

✮ *George Gibbs Dibrell* ✮

Young Dibrell was born into a farming family at Sparta, White County, Tennessee, on April 12, 1822. He managed to acquire a little more than the customary rural education, first at local common schools, and then with a year at East Tennessee University. Thereafter he returned to Sparta, first to farm and then to become a merchant. His family was predominantly Unionist in the growing sectional crisis, and in 1861 his fellow citizens in the largely loyal eastern Tennessee community sent him to the state convention as a Union delegate. The convention chose secession, however, in the wake of the firing on Fort Sumter, and Dibrell immediately bent to the majority.

In June he enlisted as a private in a company soon amalgamated into the newly formed 25th Tennessee Infantry. On August 10, when the regiment officially organized, the men chose Dibrell as their lieutenant colonel. He served with his regiment throughout most of its twelve months' enlistment, seeing fighting at Mill Springs in January 1862, where Dibrell briefly assumed command of the regiment after its colonel was wounded. Dibrell and the 25th missed Shiloh but were with the army at Corinth. There, on May 10, 1862, the regiment reorganized, and for unknown reasons Dibrell was not reelected.

That summer Dibrell received authorization to raise a regiment of partisan rangers, and in September he organized the twelve companies of what would become the 13th Tennessee Cavalry, which for most of the war would be more commonly known as the 8th Tennessee. Dibrell became its colonel and soon reorganized it in October as a regular cavalry regiment with

ten companies. All that Dibrell ever got from the War Department were six hundred sabers and four hundred old flintlock muskets; thereafter he armed his regiment by capturing weapons from the enemy.

The same month it was reorganized, the regiment went to Murfreesboro, where it and Dibrell became part of Nathan B. Forrest's brigade, commencing an association that would continue for most of the rest of the war. Dibrell led his new regiment into action almost immediately, with a skirmish on October 15, 1862, drawing first blood. He went with Forrest on the raid into west Tennessee in December, participating in the fight at Parker's Cross Roads on the last day of the year, where Dibrell briefly assumed command of his brigade.

During the rest of the winter and spring to follow, Dibrell served mainly in Middle Tennessee and northern Alabama, and in the latter service, the people of the city of Florence met in a public meeting to pay tribute to Dibrell and his men for their conduct. During Federal General Abel Streight's raid into Georgia in April and May, Dibrell and his command made diversionary thrusts to isolate Streight, helping lead to his eventual capture.

The summer of 1863 saw Dibrell occasionally in command of his brigade now that Forrest have moved on to division leadership. When Bragg's army fell back to Chattanooga in the face of General Rosecrans' advance

The only known uniformed portrait of General Dibrell shows him as a brigadier, meaning that it had to be made in February 1865 or later. It is possible that it was taken by the Nashville artist C.C. Giers within a few weeks after the surrender. (Alabama Department of Archives and History, Montgomery, Al.)

during the Tullahoma Campaign, Dibrell took his regiment to his home county and occupied the vicinity of Sparta for several weeks, skirmishing with Yankee cavalry in the preliminaries to the Chickamauga Campaign. On August 9 he and his regiment fought a successful skirmish at Sparta that concluded with the women of the neighborhood cooking and sending to their favorite son and his men a fresh breakfast, which their colonel said was "highly prized."

From August 31 on, Dibrell was almost constantly in command of a brigade, and led one first at Chickamauga, where during the battle it fought dismounted along with some of the other cavalry units. After the battle, Dibrell's brigade joined in Longstreet's Knoxville Campaign, now serving under General Joseph Wheeler. Dibrell's brigade, including the 13th (8th), the 5th, 9th, 10th, and 8th cavalry regiments, took part in most of the subsequent frustrating operations of that ill-fated campaign, seeing changes in its structure as the 11th Tennessee was added and the 4th Tennessee replaced the 8th.

There were frequent skirmishes through the end of March 1864, when Dibrell was ordered to north Georgia to join Johnston and the Army of Tennessee for the Atlanta Campaign. During Johnston's subsequent withdrawal through Georgia, Dibrell remained almost constantly engaged with the rest of the Confederate cavalry in covering the army's retreat, seeing battle at Calhoun, New Hope Church, Dallas, Kennesaw Mountain, Peachtree Creek, and more.

Following the fall of Atlanta, Dibrell and his brigade went with Wheeler on his raid into Tennessee, bringing the colonel and the men of his old regiment back to Sparta briefly, where they rested for several days with their families and friends. Wheeler's raid was broken up, however, and several of its commands isolated, including Dibrell, who wound up leading his brigade east to Saltville, Virginia, arriving just in time to take part in the October 2, 1864, battle that successfully repulsed Stephen Burbridge's Yankee raid. While none of Dibrell's Tennesseans seems to have taken part in the shameful massacre of wounded and unarmed black soldiers that took place the following day, several of them later recalled witnessing it. Dibrell finally rejoined Wheeler and helped in the unsuccessful resistance to Sherman's march from Atlanta to Savannah, Georgia. Nevertheless, on January 28, 1865, President Davis finally recognized Dibrell's long and good service with an appointment as brigadier

general. The Senate confirmed it the same day, and the appointment itself was back-dated to July 26, 1864.

In the subsequent Carolina Campaign, February–April 1865, Dibrell led his brigade in the continual retreat, and in the defeats at Averasborough and Bentonville, now in a corps commanded by General Wade Hampton. When Wheeler ceased his connection with Dibrell, he paid tribute to him for his "most valuable service to me during a long series of campaigns." Dibrell continued to earn the respect of his superiors in the last trying days of the Confederacy.

He saw his last action on April 11, 1865, at Beulah, North Carolina, and then moved to Greensboro, where his command joined the escort of President Davis and his fleeing government. Dibrell stayed with them almost to the end. Only on May 3, as the fleeing party crossed the Savannah River heading into Georgia, did the Tennessean's men refuse to go farther. On May 9 they took their parole at Washington, Georgia, making Dibrell and his men among the last commands in the East to yield. Among Dibrell's last duties had been the safeguarding of the trains carrying the archives of the Confederate War Department, the documents later used in assembling the *War of the Rebellion: Official Records of the Union and Confederate Armies.*

After the war Dibrell returned to Tennessee and immediately became a community and state leader. In 1870 he sat as a delegate in Tennessee's new constitutional convention, and thereafter served five terms in the United States Congress, 1874–1884. Like many another ex-Confederate, he took up railroading, acting as president of the Southwestern Railroad, and also helped in the development of the coal industry in his part of the state. When the veterans of his old brigade met in 1883 to form a "reunion brigade," General Dibrell became its commander, taking an active part in its meetings and affairs until his death on May 9, 1888, at his home in Sparta. Though perhaps not an outstanding commander, still Dibrell had shown mature leadership on a host of fields for almost four years, and a steadfastness in the face of the final adversity that earned him the confidence of his superiors, military and civil.

William C. Davis

Horn, Stanley, ed., *Tennesseeans in the Civil War* (Nashville, 1964).

Porter, James D., *Tennessee*, Vol. VIII in Evans, *Confederate Military History.*

✴ *Thomas Pleasant Dockery* ✴

General Dockery was photographed sometime after August 1863 for this, his only known wartime image. (Warner, *Generals in Gray*)

Thomas Pleasant Dockery was born on December 18, 1833, in North Carolina, but his family soon moved to Tennessee, and from there to Arkansas. Dockery's father established a large plantation in Columbia County, and helped to bring the first railroad to the state. When the Civil War began, Colonel Dockery raised the 5th Arkansas State Troops, but by the time of the Battle of Wilson's Creek he commanded the 19th Arkansas Infantry. (There were two regiments to bear this number—the other was captured at Arkansas Post and after exchange fought in the Army of Tennessee.)

Following Pea Ridge, Dockery crossed the Mississippi River with Earl Van Dorn, and fought in the Battle of Corinth, where he took part in the engagement at Hatchie Bridge. He was with the 19th Arkansas Regiment, and commanded the 2d Brigade, Bowen's Division, in the Vicksburg Campaign. Dockery fought at Champion's Hill, and most of the brigade was captured at Big Black Bridge. When the brigade moved into the Vicksburg defenses, it acted as reserve until May 28, when it was ordered to take position in the trenches fronting the river below the city, to support the heavy batteries and be ready to meet any attempt to storm the city. The brigade occupied this position until June 2, when it moved to the works in the rear of the city to fill a gap in the lines. Dockery reported: "This was one of the most exposed positions on the line, the enemy's guns enfilading the works from right to left, and guns of heavy caliber played upon the enemy's works from the front." When Brigadier General Martin Green was killed on June 27, Dockery assumed command of the brigade, and surrendered it on July 4.

After the exchange, he was promoted to brigadier general on August 10, 1863, to rank immediately, and ordered to report to E. Kirby Smith, where he was to reassemble the scattered and furloughed troops on the west side of the Mississippi that had been in his brigade before the surrender of Vicksburg. Dockery was instructed to collect the Arkansas troops from Port Hudson and Vicksburg, as well as reorganize his own brigade. Smith wrote, however: "I fear difficulties not anticipated will be encountered by him in the discharge of this duty, and that his success will not equal the expectations of the Department."

Dockery took charge of a camp of instruction at Washington, Arkansas, and began forming a command from the men returning from prisoner exchanges as well as conscripts. On December 5, 1863, Smith warned Dockery that his brigade should be ready for active service immediately, and at the same time informed Theophilus H. Holmes, commanding the District of Arkansas, that the men would be placed at his disposal as infantry. By December 23, Dockery was commanding around nine hundred unarmed mounted infantry. During Union General Frederick Steele's Camden Campaign in the spring of 1864, Dockery fought in the Battle of Marks' Mill on April 25 and at Jenkins' Ferry on April 30.

In November 1864 the Reserve Corps in Arkansas was placed under him, but because of trouble in keeping the men in camps he was instructed to send many of them home. In February 1865 he was still in command of the Reserve Corps, and on June 3 read the men the terms of the May 26 surrender. After the war he became a civil engineer and moved to Houston, Texas. He was in New York City when he died on February 27, 1898. His body was sent to the residence of his two daughters for burial at Natchez, Mississippi.

Anne Bailey

Kerby, Robert L., *Kirby Smith's Confederacy* (New York, 1972).

✴ *George Pierce Doles* ✴

It was Colonel George P. Doles who sat for this summer 1862 image while he commanded the 4th Georgia Infantry. No portrait as a general has come to light. (Museum of the Confederacy, Richmond, Va.)

Born in Milledgeville, Georgia, on May 14, 1830, and despite limited formal education, Doles acquired in early life a considerable knowledge of military affairs. "He was a soldier by taste, inclination, and self-education," stated one biographer. At the age of sixteen, he unsuccessfully attempted to run away to participate in the Mexican War.

Upon reaching manhood, Doles entered the mercantile business in his hometown. He was a bookkeeper in 1860, with a modest personal estate valued at $500. His family at that time included a twenty-eight-year-old wife and an eight-month-old daughter, both named Sarah.

Doles' physical appearance betrayed his military interests. He was a tall, erect individual with a staunch carriage and a springy step. His personal traits, however, revealed a gentle and polite person of unusual modesty. "No man was ever more universally admired and loved in the community," claimed one writer.

George Doles' membership in the "Baldwin Blues," a local militia unit, undoubtedly helped to fuel his military ardor. Lieutenant (later Captain) Doles was the soul of the company and its leading spirit. As drillmaster, the young officer brought his nattily attired men to a state of high proficiency. The Blues' superior training won them high praise at numerous militia encampments held throughout the late 1850s.

Captain Doles' men responded immediately to Georgia's call for troops in late April 1861. The Blues mustered into Confederate service on May 1 as Company G, 4th Georgia Volunteers. Regimental elections held on May 9 in Portsmouth, Virginia, resulted in appointment of George Doles as colonel of the regiment.

The 4th Georgia remained at Hampton Roads for nearly a year starting in late May 1861. The regiment's twelve-month enlistment expired in April 1862. In response, Doles wrote to the secretary of war on April 8 requesting authority to "raise a command for the war to consist of ten or twelve companies of infantry, one of artillery and one of cavalry." The War Department's reply is unknown, but Doles stayed with the 4th and was enthusiastically reelected colonel.

Colonel Doles received his baptism of fire at King's Schoolhouse on June 25, 1862. Six days later the 4th Georgia participated in the futile assaults against Union artillery on Malvern Hill. A shell wounded Doles during the engagement, but he remained with his men until the fighting ceased.

Doles' regiment missed the Second Battle of Manassas, but fought hard at Antietam. When General Roswell S. Ripley, the 4th's brigade commander, received a wound during the struggle, command devolved upon Doles. His subsequent handling of the brigade during the battle displeased the 3d North Carolina's Colonel William L. DeRosset. Doles, preoccupied with his own regiment and upset over the death of the 4th's major, refused at one point to issue orders to the Tarheel. DeRosset, "disgusted beyond measure," left Doles and returned to his command.

Doles retained command of Ripley's Brigade following Antietam and received a brigadiership on November 1, 1862, effective that same day. General Doles' brigade remained inactive during the December battle at Fredericksburg, but fought in the center of the maelstrom the following spring at Chancellorsville. Doles' command, consisting of the 4th, 12th, 21st, and 44th Georgia regiments, formed a portion of the front line in "Stonewall" Jackson's famed flank attack on the Union right. It also played a prominent role in the decisive struggle on May 3. Doles' performance drew praise from his division commander, Robert E. Rodes, who cited Doles in a list of officers who performed "with great gallantry and efficiency." Doles' brigade suffered heavily in the campaign, and the general himself lost a bay horse valued at eight hundred dollars.

Doles repeated his stellar performance two months later at Gettysburg. The Georgian's brigade fought well on July 1, helping to break the Federal line directly north of the town. At one point in the fighting, Doles' powerful sorrel horse panicked and galloped toward Union lines. The general escaped certain death or capture when he tumbled off the mount within fifty yards of the Federals. (The obstinate horse apparently did not survive the fight.) Doles passed through the battle unscathed and once again earned the commendations of his division commander.

General Doles' men saw only limited action during the Bristoe and Mine Run campaigns in the late fall and winter of 1863. The following spring they fought obstinately in the tangled thickets of the Wilderness. At Spotsylvania on May 10, 1864, disaster befell Doles' regiments. That afternoon a column of Federals slammed into Doles' lines and overwhelmed the Georgians, capturing hundreds of prisoners.

Doles' actions during his brigade's debacle remain unclear. One Georgian wrote on May 11 that the general fell captive during the initial confusion. When counterattacks drove back the Federals, Doles fell to the ground, feigning injury or death. When his men reached him, the general arose and resumed command. (A postwar source claims that Doles served on a cannon crew when his command collapsed.)

Doles' superiors exonerated him from blame for the mishap, but the Richmond papers were apparently not so kind. According to the editors of the Milledgeville *Confederate Union*, this harsh criticism drove their native son to unduly expose himself in subsequent actions. The unfortunate result of this recklessness occurred on June 2, 1864, at Bethesda Church, just outside of Richmond. While he was charging the Federal lines, a Minié bullet pierced Doles through the left breast and instantly killed him. One source claimed that Doles was the brigade's only fatality that day.

Several staff officers accompanied Doles' remains back to Milledgeville. The body lay in state for a day in the representative chamber of the capitol building. Townspeople then solemnly escorted the general's body to Memory Hill Cemetery.

Keith Bohannon

Bonner, James C., *Milledgeville: Georgia's Antebellum Capital* (1985).

Northen, William J., *Men of Mark in Georgia* (1974).

Thomas, Henry W., *History of the Doles-Cook Brigade* (Atlanta, 1903).

✷ *Daniel Smith Donelson* ✷

Born in Sumner County, Tennessee, on June 23, 1801, Donelson was still a child when his father died. He and his younger brother, Andrew Jackson Donelson, had their early education provided by their father's law partner and brother-in-law, General (and future president) Andrew Jackson. Daniel attended Dr. Priestley's boarding school in Nashville prior to an appointment to the United States Military Academy, which Jackson secured for both Daniel and his brother. Daniel entered West Point in 1821 and finished fifth out of the thirty-seven graduates in the class of 1825. Commissioned a 2d lieutenant in the 3d Artillery on July 1 of that year, he resigned on January 22, 1826, having served less than seven months.

Returning to Sumner County, Tennessee, Donelson engaged in planting. Financially successful from the outset, Donelson also served in the Tennessee Militia, holding the rank of major from 1827 until his promotion to brigadier general in 1829. In 1830 he married Margaret Branch, daughter of North Carolina governor John Branch, who later became the governor of Florida and Andrew Jackson's secretary of war. The Donelsons had eleven children; the two oldest sons served in the Confederate Army, while the fourth and youngest son married the niece of General John Bell Hood.

In 1834 Donelson resigned his commission in the militia and left his plantation in Tennessee for the Florida Territory, where he engaged in planting until 1836. Returning to Sumner County, he resumed planting

and entered politics. A Democrat, he served in the Tennessee legislature from 1841 to 1843. A powerful political figure in his state during the 1850s, he fervently attacked the Know-Nothings. Returning to the state legislature in 1855, he served as speaker until Tennessee seceded in 1861, an action he ardently supported, although his brother, then a prominent planter in Memphis, adhered to the Union.

A colonel in the militia at the time of secession, he was immediately appointed adjutant general of state troops upon Tennessee's withdrawal from the Union, and soon thereafter promoted to brigadier general. Governor Isham G. Harris then ordered him to select positions along the Cumberland and Tennessee rivers suitable for military fortifications. Unable to find any appropriate locations, Donelson finally settled on two sites and commenced erecting earthworks. The fort on the Cumberland was named for Donelson, while that on the Tennessee was named in honor of Tennessee Senator Gustavus A. Henry. Nature's failure to provide better topographical features for Donelson to work with was a prime factor in the Union's first major victory of the war.

Having been appointed a brigadier general in the Confederate Army on July 9, 1861, effective that same date, Donelson soon received orders to proceed to

The uniform on General Donelson shows signs of being an artist's addition. Certainly the collar insignia, suggesting a lieutenant colonel or full colonel, depicts ranks he never held, having been directly commissioned a brigadier in 1851. (Museum of the Confederacy, Richmond, Va.)

western Virginia. There he commanded a brigade under Brigadier General William W. Loring and participated in the Cheat Mountain Campaign. Early in 1862 Donelson accompanied General Robert E. Lee to Charleston, South Carolina.

Donelson departed Charleston in June for Tupelo, Mississippi, where he assisted General Braxton Bragg in rebuilding his army, which had been demoralized by its defeat at Shiloh and abandonment of Corinth. Given command of a brigade of Tennesseans, he participated in Bragg's invasion of Kentucky that fall and fought in the Battle of Perryville.

On December 31, 1862, at Murfreesboro, the sixty-one-year-old finally had an opportunity to demonstrate his military capabilities. Following the repulse of Confederate Brigadier General James R. Chalmers' brigade upon the "dense cedar brake," Donelson determined to assault the same position with his own brigade, though from a slightly different angle. His corps commander, Lieutenant General Leonidas Polk, reported:

"The brigade of General Donelson…moved with steady step upon the enemy's position and attacked it with great energy. The slaughter was terrific on both sides.

"In this charge—which resulted in breaking the enemy's line at every point except the extreme left, and driving him as every other part of his line attacked had been driven—Donelson reports the capture of 11 guns and about 1,000 prisoners….

"There was no instance of more distinguished bravery exhibited during this battle than was shown by the command of General Donelson. In the charge which it made it was brought directly under the fire of several batteries, strongly posted and supported, which it assaulted with eager resolution."

Polk concluded that the victory won by Donelson would have been secured had the four brigades of Major General John C. Breckinridge arrived sooner to relieve the brigadier's exhausted Tennesseans and press the attack—a statement which incensed Bragg, who was responsible for delaying Breckinridge's movement to support Polk.

Illness compelled Donelson's removal from active field duty, and on January 17, 1863, he was assigned to command the Department of East Tennessee. Succeeding Lieutenant General Edmund Kirby Smith, Donelson had five brigades in addition to scattered units under his command with which to maintain control of Cumberland Gap and to keep the railroad operating between Chattanooga and Virginia.

Donelson died on April 17, 1863. Although most authorities agree on the date of death, the circumstances and location vary, from natural causes to assassination, and from Arkansas to East Tennessee. On April 22 General Bragg proclaimed in general orders:

"…the death of Brig.-Gen D. S. Donelson. He died in the department of East Tennessee, which he had commanded. The regret with which his death is announced will be felt by the army and his country. He was an educated soldier, of great purity of character, singleness of purpose, and goodness of heart. Conspicuous for gallantry on the field, after the excitement had passed he was foremost in providing for the wants of his command, and devoted to the sick and wounded. His comrades in this army, and those who served under his orders, will long remember his deeds and virtues."

Considering Bragg's announcement, it is likely that Donelson died in East Tennessee, probably at Montvale Springs. Donelson's medical condition and Bragg's failure to mention specifics would indicate that he died of natural causes.

Although he had been a department commander, Donelson's death was unknown to Confederate authorities in Richmond for some time. On April 22, the same day Bragg announced the death of "Brigadier General" Donelson, the War Department promoted him to major general, to rank from January 17, 1863. He is buried in the Presbyterian Cemetery in Hendersonville, Tennessee.

Lawrence L. Hewitt

Heitman, Francis B., *Historical Register and Dictionary of the United States Army, From its Organization, September 29, 1789, to March 2, 1903*, Vol. I (Washington, 1903).

Porter, James D., *Tennessee*, Vol. VIII in Evans, *Confederate Military History*.

⋆ *Thomas Fenwick Drayton* ⋆

General Drayton probably sat for this portrait during the first two years of the war, before assignment to the Trans-Mississippi, where photographers were scarce. (U.S. Army Military History Institute, Carlisle, Pa.)

Like more than a few other future Confederate generals, Thomas F. Drayton owed his commission more to a youthful friendship with President Jefferson Davis than to any demonstrated military acumen. He was born in South Carolina, quite probably in or near Charleston, on August 24, 1808, the son of William Drayton, a distinguished officer in the United States Army, congressman, and planter, whose magnificent plantation home, "Drayton Hall," remains one of the show places of the Old South. Young Thomas Drayton, like his brother Percival, showed an early interest in life in uniform, and his father's influence easily gained him an appointment to the U.S. Military Academy in 1824. Here he made an early friendship with a young cadet from Mississippi, Jefferson Davis, and the two remained close for years. Drayton graduated along with Davis in 1828, ranking an unimpressive twenty-eighth out of a class of thirty-three, and received his brevet commission as second lieutenant and assignment to the 6th Infantry. Perhaps evidencing a disinterest in the actuality of military life that accounted for his poor performance at West Point, Drayton only remained in uniform for eight years, chiefly seeing duty at eastern garrisons.

In 1836 he returned to Drayton Hall plantation, near Charleston, and there engaged in farming off and on until the outbreak of war. At the same time he took an active role in local and state affairs, serving as a militia captain; as a state senator, 1853–1861; and on state militia boards. He also worked as a civil engineer in Kentucky, Ohio, and South Carolina briefly, and spent three years as president of the Charleston & Savannah Railroad, 1853–56.

The outbreak of the war divided the Drayton brothers. Percival, who had become a career officer in the Navy, remained with the Union in spite of his South Carolina nativity. Thomas, however, offered his services to the Confederacy, though not in the first rush of enthusiastic enlistments. Nevertheless, his old friend President Davis appointed him brigadier general on September 25, 1861, effective immediately, and Drayton accepted the appointment eight days later. The Senate confirmed the commission on December 13.

By the time Drayton's commission was confirmed, he had already become branded as something of a loser. His first assignment was command of the defenses of Port Royal Sound in South Carolina, and it became his lot to be the object of the first serious Yankee thrust to gain a foothold on the Confederate Atlantic coastline. On November 7, 1861, a Federal fleet appeared off Forts Beauregard and Walker, and after a heavy bombardment, Drayton was forced to withdraw. One of the ironies of the event is that his brother, Percival, commanded one of the attacking Union ships and actually took his vessel closer in toward the forts, and fired more heavily, than any other vessel, fearing that to do otherwise might open him to charges of being reluctant to fire on his own brother.

Drayton held other district commands in South Carolina through the spring of 1862 and was then given command of a brigade and sent to Virginia to join with a Georgia brigade in forming D. R. Jones' Division in Longstreet's wing of the Army of Northern Virginia. Drayton's was a troubled brigade from the start, in part perhaps because he had two Georgia regiments, the 50th and 51st, making it one of only four mixed brigades in Longstreet's command. Furthermore, Drayton's handling of the brigade in action seems to have impressed no one. He saw action first at Thoroughfare Gap on August 28 and thereafter was at Second Manassas, in which campaign his brigade incurred the smallest losses of any brigade in the army. His division commander, Jones, hinted rather openly in his report of the campaign that Drayton was slow, and perhaps even lacking in intelligence.

Drayton went on to the engagements at South Mountain and Antietam and again did not emerge with compliments from his commanders. This time he saw much heavier action, his brigade suffering the fifth highest rate of casualties for the campaign. Drayton was posted on the far right of Lee's line at Antietam and he held his ground during the early part of the fight, but later his brigade gave way in the face of Yankee attacks. This all but ended Drayton's active field service; owing to a lack of enthusiastic support from his commanders—and open criticism from some—he was sidetracked to other duty. His regiments were reassigned to other brigades, and he himself went on court-martial duty. In 1863 the War Department sent him to the Trans-Mississippi, apparently at the suggestion of Lee, who felt kindly towards the South Carolinian and hoped that "some duty may be found for him…which he may be able to perform." Drayton arrived in Little Rock, Arkansas, in August 1863 and spent the rest of the war in that theater. At first he commanded a brigade at Shreveport, but in March 1864, with the Red River Campaign about to open, he was relieved by department commander Kirby Smith and sent to a noncombatant post drilling troops in Texas, and obviously to prevent him from commanding soldiers in the field. In May he took command of two districts headquartered at Columbus, and the following month took command of the Western Sub-District of Texas, comprising territory west of the Colorado River. Most of these positions were essentially banishment from active field command for Drayton (and for many other failed commanders), though by year's end he did have a command of about one thousand in southwestern Texas. The end of the war found him sitting on a court of inquiry looking into the conduct of Sterling Price's Missouri Campaign of the year before.

Drayton first went to Georgia after the war, even though Drayton Hall, in South Carolina, had survived the ravages of the conflict. He farmed in Dolly County until 1872, then took the presidency of the South Carolina Immigrant Society, in addition acting as an insurance agent briefly in Charlotte, North Carolina. He died on February 18, 1891, in Florence, South Carolina, but was returned to Charlotte for burial.

Robert E. Lee passed the verdict on Drayton. Writing late in 1862 of how the South Carolinian's brigade had been "a source of delay and embarrassment from the time the army left Richmond," he complained of its sloth at Second Manassas, its rout at Antietam, and its habitual lack of discipline. Drayton could not keep it organized, and was a cause of complaint from Generals Jones, McLaws, and even Longstreet. "He is a gentleman, and in his own person a soldier," said Lee, "but seems to lack the capacity to command."

William C. Davis

Capers, Ellison, *South Carolina*, Vol. V in Evans, *Confederate Military History*.

✯ *Dudley McIver DuBose* ✯

No uniformed image of DuBose has been found to date, and this portrait is of undoubted postwar origin. (Warner, *Generals in Gray*)

Born October 28, 1834, in Shelby County, Tennessee, DuBose attended the University of Mississippi and then graduated from Lebanon Law School in Tennessee and was admitted to the bar in 1857. By 1860 he had relocated to Augusta, Georgia, where he met and married a daughter of United States Senator Robert Toombs.

When the Civil War began, DuBose was appointed a lieutenant in the 15th Georgia but eventually joined the staff of his father-in-law, rising to the rank of captain. He served under Toombs throughout the early campaigns of 1862. In January 1863 he accepted the colonelcy of the 15th Georgia in the brigade of Henry Benning in John Hood's Division. His regiment participated in James Longstreet's Suffolk Campaign April–May 1863 before rejoining the Army of Northern Virginia for the Gettysburg Campaign.

On the afternoon of July 3, 1863, at Gettysburg, Hood's and Lafayette McLaws' divisions attacked the Union line in the Peach Orchard–Little Round Top area. For three hours the opponents engaged in some of the fiercest combat of the war. Benning's brigade fought among the rocks and woods of Devil's Den. In his report Benning praised DuBose, writing: "Colonel DuBose not only drove back the enemy's line, but repulsed repeated attacks made to recover it, taking over 100 prisoners."

On July 3 the two divisions maintained their lines while other Confederate units assailed the Union center. Late in the afternoon, Hood's troops were pulled back, but because of a mistake in orders, DuBose's regiment was left isolated. Two Federal brigades charged the Georgians, inflicting heavy casualties. In

Benning's words, DuBose "was fortunate to escape at all. His escape is high evidence both of his skill and courage." The regiment lost over half its members during the two days of combat.

DuBose suffered a wound in the Battle of Chickamauga in September but retained his command, participating in the fall and winter operations around Chattanooga and Knoxville, Tennessee. Ambitious and capable, DuBose was a demanding officer who earned the respect of his men.

By the spring of 1864 Longstreet's two divisions had returned to Virginia. Charles Field now led Hood's Division, and in the Battle of the Wilderness Benning fell wounded. DuBose assumed temporary command of the brigade, leading it with skill and valor in the fighting at Spotsylvania and Cold Harbor. During Ulysses S. Grant's so-called Fifth Offensive against the Richmond-Petersburg works September 29–October 2, DuBose continued to prove his worth as a brigade commander.

On December 5, 1864, DuBose was promoted to brigadier general, to rank from November 16, and assigned a brigade in the division of Joseph Kershaw. His command consisted of the 16th, 18th, and 24th Georgia and the 3d Georgia Battalion. During the Confederate retreat from Petersburg in April 1865, DuBose was captured in the debacle at Sayler's Creek on the 6th. Union authorities placed him along with other captive officers in Fort Warren in Boston. He was finally released in July.

DuBose opened a law office in Washington, Georgia, after the war. He served one term, 1871–73, in the United States House of Representatives. Resuming his profession, he lived only ten more years, dying at the age of forty-eight on March 2, 1883. He was buried in Rest Haven Cemetery in Washington.

Jeffry D. Wert

Pfanz, Henry W., *Gettysburg: The Second Day* (Chapel Hill, 1987).
Sommers, Richard J., *Richmond Redeemed: The Siege At Petersburg* (New York, 1981).

✶ *Basil Wilson Duke* ✶

It is possible that this portrait of Basil Duke was made at Fort Delaware by Philadelphia photographer J.L. Gihon during Duke's captivity. If so, then it was made in May 1864. (Museum of the Confederacy, Richmond, Va.)

Duke was born in Scott County, Kentucky, on May 28, 1838. The son of a naval officer, Duke was well educated at Centre College and Transylvania University Law School. After being admitted to the bar in 1858, he moved to St. Louis to set up his practice. There in 1861 Duke became actively involved in a prosecessionist organization known as the Minute Men. Appointed chairman of the group's military committee, he had several tense clashes with the Unionist Wide Awakes. In March Governor Claiborne Jackson appointed Duke to the St. Louis Board of Police Commissioners and in April sent him to meet Jefferson Davis in Montgomery to try and secure a cannon for the secessionist militia. The mission was a success, but Duke was indicted for treason by Federal authorities in Missouri because of his activities.

In June 1861 Duke left Missouri and returned to Kentucky, where he married Henrietta Hunt Morgan, sister of famed Confederate cavalry raider John Hunt Morgan. After the wedding Duke slipped into northern Arkansas and served as a volunteer aide to Colonel Thomas C. Hindman. He also volunteered for scouting missions for William Hardee and served briefly with M. Jeff Thompson. Returning to Kentucky, Duke tried to raise his own command but failed because, he claimed, every Kentuckian wanted to be a captain. He finally joined brother-in-law John Hunt Morgan's Lexington Rifles as a private, but was soon elected 2d lieutenant. For several months Morgan's men performed scouting duty in southern Kentucky. During this time Duke displayed his considerable skill in training and drilling soldiers.

Duke's first real battle occurred at Shiloh. By then the famed 2d Kentucky Cavalry was organized with Morgan serving as colonel and Duke lieutenant colonel. At Shiloh Morgan commanded a brigade of cavalry on the Confederate left flank and attacked the Yankees on April 6. In the assault Duke was badly wounded in both shoulders and was put out of action for some time. Still, his bravery and constant cheerfulness inspired his men. Although small in stature, weighing only 130 pounds, Duke was greatly admired. One of his men said he was "the coolest and always most self-possessed officer that we encountered during the war."

In July 1862 Morgan and Duke launched the first of several raids that made them the terror of Union commanders. Slashing through Kentucky, the small force destroyed valuable supplies and railroads, and captured seventeen towns and twelve thousand prisoners. In addition, three hundred new recruits joined Morgan's cavalry. In this and other raids Duke earned the reputation of being the mastermind behind Morgan's successes. General Edmund Kirby Smith wrote Davis, "I know him to be the man of that command. He is said by all to do all the drilling, planning and fighting which has gained his regiment such *eclat*." During the war Braxton Bragg echoed Kirby Smith by referring to Duke as "the man of Morgan's regiment." Even Union General Ambrose Burnside would agree when he wrote that Duke "has been the managing man of all Morgan's raids."

When Bragg and Kirby Smith invaded Kentucky in the autumn of 1862, Duke took six hundred of Morgan's cavalry to observe Federal activities near Cincinnati. Duke hoped to cross the Ohio River upstream from Cincinnati at Augusta, Kentucky, but found a tenacious militia force blocking his way. In savage street fighting, Duke ordered houses burned if the enemy fired from them. After much destruction and the loss of thirty-nine men, Duke decided not to force the crossing and withdrew with several hundred prisoners. Rejoining Morgan, Duke helped cover Bragg's retreat from Perryville—a retreat he bitterly opposed. He and Morgan then again grabbed headlines by circling around the Federal Army, spreading fear and destruction before returning to Tennessee in November.

Duke next accompanied Morgan and twenty-two hundred men on a raid against Hartsville, Tennessee. On December 8, Duke led a decisive attack against the Yankee defenders and overwhelmed them. At a loss of 139 men, the raiders captured two thousand prisoners and burned the enemy's supplies. Morgan praised Duke's role in the fight, saying he was "as he always has been, 'the right man in the right place.' Wise in counsel, gallant in the field, his services have ever been invaluable to me."

Shortly after the Hartsville raid, Morgan was promoted to brigadier general and Duke to colonel of the 2d Kentucky Cavalry, with command of Morgan's 1st Brigade. Without a respite, the cavalry launched a "Christmas raid" to cut the supply line of Union General William Rosecrans. After burning a railroad bridge at Elizabethtown, Kentucky, Duke was commanding the rear guard in a hot fight at Rolling Fork River on December 29 when he was hit behind the ear by shrapnel. Falling from his horse, Duke was carried across the river to safety but was out of action for two months.

Morgan's and Duke's string of successful raids ended in the summer of 1863. With approximately twenty-five hundred men, they rode into Kentucky in July and promptly disobeyed orders by crossing the Ohio River. Determined to capture the horsemen, the Union regulars, militia, and Home Guards pursued and closed in on them. The raid became a nightmare of ambushes, skirmishes, and constant riding. Duke claimed the men rode twenty-one hours a day and often fell asleep in their saddles. Finally on July 19, Union forces caught the raiders at Buffington Island on the Ohio River. Duke held them at bay while Morgan escaped with about one thousand men. Then, exhausted and out of ammunition, Duke surrendered with seven hundred troopers. Morgan was captured soon afterwards. For the next year, Duke was held at such prisons as Johnson's Island, the Ohio penitentiary, Camp Chase, and Fort Delaware. He even spent several weeks aboard a prison ship before being exchanged in the summer of 1864.

After Morgan's death, Duke was promoted to brigadier general on September 15, 1864, to rank from September 15, and was given command of Morgan's cavalry. For the next two months Duke's brigade skirmished in East Tennessee and then moved into southwest Virginia to protect the salt and lead mines there. Serving under General John C. Vaughn, Duke saw brutal service during December when Yankee raiders rode through the area. At Wytheville he held off Federal raiders with only 220 men for an entire day and managed to kill 187 of the enemy. When the Yankees raided Saltville, Duke chased them through bitterly cold weather that killed men and mounts. He later claimed his men counted two hundred dead horses on a one-mile stretch of road. After the Union raid, forage was so scarce that Duke's horses were sent to North Carolina for the winter and his proud cavalry served as infantry.

When Robert E. Lee surrendered in April 1865, Duke's and Vaughn's brigades were mounted on mules and ordered to join Johnston's army in North Carolina. After finally retrieving their horses, the cavalry linked up with the fleeing Confederate government and Duke helped escort President Davis to Washington, Georgia. For part of the journey Duke was responsible for guarding the remaining gold in the Confederate treasury—a duty that made him understandably nervous. Duke's final mission was to lead two hundred men away from the Davis party in an attempt to draw off the pursuing Federals. He did so and finally surrendered at Augusta, Georgia.

Following the war, Duke became a model citizen and a leading moderate who counseled reconciliation. He resumed his law practice in Louisville, Kentucky, and was elected to the Kentucky legislature in 1869. Duke also found the time to write two popular accounts of the war and became the editor of *Southern Bivouac*, a Confederate veterans' magazine. His last tie to the Civil War was when he served as a commissioner for the Shiloh National Military Park. Duke died in New York City on September 16, 1916, and is buried in Lexington, Kentucky.

Terry L. Jones

Duke, Basil W., *History of Morgan's Cavalry* (New York, 1906).

Duke, Basil W., *Reminiscences of General Basil W. Duke, C.S.A.* (New York, 1911).

Gihon certainly made this image at Fort Delaware, showing Duke standing second from the right, in May 1864. (Albert Shaw Collection, Courtesy of Mr. and Mrs. Bruce English, U.S. Army Military History Institute, Carlisle, Pa.)

☆ *Johnson Kelly Duncan* ☆

Duncan was born on March 19, 1827, in York, Pennsylvania. Little is known of his early life except that he attended West Point and graduated fifth in the class of 1849. Assigned to the 2d Artillery, Duncan fought the Seminoles in Florida 1849–50. After the Indian War he served on garrison duty in Maine and 1853–54 helped to explore and map a railroad route for the Northern Pacific Railroad across the rugged northwest. On January 31, 1855, 1st Lieutenant Duncan of the 3d Artillery resigned his commission in order to accept the position of superintendent of government construction for New Orleans.

For the next six years Duncan served as a civil engineer, surveyor, and architect in the South's largest city. By 1861 he had risen to the post of chief engineer for the Louisiana Board of Public Works. When the Civil War began, Duncan chose to support his adopted state. Commissioned a colonel of artillery by Jefferson Davis, he was put in temporary command of the fortifications on Ship Island in September 1861. His experienced eye revealed the island to be a poor defensive position, and Duncan recommended it be abandoned for a stronger one. His recommendation was acted upon, and Duncan quickly supervised the evacuation of men and material.

Major General Mansfield Lovell, commander of the New Orleans area, elevated Duncan to command the coastal defenses of the city. In October Lovell recommended to Davis that Duncan be promoted to

brigadier general. Lovell wrote that Duncan had "rendered most efficient service, with a zeal, untiring industry, and ability which entitle him to your consideration." Lovell stated that the five thousand men on the coastal defensive line needed a general grade officer in command, and Duncan's familiarity with artillery and the coast made him a logical choice. Davis accepted the recommendation, and on January 7, 1862, Duncan received his promotion, effective immediately.

Duncan's main defense relied on Forts Jackson and St. Philip lying seventy-five miles downstream from New Orleans. In March 1862 a large Union flotilla under David Farragut appeared at the mouth of the Mississippi River to attack the Confederate forts and capture New Orleans. On March 28 Duncan arrived at Fort Jackson to supervise the defense. Fort Jackson, the stronger of the two, was located on the west bank, with Fort St. Philip across the river just upstream. A boom was constructed across the river by chaining schooners together. Chains and riggings were trailed behind the boats to foul the Yankees' propellers. Placed across the river three hundred yards below Fort Jackson, this barrier was expected to keep the Union fleet from running past the forts. Unfortunately, a storm had torn a gap through it near Fort Jackson. Duncan had about five hundred men and eighty guns

---

This engraving of General Duncan is all that has been found thus far. (Museum of the Confederacy, Richmond, Va.)

to man the fort, but most of his guns were too light to be very effective. In addition, the fort was badly flooded by high water and the Confederate powder proved to be defective. Duncan requested larger guns but received little help from the government. The only material aid he received was a River Fleet consisting of nine small gunboats. The River Fleet stood by upstream with dozens of fire rafts filled with pine knots. The rafts were supposed to light up the river at night and hopefully set fire to the Yankees' ships. Unfortunately, the River Fleet and fire rafts were under the Confederate Navy's command. During the siege Duncan was repeatedly foiled in his attempts to get the Navy to cooperate with his defense.

On Good Friday morning, April 18, 1862, Captain David Porter's mortar boats began raining shells down upon the forts. Since Fort Jackson was the nearest and most powerful of the two, almost all of the shells were dropped on it. For days the fort was continually battered, and much of it was consumed by fires. Duncan repeatedly asked the Confederate Navy to send down fire rafts, but his requests were frequently ignored or the rafts were improperly released and harmlessly ran ashore to burn themselves out. On April 21 the garrison was encouraged by the arrival of the *Louisiana*, a massive ironclad from New Orleans. Since the engines were inoperable, it was decided to use the ship as a floating battery. Duncan desperately tried to get it placed below the boom in order to be in position to fire broadsides into the enemy vessels as they slowed down at the barrier. But the Navy feared the high angle mortar fire would penetrate the *Louisiana*'s thin top deck and refused. Instead it was placed upstream near Fort St. Philip.

In the predawn hours of April 24 Farragut's fleet ran past the forts. Duncan expected such an attempt and urgently requested that fire rafts be sent down the river regularly to light it up. Apparently none were sent. As a result, the Yankees steamed up through a hole in the boom, raked the forts with broadsides, and passed by. The River Fleet was either destroyed or retreated, and New Orleans fell within days. An aide to Duncan declared, "It was the opinion of everyone with in [sic] the Fort, that had Gen. Duncan's request been complied with...not one of the enemy's vessels would have succeeded in passing." Duncan also blamed the Navy's lack of cooperation for the passage. He wrote of the River Fleet, "Unable to govern themselves, and unwilling to be governed by others,

their almost total want of system, vigalence [sic], and discipline, rendered them nearly useless and helpless when the enemy finally dashed upon them." The Navy's failure to send down fire rafts, Duncan claimed, was "criminal negligence."

On April 27 Porter demanded that Duncan surrender the forts, but he declined, saying he would defend them "so long as his men would stand by him." But his men did not. Later in the day most of the Fort Jackson garrison mutinied. Under the impression that Duncan intended to fight until provisions ran out and then blow up the men and fort, they disarmed the loyal soldiers, left the fort, and surrendered to Porter. With no hope left, Duncan then surrendered the remaining men on April 28. During the surrender, the crew of the *Louisiana* blew up the ship rather than let it fall into enemy hands. During the siege several thousand two-hundred-pound shells exploded within Fort Jackson, but they inflicted surprisingly few casualties. Duncan's entire force lost only eleven dead and thirty-seven wounded.

Duncan was not blamed for the disaster. The people of New Orleans welcomed him as a hero and placed blame on the Navy and Lovell. Duncan was quickly exchanged and was given command of a brigade of infantry in Leonidas Polk's reserve division. He served in the 1862 invasion of Kentucky but saw little action. In October he briefly commanded Polk's reserve division but was appointed Braxton Bragg's chief of staff on November 20, 1862. Illness prevented Duncan from ever assuming his duties, and he died of fever in Knoxville, Tennessee, on December 18, 1862. He is buried in the McGavock Cemetery in Franklin, Tennessee.

Terry L. Jones

Jones, Terry L., ed., *The Civil War Memoirs of Capt. William J. Seymour: Reminiscences of a Louisiana Tiger* (Baton Rouge, 1991).

✶ *John Dunovant* ✶

Born in Chester, South Carolina, on March 5, 1825, Dunovant served as sergeant in the Palmetto Regiment from 1846 to 1847, and captain of Company A, 10th U.S. Infantry Regiment from 1855 to 1860. He was "saturated with the war fever," according to a fellow captain, Henry Heth. An ardent secessionist, Dunovant resigned on December 20, 1860.

Commissioned major of the 1st South Carolina Regular Infantry Regiment on January 19, 1861, he became colonel of that regiment. Disgrace soon followed, due partly to his drunkenness and partly to the hostility of his superiors, who ironically were two of the most notorious drunkards in the Confederate Army—Roswell Ripley and Nathan G. Evans. Ripley, who reportedly resented Dunovant, transferred him from Sullivan's Island to Stono River in May of 1862.

There during the Secessionville Campaign, Evans directed Dunovant to storm Legareville on June 9. However, the colonel—allegedly "lying drunk by the roadside," in full view of his officers and men—was too inebriated to attack. He was arrested, court-martialed in August, and convicted. War Department General Order 83, November 8, 1862, quoted Jefferson Davis' approval of the verdict: "The offense is of too grave a character to be overlooked in an officer of such high rank and is aggravated by the circumstances under which it was committed. Col. Dunovant will be dismissed from the service."

The sentence surprised the court. Its members—Johnson Hagood, Ambrosio Gonzales, and James McCullough—petitioned for Dunovant's restoration. The disgraced officer's former colonel, Richard H. Anderson, and his influential brother, General Richard Dunovant, sent separate appeals for his reprieve. Not until mid-1863 did Davis relent. He would not restore Dunovant to the Regulars but did appoint him colonel of the 5th South Carolina Cavalry Regiment on July 25, 1863. Throughout the Siege of Charleston that summer and fall, Dunovant commanded the battalion of his regiment on James Island.

Standing siege was not the best use for cavalry when graver dangers threatened the Confederacy in 1864. Accordingly, on March 18, the 5th was ordered to Virginia, but footdragging by the Charleston headquarters and the unprepared condition of the regiment—numerically full but poorly equipped—delayed its departure. Not until April 25 did the 5th leave Columbia for Richmond, the troopers by train and the horses by road. Before the animals arrived, Dunovant's men served as infantry in the Bermuda Hundred Campaign, patrolling flanks at First Ware Bottom Church and Second Drewry's Bluff and pursuing to Bermuda Hundred.

With Richmond saved, Dunovant's regiment reinforced the Army of Northern Virginia. Now mounted, it participated in Fitzhugh Lee's repulse at Fort Pocahontas. Four days later the 5th fought in Wade Hampton's great cavalry battle with Philip Sheridan at Haw's Shop. Because the new brigadier, Matthew C. Butler, had not yet assumed command, senior colonel Dunovant evidently led both the 4th and 5th South Carolina Cavalry Regiments on May 28. Their full ranks, redoubtable Enfield rifles, and ardent determination made his Carolinians formidable fighters that

---

John Dunovant may not have left behind any uniformed portraits. This one is almost certainly prewar. (*Confederate Veteran*, XVI, April 1908)

day—almost too steadfast, for they did not retreat when ordered and were nearly trapped. In this battle Dunovant was shot through the left hand.

Hospitalized until July 8, he missed the 5th's many battles from May 30 to June 29. Even after returning to the front, he was too unhealthy to assume command at First Gravelly Run or Lee's Mill, and his outfit was not engaged at Second Reams' Station.

In those August affairs, Dunovant held higher office. Hampton recommended him for brigadier general on July 18. The request was seconded not only by Butler but also by the other two cavalry division commanders and by Anderson, Heth, Joseph B. Kershaw, and A. P. Hill. A week later R. E. Lee commented, "I wish there was a brigade of cavalry to which he could be assigned." President Davis suggested Dunovant to command the Tramp Brigade, ironically Evans' old infantry. Dunovant, however, remained with mounted troops. The elevation of Hampton and Butler in August created a vacancy. On August 22 Dunovant was promoted to brigadier general, to rank immediately, and assigned to command the brigade containing the 4th, 5th, and 6th South Carolina Cavalry Regiments.

His first combat with the brigade was Poplar Spring Church. At McDowell's Farm on September 29 he helped drive the Yankees, but at Armstrong's Hill on September 30 he was surprised and stampeded, and his adjutant (Butler's cousin) was captured. That humiliation, on top of his 1862 disgrace, may have made him rash for redemption in the Vaughn Road fighting on October 1.

"Dunovant seemed to be very impatient," recalled his courier, "and when Butler gave him this order [for a flank attack] he saluted and replied, 'Oh, General, let me charge 'em, we've got 'em going and let us keep 'em going.' [The brigadier kept urging a frontal assault until Butler angrily consented.] Instantly Dunovant wheeled his horse, and his voice rang out...'Forward, charge!'...Dunovant rushed out into the road and down to the creek, shouting to his men to charge, and just as he reached the creek, I saw him fall from his horse." Shot through the heart, Dunovant died instantly. Horrified, his brigade was repulsed. He is buried near Chester, South Carolina.

Hampton promptly termed Dunovant "admirable...zealous in the performance of...duties." Thirty years later, in the afterglow of the Lost Cause, Butler called him "the beau ideal of a soldier, a knightly, chivalric gentleman,

thorough in...discipline and order, exacting, but always just, guarding...the interests of his soldiers, demanding of all...the full measure of their duty...his command was always ready to respond promptly to his orders. He was...a model of promptness and precision, both in obeying and executing orders. [He was exceptional] in the organization, discipline, and command of troops in battle."

Actually Dunovant commanded troops in heavy fighting only four days of the entire war, three of them defeats. It is difficult reconciling Butler's recollection with the reality of Dunovant lying drunk on the Legareville Road and lying dead after a foolhardy frontal foray on the Vaughn Road. Brave the brigadier unquestionably was, but his bravery was the rashness of irresponsibility.

Richard J. Sommers

Brooks, Ulysses R., *Butler and His Cavalry in the War of Secession* (Columbia, 1909).

Dunovant, Adelia A., "Gen. John Dunovant, Houston, Tex.," *Confederate Veteran*, Vol. XVI: 183–184, 1908.

Wells, Edward L., *Hampton and His Cavalry in '64* (Richmond, 1899).

⋆ *Jubal Anderson Early* ⋆

The cantankerous old Jubal A. Early seems to have been informal about uniform, as about everything else. Only his military vest and the star on his hat suggest this to be a wartime uniformed view. (William Turner Collection)

Early was born near Rocky Mount, Franklin County, Virginia, on November 3, 1816. Reared in comfortable circumstances and educated at the best local schools, he secured an appointment to West Point and graduated eighteenth in the class of 1837. As a newly commissioned 2d lieutenant in the 3d Artillery he campaigned against the Seminoles during 1837 and 1838, after which he accompanied his unit to Ross' Landing (now Chattanooga), Tennessee. "It had not been my purpose to remain permanently in the army," Early later explained, and he resigned effective July 31, 1878, to study law in Franklin County. Admitted to the bar in 1840, he practiced law for the next two decades, winning election as a Whig to the lower house of the Virginia legislature for a single term, 1841–42, and serving as commonwealth's attorney for Franklin County between 1842 and 1852. The war with Mexico temporarily interrupted Early's civilian pursuits. Commissioned a major in the 1st Virginia Regiment on December 22, 1846, he performed garrison duty with Zachary Taylor's army in northern Mexico before being mustered out on August 3, 1848.

The crisis of 1860–61 found Early a successful lawyer in Franklin County. As a delegate to the Virginia state convention in 1861, he voted against the ordinance of secession. "The adoption of that ordinance wrung from me bitter tears of grief," Early wrote, "but I at once recognized my duty to abide by the decision of my native State, and to defend her soil against invasion." Offering his services to Governor John Letcher on May 1, he was commissioned a colonel of Virginia state troops and soon took command of the 24th Virginia Infantry at Lynchburg.

Over the next four years, Early compiled one of the finest combat records in the Army of Northern Virginia and earned a reputation as one of its great characters. Nearly six feet tall and weighing about 170 pounds, he appeared older than his years because painful arthritis caused a pronounced stoop. Constant pain may have contributed to what one staff officer called a "snarling, raspy disposition." Another witness recalled that his "wit was quick, his satire biting, his expressions vigorous, and he was interestingly lurid and picturesque." His men called him "Old Jube" or "Old Jubilee"; R. E. Lee, who developed a true fondness for his prickly lieutenant, referred to him affectionately as "my bad old man."

Early commanded a brigade at First Manassas, where his soldiers played a crucial role late in the day.

Promoted brigadier general on August 28, 1861 (to rank from July 21, 1861), he suffered a severe wound on May 5, 1862, at the Battle of Williamsburg but recovered in time to fight at Malvern Hill. He subsequently led a brigade in Richard S. Ewell's division of "Stonewall" Jackson's command during the campaigns of Second Manassas and Antietam. Both Lee and Jackson praised his conduct in those operations, for a portion of which he commanded Ewell's Division. Lee believed that his subordinate's record justified advancement (Early made no secret of his desire for promotion); however, Early continued as a brigadier leading a division. Deft handling of his troops at Fredericksburg on December 13, 1862, enabled Early to seal a serious break on Jackson's front, a contribution that helped to bring him to a major, generalship on April 23, to rank from January 17, 1863.

At Chancellorsville, Lee selected Early to hold the lines at Fredericksburg while the bulk of the army marched west to meet Joseph Hooker's flanking movement. Two months later he struck hard against the Union XI Corps on the afternoon of July 1 at Gettysburg, and that evening advocated a joint assault by Ewell and A. P. Hill against Cemetery Hill. He suffered a reverse at Rappahannock Bridge on November 8, 1863, led the II Corps at Mine Run when Ewell fell ill, and commanded his division again at the Wilderness. Despite Early's occasional lapses of judgment and execution at the divisional level, Lee watched his progress with pleasure and concluded that he "would make a fine corps commander." When A. P. Hill reported himself sick on May 8, 1864, Lee placed Early in charge of the III Corps for the operations near Spotsylvania. Early returned to his division briefly in mid-May before assuming command of Ewell's II Corps on May 27; appointment to lieutenant general followed on May 31, to rank immediately.

Lee had used Ewell's latest illness as a pretext to remove him, an action that caused bitterness among friends of Ewell who thought Early had schemed to supplant their chief. Campbell Brown, Ewell's stepson and aide, wrote that Early "looks at me like a sheep-stealing dog"; Early protested his innocence to Ewell and said he would "regret excessively if any misunderstanding between ourselves should result."

On June 12, 1864, Early received his greatest orders. A Federal army under David Hunter had taken control of the lower Shenandoah Valley and was closing on Lynchburg. Lee told Early that he and the II Corps must save Lynchburg and regain the valley; if possible, they should menace Washington and compel U. S. Grant to weaken the Army of the Potomac by sending units to counter Early's movements. Assigned a task fully equal to that given Jackson in the spring of 1862, Early embarked on a campaign that brought glory and then tragedy in ample measure.

Early's small force, soon christened the Army of the Valley, drove Hunter away from Lynchburg on June 18 and 19, cleared the Shenandoah of Federals, and crossed the Potomac River. Early won the Battle of the Monocacy outside Frederick, Maryland, on July 9, and pushed on to the suburbs of Washington, D.C., where reinforcements from Grant's army blocked passage into the city. During late July and August, he maneuvered in the lower valley, ordered the burning of Chambersburg, Pennsylvania, and threatened lines of communication between Washington and the West.

Grant responded to Early's diversion by sending Philip H. Sheridan to the valley with orders to collect an army of forty thousand men, defeat Early, and lay waste to the countryside. Between mid-September and mid-October 1864, Early's army, which never numbered as many as twenty thousand troops and usually contained fewer than fifteen thousand, suffered three crushing defeats at the hands of Sheridan's immensely superior Army of the Shenandoah. Stubborn Southern resistance collapsed in the face of overwhelming Union strength at Third Winchester on September 19; three days later Sheridan pummeled the Army of the Valley a second time at Fisher's Hill. Early withdrew southward, while Sheridan systematically burned much of the beautiful lower valley. Reinforced by Lee in October, Early pursued Sheridan to the vicinity of Middletown, Virginia. In the Battle of Cedar Creek on October 19, he overcame daunting obstacles to deliver the most audacious surprise attack of the entire war. His men routed two-thirds of Sheridan's army before losing momentum; late in the day a Union counterattack broke Early's army. This defeat effectively closed major operations in the Shenandoah Valley.

Early lingered in the valley until March 2, 1865, when he and about a thousand men suffered a final reverse at Waynesboro. Shortly thereafter Early returned to the Army of Northern Virginia, where Lee gently informed him that although he retained confidence in him, the Southern people demanded his removal. On March 30, Lee instructed Early to go home and await further orders. Appomattox brought an end to the war in Virginia ten days later.

Most Southerners blamed Early for the loss of the valley. Certainly he had made mistakes, both tactical and strategic. For example, he habitually underestimated Sheridan's ability, deployed his army poorly at Fisher's Hill, and feuded with officers of the unreliable valley cavalry. All things considered, however, he had conducted a remarkable campaign. He marched farther, fought harder against a larger and better-commanded enemy, and tied down as many Federals for a longer time than had Jackson in his fabled valley campaign. Early's operations in the summer and fall of 1864 revealed skills that placed him only behind Jackson and Longstreet on the roster of Confederate corps commanders. Lee aptly summed up Early's career in a letter written shortly after the war: "He was in all battles of the Army of Northern Virginia except when absent on account of severe wounds. He exhibited during his whole service high intelligence, sagacity, bravery and untiring devotion to the cause in which he had enlisted."

After Appomattox, Early traveled first to Mexico and eventually to Canada, where he wrote his memoirs and remained until 1869. Once back in the United States, he settled in Lynchburg and resumed the practice of law. His appointment as commissioner of the Louisiana Lottery in 1877 afforded financial security and freedom to pursue his deep interest in the war. He wrote and lectured extensively, served as president of the Southern Historical Society, and helped to shape the Lost Cause explanation for Confederate defeat. Always he defended Lee, and by the time of his death enjoyed a reputation as the foremost Southern authority on the war. He died in Lynchburg on March 2, 1894, and was buried in Spring Hill Cemetery.

Gary W. Gallagher

Bushong, Millard K., *Old Jube: A Biography of General Jubal A. Early* (Boyce, 1955).

Early, Jubal, *Autobiographical Sketch and Narrative of the War between the States* (Philadelphia, 1912).

Early's best known wartime portrait shows his general's insignia on the inside of his collar, though it is possible this is an artist's addition. (Museum of the Confederacy, Richmond, Va.)

⋆ *John Echols* ⋆

General Echols' only known wartime photo shows him with a general's arrangement of buttons, but a colonel's collar insignia. In either case, it must date from 1862. (U.S. Army Military History Institute, Carlisle, Pa.)

Born March 20, 1823, in Lynchburg, Virginia, Echols graduated from Washington College in Lexington, then studied law at Harvard and was admitted to the Virginia bar in 1843. He then served as a commonwealth's attorney and as a member of the Virginia general assembly. In April 1861 he attended the state's secession convention that voted Virginia out of the Union.

Echols initially performed recruiting duties in western Virginia before accepting the lieutenant colonelcy of the 27th Virginia. At First Manassas, on July 21, Echols commanded the regiment as it and four other Virginia regiments won enduring fame for themselves and their brigade commander, Thomas J. "Stonewall" Jackson. Promotion to colonel followed shortly for Echols, and he retained command through the fall and winter.

On March 23, 1862, the 27th Virginia opened the Battle of Kernstown for Jackson by advancing against the Federal lines. Echols' men repulsed two charges before additional Confederate units came to their assistance. Echols, however, fell severely wounded in the combat. In his report Jackson described Echols as the "noble leader of the Twenty-seventh." His conduct secured him promotion to brigadier general on April 18, to rank from April 16.

Echols was an imposing man, standing six feet, four inches tall and weighing approximately 260 pounds. He was also an amiable man, a capable officer and, as he soon demonstrated, a gifted organizer. Health problems, however, plagued him throughout the war and perhaps limited his potential.

By September 1862, Echols had returned to active duty, commanding a brigade under William W. Loring in western Virginia. On October 16 he replaced Loring as commander of the Department of Southwestern Virginia but resigned the post within a month. Less than four weeks later Echols relinquished field command, citing ill health as the cause. His physical ailments evidently persisted, as Echols did not return to active duty for several months.

During the summer of 1863 the Confederate government assigned him, Howell Cobb, and Robert Ransom to a court of inquiry to investigate the surrender of a Confederate army at Vicksburg, Mississippi, in July. Following this duty, Echols assumed command of a brigade in the Army of Western Virginia and East Tennessee. His unit consisted of the 22d Virginia and the 23d and 26th Virginia battalions.

On November 6, 1863, Echols, directing a force consisting of his brigade, a six-gun battery, and several hundred cavalrymen, met a five-thousand-man Union force under William W. Averell at Droop Mountain, West Virginia. Outnumbered roughly two to one, Echols deployed his men on the summit. Early in the afternoon, the Federals hit the Confederate cavalrymen on Echols' left front. The Southern horsemen broke under the onslaught, but the infantry held for over an hour before Echols abandoned the field. Despite the defeat, the brigadier had performed capably.

When a Union army advanced southward up the Shenandoah Valley in the spring of 1864, Echols' brigade joined the forces of John C. Breckinridge. On May 15 the armies met at New Market, and Breckinridge won a critical victory. Echols' three regiments fought well, attacking on the Confederate right and repulsing a Union counterthrust. Shortly after the battle, however, Echols relinquished command of the brigade because of illness, suffering from "neuralgia of the heart."

On August 22, 1864, Echols assumed command of the District of Southwest Virginia. He demonstrated fully his organizational skills while in command of the district. On October 2, a contingent of his forces defeated a Union raiding force at Saltville, a village on the Virginia & Tennessee Railroad that supplied Confederate armies with vital salt supplies. Echols served as district commander until March 30, 1865, when he replaced Jubal Early as commander of the Department of Western Virginia.

A few days later Echols learned of Robert E. Lee's retreat from Petersburg and, gathering together a force of roughly seven thousand men, marched eastward to join Lee. On April 10 while at Christiansburg, he was informed of Lee's surrender to Ulysses S. Grant at Appomattox on the previous day. He then headed toward North Carolina, where he joined Joseph Johnston's Confederate army. When Johnston surrendered on the 24th, Echols fled into Georgia, finally surrendering at Augusta with members of the fleeing government who were endeavoring to leave the country.

Echols settled in Staunton, Virginia, after the war. He became president of a local bank and organized the Chesapeake & Virginia Railway. He also served on the board of visitors of Washington and Lee University and the Virginia Military Institute. For a number of years he lived in Louisville, Kentucky, prospering there as a businessman. Echols, who had served the Confederacy well both as a combat officer and departmental commander, died in Staunton on May 24, 1896, and was buried there.

Jeffry D. Wert

Davis, William C., *The Battle of New Market* (New York, 1975).
Tanner, Robert G., *Stonewall in the Valley: Thomas J. "Stonewall" Jackson's Shenadoah Valley Campaign Spring 1862* (New York, 1976).

⋆ *Matthew Duncan Ector* ⋆

In the absence of any uniformed photograph of Ector being known, this postwar civilian view must suffice. (Texas State Archives, Austin, Tex.)

Ector was born in Putnam County, Georgia, on February 28, 1822. Educated in La Grange, Georgia, and at Centre College in Danville, Kentucky, he gained admittance to the Georgia bar in 1844. In addition to his law practice, he served one term, 1845–47, in the Georgia legislature. Either as a private or noncommissioned officer, Ector served in a Georgia regiment during the Mexican War and, apparently while stationed in Texas, developed a fondness for that state. He moved to Henderson, Texas, in 1849 and practiced law, then represented his district in the Texas legislature from 1855 until he resigned his office following the attack on Fort Sumter in April 1861.

Enlisting as a private in the Confederate Army, Ector soon became a lieutenant in Company B and regimental adjutant for the Texas Cavalry. Recruited with the intention of invading southern Kansas, the regiment departed for Missouri. It participated in the Battle of Wilson's Creek on August 10, and Ector's regimental commander reported that he "acted with great gallantry during the whole battle." Lieutenant Ector commanded his company in the engagement at Chustenahlah, Cherokee Nation, on December 26. Again serving as regimental adjutant during the Battle of Pea Ridge in March 1862, Ector demonstrated "gallant bearing and conduct throughout the entire engagement."

By mid-April Ector was serving as adjutant on the staff of Brigadier General Joseph L. Hogg, whose brigade was stationed at Corinth, Mississippi. Following Hogg's death from disease in May, the men of the 14th Texas Dismounted Cavalry elected Ector their colonel. His new regiment formed part of a brigade sent to reinforce Major General Edmund Kirby Smith in East Tennessee prior to the transfer of the main army from Mississippi to Tennessee.

Ector advanced into eastern Kentucky in August in Colonel Thomas H. McCray's brigade of Brigadier General Thomas J. Churchill's division. Participating in the Battle of Richmond, Kentucky, on August 30, "Ector particularly distinguished himself, being in the front of the battle and cheering on his men," according to his brigade commander.

After the invasion of Kentucky concluded in October, Ector was promoted to brigadier general on September 27, apparently for his conduct at Richmond; his commission was dated from August 23. Although they would eventually outrank him, Ector's date of commission gave him seniority over several brigadiers in the Western Department in the fall of 1862, including Joseph Wheeler and Stephen D. Lee. By the end of October, Ector had replaced McCray in command of the brigade, which now comprised part of Major General John P. McCown's division.

December 31 found Ector leading his brigade in a surprise dawn attack by the Confederate left against Union Major General Alexander M. McCook's troops near Murfreesboro, Tennessee. McCown praised Ector for his conduct during the assault:

"General Ector came under a galling fire from the infantry, sheltered in a cedar brake, and artillery. General Ector at once charged them, forcing their first line of infantry beyond their second, and their cannoneers from their guns in their front...[he] exhibited cool and dauntless courage, as well as skill, in the handling of his brigade."

A major in the brigade adjacent to Ector's in the assault reported that Ector "pursued the fleeing enemy for the distance of some 4 miles, until recalled." The Confederate center had failed to equal the success achieved by Ector and others on the left, in this case forcing the left to break off the attack.

In early May Ector's brigade was one of two transferred from Middle Tennessee to central Mississippi, and among the first troops to arrive in Jackson. Union forces had already effectively isolated Lieutenant General John C. Pemberton at Vicksburg; however, Ector remained in central Mississippi during the summer of 1863, where his brigade participated in General Joseph E. Johnston's imaginary efforts to relieve the Confederates besieged in Vicksburg and in the abortive fighting around Jackson.

Ector and his brigade returned to Bragg's army with Major General William T. Walker's division in time to participate in the Battle of Chickamauga, Georgia, September 19–20. Ordered back to central Mississippi on September 22, the brigade remained there until May 1864, despite evidence indicating its transfer to Mobile in February. The brigade accompanied Lieutenant General Leonidas Polk to Georgia in May of 1864 to participate in the Atlanta Campaign.

On July 27 near the outskirts of Atlanta, "while in a redan occupied by Ward's battery and directing the fire of the same...[Ector] received, by a piece of shell which exploded in the redan, a painful wound above the left knee." Colonel William H. Young succeeded him and gave the following description of Ector's participation in the struggle for Atlanta:

"During most of the campaign, having but a single staff officer, he had borne upon his own shoulders to an unusual degree the burden of the management of the brigade. Yet, though often feeble, by his patriotic zeal, his tireless energy, his undaunted bravery, he was able to conduct his brigade through every contest and trial with great credit and honor."

Despite the amputation of his leg and the Mississippi River being under Union control, Ector apparently managed to return to Texas to convalesce.

Considering the seriousness of his operation and the distance traveled, his recovery and return to duty seem almost miraculous. Although evidence is sketchy, it seems certain that he had rejoined his brigade by April 1865, when he participated in the defense of Spanish Fort and in the evacuation of Mobile. He and his brigade formally surrendered with Lieutenant General Richard Taylor the following month.

Paroled shortly thereafter, Ector returned to Texas and resumed his law practice. From 1866 until his removal the following year, Ector served as judge of the Sixth Judicial District of Texas. Prohibited from holding public office during Reconstruction, Ector was limited to the practice of law in Marshall. In 1874 he was elected judge of the Seventh Judicial District and from 1876 until his death in Tyler on October 29, 1879, held the post of presiding justice on the Texas Court of Appeals. He is buried in Marshall.

Lawrence L. Hewitt
Roberts, O.M, *Texas*, Vol. XI in Evans, *Confederate Military History*.

⭐ *Stephen Elliott, Jr.* ⭐

Born in Beaufort, South Carolina, on October 26, 1830, Elliott became a Parris Island planter, state legislator (1859–66), and captain of the Beaufort Volunteer Artillery (1856–63).

This sea-island life of luxury and leadership prepared him well for war. Even before secession, his unit volunteered for state service on November 24, 1860, and he personally helped capture Fort Sumter. His militia battery became Company A, 11th South Carolina Infantry Regiment on June 12, 1861, with himself as captain. While commanding embattled Fort Beauregard on November 7, 1861, he was slightly wounded in the leg.

Despite that Port Royal defeat, Elliott contributed significantly to containing the Federal foothold. Detached from the 11th as the 5th District's "Siege Train" in February 1862, his Beaufort company reenlisted as artillery on March 17 and became a twelve-pound howitzer battery in May. It fought valiantly in both Pocataligo victories. He commanded all artillery there on October 22 and became the 3d District's chief of artillery on November 15.

On October 8 district commander William S. Walker urged Elliott's promotion to colonel of the 11th. The captain's commendations were impressive. Walker reported, "Elliott, whose name is identified with the history of the defense of this coast by many a daring exploit, behaved with his accustomed coolness, skill, and determination." Robert E. Lee himself, on April 10, 1863, called Elliott "one of the best officers in the Department...he showed good judgment and exhibited intelligence, boldness, and sagacity." Although the colonelcy proved unattainable, Richmond promoted him artillery major on April 30, ranking from November 15, 1862.

The Virginian recalled his own Carolina service when Elliott scouted Yankee positions. The subordinate's knowledge of the coast and his prewar prowess as a swimmer and boatsman made him a Civil War counterpart of "Swamp Fox" Francis Marion. His red-shirted artillerists repeatedly bombarded Port Royal Ferry, raided outposts, and even captured ships off Savannah (May 19, 1861) and in Coosaw River (April 9, 1863). Innovative as well as daring, he experimented with home-made torpedoes, which sank at least one Union vessel in Stono Inlet on August 10, 1863, and which posed threats to the Northern fleet off Charleston.

Defending that citadel of secession earned Elliott his greatest fame. On September 3, 1863, with Morris Island virtually lost, P. G. T. Beauregard, who considered Elliott "a young officer of well-earned esteem, modest, thoroughly self-possessed, and dauntless," offered him command of Fort Sumter. Elliott proved worthy of the trust. He made that battered ruin an impregnable stronghold that withstood tremendous bombardment (nineteen thousand shells, October 26–December 11), repulsed landing parties on September 9 and November 20, and defied the Federal fleet. Although wounded in the head and ankle when a magazine exploded on December 11, Elliott held command continuously from September 5 to May 4, minus only seventeen days' leave. Saving symbolic Sumter made him a Southern hero. Elliott's "energy, judgment, and coolness, under

---

Stephen Elliott appears as a lieutenant colonel in the Holcombe Legion in this image made probably in 1863. (Museum of the Confederacy, Richmond, Va.)

all circumstances," wrote Beauregard's second-in-command, Jeremy F. Gilmer, "call forth the admiration of all the brave troops now engaged in the defense of Charleston."

Beauregard detailed the garrison from several units so that no officer outranking Elliott could claim command. The general also sought higher rank for his brilliant subordinate. "Brave, zealous, and efficient," Beauregard called the Carolinian in recommending his promotion for the September 9 victory. Although James A. Seddon considered the artillerist "a vigilant, zealous officer," the recommendation miscarried into files concerning Elliott's father, Chaplain Stephen Elliott, Sr. Once the document was located, Jefferson Davis promoted him to artillery lieutenant colonel on November 21, ranking from September 9. Then on April 25, 1864, Elliott was appointed colonel of the Holcombe Legion, as of April 20. He accepted on May 2 and left Fort Sumter two days later.

He soon left South Carolina as well, for promotion brought service in the main theater. The Tramp Brigade, including the legion, had already started north. When he overtook his regiment on May 14, it was protecting Stony Creek Depot, Virginia. Although the legion continued guarding the Weldon Railroad, Elliott himself came to Bermuda Hundred to command the brigade after Walker was captured on May 20. Beauregard recommended him for brigadier general on May 25. He was promoted on May 28, ranking from May 24, and accepted June 9. In one month, Elliott rose two grades and led a brigade instead of a battalion.

Now commanding the 17th, 18th, 22d, 23d, and 26th South Carolina infantry regiments in Bushrod Johnson's Division, Elliott fought at Bermuda Hundred and Petersburg. He helped repulse assaults June 17–18 and supported the counterattack which saved the Weldon Railroad on June 22. The most notorious Union attack, however, proved more disruptive, as the Crater exploded under his 18th and 22d regiments on July 30. He attempted to counterattack with the 17th and 26th but was severely wounded through the left lung.

This nearly fatal shot paralyzed his left arm and disabled him until December, but commitment and constitution brought him back to duty. By then, South Carolina (where he convalesced) was seriously threatened, so he took over its third subdistrict on December 9. His forces repulsed probes on James Island in February. Although his health was failing, he accompanied William B. Taliaferro's Division when it abandoned Charleston.

His now mobile brigade contained the 22d and 28th Georgia heavy artillery battalions, 2d Regiment and 18th Battalion of South Carolina Heavy Artillery, Citadel Cadet Battalion, and probably some South Carolina Junior Reserves. The cadets and reserves remained in their state, but the 2d North Carolina Local Defense Battalion joined him in Fayetteville. He fought at Averasborough and Bentonville and was again wounded, apparently on March 20 or 21. That blow, plus the eruption of his lung wound, compelled his return to South Carolina. His final service was taking the field to oppose Edward Potter's Camden Raid. Though pardoned and reelected a state legislator, Elliott did not long survive the war. Combat, especially the Crater, had shattered his health. He died at Aiken on February 21, 1866, and is buried in Beaufort. Versatile, resourceful, and brave, Elliott proved equally adept raiding with light artillery or defending with heavy artillery. Although his service as brigadier was too abbreviated to permit full evaluation, his great success at lower grades suggests that if he had come to Virginia in 1862, he would rank with Wade Hampton and Joseph Kershaw as the great citizen-soldiers of South Carolina.

Richard J. Sommers

"Brigadier General Stephen Elliott, C.S.A," *The Land We Love*, Vol. IV, no. 6: 453–458 (April 1868).

Capers, Ellison, *South Carolina*, Vol. V in Evans, *Confederate Military History*.

Hamilton, John A., "Stephen Elliott" and "General Stephen Elliott, Lieutenant James A. Hamilton, and Elliott's Torpedoes," *Southern Historical Society Papers*, Vols. IX–X (1881–82).

Selby, Julian A., *In Memoriam: General Stephen Elliott* (Columbia, 1866).

✶ Arnold Elzey ✶

For reasons never entirely clear, Arnold Elzey Jones dropped his last name when he was at West Point and spent the rest of his life using his paternal grandmother's maiden name, and his own middle name. He was born in Maryland at the family home, "Elmwood," in Somerset County on December 18, 1816, and attended the U.S. Military Academy until his graduation in 1837. Entering the artillery, he spent the next twenty-four years in the United States service, winning plaudits in the Seminole War and later promotion for his bravery in Mexico. By 1861 he had become a captain in the 2d Artillery commanding the Augusta, Georgia, arsenal.

Despite his birth in a border state, Elzey sided with the Confederacy from the onset. Resigning his commission on April 25, 1861, he was quickly made colonel of the newly raised 1st Maryland Infantry. The War Department assigned him to the small army being raised in the Shenandoah under Joseph E. Johnston, and Elzey was quickly put in command of a brigade containing his own regiment, the 10th and 13th Virginia, and the 3d Tennessee.

Officially designated the 4th Brigade of the Army of the Shenandoah, it was destined not to go into battle under Elzey's command. He was an unlucky commander, his ill fortune starting when Johnston moved to Manassas to join with Beauregard in meeting McDowell. Brigadier General E. Kirby Smith could not get his own brigade in motion in time, so he attached himself to Elzey's brigade instead, effectively superseding him in command. Once they reached the battle, however, Smith soon fell with a wound and Elzey resumed command. Determined not ever to be superseded in command by a brigadier again, Elzey vowed as he went into the fight that he would have "a yellow sash or six feet of ground."

He got the yellow sash. He hit McDowell's right just in time to crumble that wavering flank of the Union Army, helping to start the retreat that turned into rout. "Hail, Elzey! Thou art Blucher of the day," Beauregard said when he saw him. A few weeks later, probably on August 28, 1861, Elzey got his commission as brigadier, to date from July 21, the day of his first battle.

Following the several months of inactivity that postdated First Manassas, Elzey and his brigade went back to the Shenandoah with Jackson to participate in the fabled Valley Campaign. There he distinguished himself, then came east of the Blue Ridge once more when Lee summoned Jackson to join him in the Seven Days' battles. There at Gaines' Mill, on June 27, his luck failed him yet again as he took a horrible wound in the face and head. For the rest of the year Elzey recuperated, not going back to active duty until December. On the fourth of that month he was promoted to major general and then assigned to James Longstreet's Department of Southern Virginia and North Carolina. On March 7, 1863, Lee requested that Elzey be assigned to him as chief of artillery of the Army of Northern Virginia, but his still-precarious health apparently preempted such an appointment. Instead, in April 1863 Elzey was put in command of the newly designated Department of Richmond, his mission essentially the organization and maintenance of civilian home guards—largely raised from the clerks in the several government bureaus. On July 1 Elzey temporarily relinquished his command to D. H. Hill, when at his request he was ordered to active artillery duty with Lee's army, then in Pennsylvania, but the next day President Davis countermanded the order, preferring to keep Elzey in command of the city defenses.

Elzey was not popular in Richmond, especially among the clerks whom he sometimes virtually commandeered into service, or with their managers who had to fight with him to keep their employees out of the field. Meanwhile, Elzey frequently strove to get back into the field, but did not succeed until June 1864. John C. Breckinridge, then defending Lynchburg against the invasion of David Hunter, requested that Elzey be sent to replace the inefficient General John Vaughn in command of his infantry. On June 18 Elzey assumed his new position, a "division" that in fact

The handsomest of General Arnold Elzey's several wartime portraits, this may have been taken by the Richmond photographer Julian Vannerson almost any time after First Manassas. (Bradley T. Johnson Papers, Duke University Library, Durham, N.C.)

Probably Elzey's first war portrait, this shows a not unusual confusion of insignia buttons and cuff braid of a brigadier, collar stars of a colonel, and a curious stripe on the shoulder, which was entirely non-regulation. (U.S. Army Military History Institute, Carlisle, Pa.)

A slight variant made obviously at the same sitting. (William A. Turner Collection)

An excellent portrait quite possibly by either Vannerson or Cook. (Cook Collection, Valentine Museum, Richmond, Va.)

numbered barely more than one thousand, but he did not hold the command for long. On September 8, 1864, the War Department assigned him to John B. Hood as chief of artillery for the Army of Tennessee, but apparently his health—his recovery from his wound was never entirely complete—kept him from serving in the aborted Franklin-Nashville Campaign.

Elzey was relieved of his position on February 17, 1865, and returned to Richmond, where he again was involved with the local defense forces, and accompanied the fleeing government on its retreat south after the fall of the capital. He finally gave his parole on May 9, 1865, at Washington, Georgia, where most of the remnant of the government officers and the flotsam from Joseph E. Johnston's army ceased their resistance.

Elzey had but a short time left to live. He removed to Anne Arundel County in his native Maryland and farmed for a few years before his February 21, 1871, death in Baltimore. He is buried in Greenmount Cemetery, along with such other notables as John Wilkes Booth and Edgar Allan Poe. The opportunity to become a distinguished soldier eluded Elzey thanks to circumstances and poor luck, though he was also a troublesome subordinate at times, and too arbitrary to win the lasting affection of soldiers and civilians.

William C. Davis

Davis, William C., *Battle at Bull Run* (New York, 1977).
Dowdey, Clifford, *The Seven Days* (Boston, 1964).
Jones, John B., *A Rebel War Clerk's Diary* (Philadelphia, 1866).

An unusual profile of Elzey by an unknown photographer. (William A. Turner Collection)

✷ *Clement Anselm Evans* ✷

Quite amazingly, considering his extensive work in Confederate history after the war, no wartime uniformed portrait of Clement A. Evans has yet surfaced. This is taken from a rather crude portrait. (Museum of the Confederacy, Richmond, Va.)

Evans was born in Stewart County, Georgia, on February 25, 1833. He attended the public schools of Lumpkin, Georgia, and William Tracy Gould's school of law in Augusta. Licensed on January 30, 1852, he commenced his practice in Lumpkin and entered public life in 1855 as a judge in his home county. Evans served in the Georgia senate 1859–61, and cast his vote for John C. Breckinridge as an elector in the presidential canvass of 1860. During the secession crisis of December 1860, he helped organize a company of infantry in Stewart County that became part of the 2d Georgia Infantry, though he never took the field with the regiment. He was commissioned major in the 31st Georgia Infantry on April 17, 1862 (to rank from November 18, 1861), and colonel of that unit on March 13, 1863 (to rank from May 13, 1862). Despite the official date of his appointment, Evans functioned as colonel of the 31st, and appears in correspondence and reports as such, from late spring 1862 forward.

Evans participated in most of the campaigns of the Army of Northern Virginia. He and his regiment joined A. R. Lawton's Georgia brigade of "Stonewall" Jackson's Division prior to the Seven Days' Campaign (John B. Gordon and Evans himself would later command this brigade), and Evans suffered a slight wound at Gaines' Mill on July 27, 1862. Attrition among officers in the brigade left Evans temporarily in command at Fredericksburg, where he performed well and received praise in Jubal A. Early's divisional report. At Chancellorsville, his regiment helped to recapture Marye's Heights on May 4. A controversy arose after the battle about whether the Heights had been vacant, prompting Evans to observe sarcastically that it was "Very strange indeed, that my Regiment should be under a hot fire, capture prisoners, wagons, horses, mules, and drive Yankees off an evacuated hill." Evans' principal activity at Gettysburg came on July 1 during Early's assault against the Union XI Corps north of town. Grazed in the side by a shell fragment, he remained with his unit for the rest of the battle despite severe pain. During the balance of 1863, Evans participated in the Bristoe and Mine Run campaigns. He fought his last battle as a regimental commander the following spring in the Wilderness, where his troops saw light action on May 5 and took part in Gordon's flank attack the next evening.

Evans replaced Gordon in brigade command on May 8, 1864, when the latter advanced to the divisional level. Called forward at a moment of crisis on May 12 at Spotsylvania, his brigade helped seal the break along the east side of the Mule Shoe salient. Evans received promotion to brigadier general on May 20, 1864 (to rank from the previous day); three weeks later he and his brigade accompanied the II Corps to Lynchburg in the initial stage of Jubal Early's 1864 Shenandoah Valley campaign.

The first hard fighting of the campaign came on July 9 at the Monocacy, where Evans' brigade sustained heavy casualties. Evans himself suffered a severe wound that Gordon described in a postwar account: "A Minié bullet struck him in his left side, passing through a pocket of his coat, and carrying with it a number of pins, which were so deeply imbedded that they were not all extracted for a number of years." The wound kept Evans out of action for several weeks, during the course of which Early lost the battles of Third Winchester and Fisher's Hill. "I am sorry that I have to rejoin my command under circumstances so discouraging," wrote Evans as he prepared to return to the army in late September, "but as I have never yet participated in a defeat perhaps the tide will turn when I arrive." He fought at Cedar Creek on October 19, a Confederate disaster that contributed to his low opinion of Early's generalship. Evans gave full credit for the successful morning phase of that battle to Gordon, blaming Early for failing to press the attack when he had the Federals off balance. R. E. Lee recalled the bulk of the II Corps from the Shenandoah in late 1864; Evans departed Waynesboro in early December, leaving behind Jubal Early and the bad memories of the Valley campaign.

From late fall 1864 through the end of the war, Evans commanded Gordon's Division as a brigadier general while Gordon led the II Corps. He was not promoted to major general because of the expectation that Gordon, who continued at that rank, would return to his division if Early resumed control over the corps. Active to the very end, Evans saw action at Appomattox on April 9, 1865, and later claimed that his division mounted the final Southern resistance. "There is no question in my mind of the fact that the last shot fired and the last capture made by the army under Gen. Lee were through you and your picked sharpshooters," he wrote one of his subordinates. "It is one of the proudest of my thoughts that we were shooting with all our might when the army was surrendered; and I have not the slightest doubt…that you burned the last grain of powder and directed the last Confederate bullet from the great old army of Gen. Lee."

The postwar years were productive for Evans. He had decided in 1863 to enter the ministry if he survived the war, and upon returning to Georgia sought admission to the North Georgia Conference of the Methodist Episcopal Church, South. In 1866 he began a career as a clergyman that lasted until 1892. He lived in Augusta for many years, where, in addition to his ministry, he engaged in a number of business ventures. Always a devoted ex-Confederate, he played a leading role in the affairs of the United Confederate Veterans from its organization in 1889 until his death, serving as commander in chief 1908–10. His interest in the war led Evans to assume an active role in the movement to raise money for the Confederate Memorial Institute in Richmond (completed after his death, the museum became known as the Confederate Battle Abbey). He also published widely; his literary efforts included *Military History of Georgia* (1895) and editorship of *Confederate Military History* (1899), a twelve-volume cooperative work that focused on military affairs. Evans died on July 2, 1911, and is buried in Atlanta, where he had lived the last years of his life.

Gary W. Gallagher

Derry, Joseph T., *Georgia*, Vol. VII in Evans, *Confederate Military History*.

Nathan G. Evans' fierce nature shows in this excellent portrait. (Library of Congress, Washington, D.C.)

⭐ Nathan George Evans ⭐

Nathan George Evans was born on February 3, 1824, at Marion, South Carolina. After attending Randolph-Macon College in Virginia, he received an appointment to the United States Military Academy in 1844. While at West Point he acquired the nickname "Shanks," because of his conspicuously skinny legs. Graduating near the bottom of the class of 1848, he was assigned to the dragoons, spending his entire antebellum career on the frontier. He earned a reputation for bravery in combat with the Plains Indians, securing promotion to 1st lieutenant and captain of the 2d U.S. Cavalry.

With the secession of South Carolina and with the dissolution of the Union during the winter of 1861, Evans resigned his commission in February and returned to his native state. He served as adjutant general of the state's troops at Fort Sumter before securing a commission of colonel and command of the 4th South Carolina. Subsequently, Evans and his regiment were transferred to Virginia and joined the army of P.G.T. Beauregard at Manassas. The South Carolinian was given command of a demi-brigade comprised of his regiment and the 1st Louisiana Battalion.

Evans and his 1,100 man command played a pivotal role in the Battle of First Manassas on July 21. Posted to guard the Stone Bridge crossing of Bull Run Creek, Evans' pickets initiated the combat by engaging Federal skirmishers before daylight. When Evans learned of the enemy movement beyond the Confederate left flank, he left a guard at the brigade, informed his superior officer, and marched to meet the Federals. He deployed his troops on Matthews Hill and waited for the Northerners.

When the Federals advanced up the slope, the South Carolinians and Louisianans lashed into them. Evans skillfully concealed his few numbers while stopping the enemy with defense and counterattacks. Additional Confederate brigades came to his support, and the Southerners held for a couple of hours until overwhelmed by Union strength. Evans' units broke under the pressure, but he later rallied the 4th South Carolina which fought during the afternoon.

Evans lost a total of 144 men in the battle. His performance elicited praise from both Beauregard and Joseph E. Johnston. Beauregard cited Evans for "dauntless conduct and imperturbable coolness,." while Johnston in his report wrote that Evans demonstrated "skill and unshrinkable courage." He seemed to be worthy of immediate promotion and more responsibility.

Evans' character and reputation, however, evidently delayed the promotion. He was a man of medium height, balding, with a black mustache and beard and small, dark eyes. Evans also possessed crudeness and conceit. He spoke his mind and made opponents. More importantly, perhaps, he enjoyed whiskey, so much so, in fact, that one of his aides shadowed him, carrying a one-gallon jug of the liquor that Evans dubbed his "barellita."

Following First Manassas, Evans was stationed at Leesburg, Virginia, to guard crossings of the Potomac River. He commanded three regiments of Mississippians and one of Virginians. On October 21, a Union force, under Colonel Edward D. Baker, landed on the

Evans is seated at left in this image of unknown date. While possibly prewar, it may also date from the days immediately around the firing on Fort Sumter. (Oakley Park, Edgefield, S.C.)

southern bank, advancing toward Leesburg. While Evans was not present on the field, his troops performed superbly, ravaging the Federals, killing Baker, and inflicting a disaster upon the Northerners. The Battle of Ball's Bluff, as it was called, earned Evans "Thanks of Congress" and promotion to brigadier general, to date from the 21st.

At the request of the governor, Evans was transferred to South Carolina, where he assumed command of a brigade comprised of four regiments and a legion. By the summer of 1862, Evans and his brigade had returned to Virginia, arriving in time for the Battle of Second Manassas, on August 29-30. Formally listed as an Independent Brigade, Evans' troops fought with James Longstreet's wing of the army, losing nearly six hundred men in the counterattack of the 30th.

At the Battle of Sharpsburg, on September 17, Evans held a position near the so-called Middle Bridge. During the bloody combat, he lost another 232 men. Within two months, Evans' command was en route southward to North Carolina to guard the Weldon Railroad. There, in December, Evans lost four hundred men and six cannon to a Union force that outnumbered him five-to-one.

During the winter of 1863, Evans' troubles with superiors began to arise. General William H. C. Whiting, Evans' commander in North Carolina, reported that "I place but little reliance on Evans' brigade, which is certainly in worse condition than any I have ever seen. It had but about one thousand five hundred men for duty, a very large number of field officers absent or under arrest." Shortly thereafter, Evans' regiments, who were known as the "Tramp Brigade" because of their travels, were ordered to the West, where the unit served under Johnston in the Vicksburg Campaign.

By the end of 1863, Evans' career had reached its nadir. Twice authorities charged him with intoxication and disobedience of orders. Although acquitted by the courts martial, he lost command of his brigade. Returning to duty in the spring of 1864, Evans fell from his horse and was incapacitated for future field service. He was in Richmond in April 1865, fleeing with the Confederate government before surrendering.

After the war, Evans settled in Midway, Alabama, where he served as principal of a high school. He died on November 23, 1868, and was buried in Cokesbury, South Carolina. "Shanks" Evans had a checkered Confederate career that declined from the fields of

First Manassas to a flight from a burning capital. In the end, his training, skill, and bravery could not overcome his drinking problem.

Jeffry D. Wert

Davis, William C., *Battle at Bull Run* (1977).

Freeman, Douglas Southall, *Lee's Lieutenants: A Study in Command* (1942-44).

Hennessy, John, *The First Battle of Manassas* (1989).

Hollen, Kim B., *Battle At Ball's Bluff* (1985).

Another possibly very early war portrait of Evans. (Museum of the
Confederacy, Richmond, Va.)

Richard S. Ewell was one of Lee's least-photographed principal commanders, leaving behind only this excellent image and a slight variant that follows. (Cook Collection, Valentine Museum, Richmond, Va.)

✷ *Richard Stoddert Ewell* ✷

Born in Georgetown, District of Columbia, on February 8, 1817, he was the third son and fifth surviving child of Thomas and Elizabeth Ewell. Thomas' father, Jesse Ewell, had served as a colonel in the American Revolution and owned a sizeable plantation in northern Virginia, while Elizabeth's father, Benjamin Stoddert, had been one of the country's foremost merchants and its first secretary of the navy.

Despite his illustrious roots, Ewell's childhood was spent in poverty on the family plantation, Stony Lonesome, in Prince William County, Virginia. His father died when he was just nine years old. Unable to finance a college education for Richard, Elizabeth Ewell arranged to have him appointed to the United States Military Academy. He graduated there in 1840, thirteenth of forty-two in a class that included William T. Sherman, George Thomas, and George Getty.

From West Point Ewell entered service in the 1st U.S. Dragoons, a regiment with which he would serve until the Civil War. His first assignments were on the Western plains, on what was then optimistically termed the "Permanent Indian Frontier." After a brief tour of duty at Fort Wayne in the present state of Oklahoma, Ewell's company transferred to Fort Scott, near the Oklahoma-Arkansas border. His service at Fort Scott was punctuated by recruiting service in the East as well as participation in two famous journeys to the West: Colonel Philip St. George Cooke's 1843 Santa Fe Trail expedition, and Colonel Stephen Kearny's 1845 Oregon Trail expedition.

Ewell's first combat experience came in the Mexican War, where his company served as mounted escort to General Winfield Scott. In August 1847, Ewell's company charged a Mexican battery near the town of Churubusco, outside Mexico City. In the attack Ewell's horse was shot from under him and his company commander, Captain Philip Kearny, was wounded in the arm. Ewell assisted the wounded Kearny from the field, and was brevetted captain for "brave and meritorious services" there.

Ewell left Mexico in 1848 and after a brief period of recruiting duty in the East went west, where for the next ten years he would serve at a variety of frontier posts in the Arizona and New Mexico territories, including Rayado (1850–51), Los Lunas (1851–56), and Fort Buchanan (1857–60). During these years he participated in numerous expeditions against the Apache Indians, gaining a reputation as one of the army's foremost frontier officers. In recognition of his services, delegates to the 1860 Arizona Constitutional Convention granted Ewell an honorary seat on the floor of the convention and named one of the territory's first four counties in his honor. (The name was later changed when Ewell threw his allegiance to the Confederacy.)

The Civil War ended Ewell's career in the United States Army. Like most army officers, he had strong ties to the Federal government, but when the state of Virginia left the Union in April 1861, Ewell felt he had no choice but to join her. He tendered his sword to the Confederacy and was appointed lieutenant colonel of cavalry. By the summer of 1861 he was commanding an outpost at Fairfax Court House, Virginia. When Union horsemen attacked the town on June 1, Ewell received a bullet injury to his arm, making him perhaps the first Confederate field officer wounded in the war.

Shortly thereafter, on June 17, he won promotion to brigadier general, to rank immediately, and was placed in command of a brigade. His unit held the right end of the Confederate line at the First Battle of Manassas. In that battle Ewell was designated to lead an assault on the Federal left, but the order telling him to advance miscarried and his brigade remained in idleness for the better part of the day. Although some newspapers attached blame to him for this failure, evidence conclusively shows he was not at fault.

Certainly the War Department did not find him so, for on January 24, 1862, he was made a major general, effective immediately, and placed in charge of a division. Ewell's Division soon joined Major General Thomas J. "Stonewall" Jackson in the Shenandoah Valley. In a three-week campaign Jackson and Ewell repeatedly defeated the forces sent against them, upsetting Federal military plans in the East and giving the struggling Confederacy new life.

Ewell continued to serve capably under Jackson throughout the Seven Days' fighting, at Cedar Mountain, and at Groveton. In the battle at Groveton, Ewell's knee was shattered by a Union Minié bullet, necessitating amputation of his left leg. He was ultimately taken to Richmond, where he recuperated from his wound under the care of his first cousin and fiancée, Lizinka Campbell Brown. When Jackson died as a result of wounds received at the Battle of Chancellorsville in May 1863, General Robert E. Lee appointed Ewell to command Jackson's II Corps, and promotion to lieutenant general came on May 23, to rank from that date. Before taking command, Ewell married the widow Brown, an action which, taken together with the amputation of his leg, may have impaired his efficiency as a general.

In the Gettysburg Campaign, Ewell led the advance into Pennsylvania, defeating en route a large Federal force at Winchester. His attack on the Union Army at Gettysburg on July 1, 1863, was a great success, but he failed to press on and capture Cemetery Hill, a decision for which he has been severely and perhaps unfairly criticized. When attacks on July 2 and 3 failed to pry the Union Army from its strong position, Lee retreated to Virginia. In subsequent campaigning that fall, Ewell played but a minor role.

The 1864 campaign brought fighting even more severe than that which had preceded it. At the Wilderness in May, Ewell held the Confederate left and successfully beat back the attacks of two Union corps on the Orange Turnpike. At Spotsylvania Court House later that month, Ewell's corps held the Muleshoe Salient in the center of the line. On May 12 the Federals attacked the Muleshoe and broke Ewell's line, but the Confederates successfully patched the breach in savage hand-to-hand fighting.

The constant day-to-day combat broke Ewell's feeble health, and in late May Lee relieved him of corps command and ordered him to report to the Department of Richmond. From June 1864 until April 1865, he supervised the defenses of the Confederate capital, and in September 1864 prevented Federal forces from capturing the city by gallant fighting near Fort Harrison.

The rupture of Lee's lines at Petersburg in April 1865 necessitated the evacuation of Richmond. In the retreat toward Appomattox, Ewell commanded a heterogeneous corps of sailors, marines, government clerks, heavy artillery, and infantry. At Sayler's Creek, Ewell's corps was assailed in front and flank by the Federal army, surrounded, and forced to surrender. Ewell was taken as prisoner to Fort Warren in Boston harbor, where he remained until July.

After the war Ewell moved to Maury County, Tennessee, where he successfully operated his wife's Spring Hill plantation. He died there of pneumonia on January 25, 1872, at the age of fifty-five, just three days after his wife had succumbed to the same ailment. They are buried side-by-side at the Old City Cemetery in Nashville.

Ewell stood five feet, eight inches tall, had grey eyes, a prominent nose, and a bushy brown beard that offset a largely bald head. Although irritable and prone to swearing, he was a likeable character with a wry sense of humor. As an officer he showed great attention to detail, was a strict disciplinarian, and had excellent military instincts; however, he lacked the self-confidence necessary to exercise independent command. Although the Confederacy produced officers of greater ability than Ewell, none fought more faithfully in its defense. As General James Longstreet commented, "A truer and nobler spirit than Ewell never drew sword."

Donald C. Pfanz

Hamlin, Percy Gatling, *"Old Bald Head" (General R. S. Ewell): The Portrait of a Soldier* (Strasburg, 1940).

Hamlin, Percy Gatling, *The Making of a Soldier: Letters of General R. S. Ewell* (Richmond, 1935).

Several very subtle differences suggest that this may be a variant of the previous portrait of Ewell. (William A. Turner Collection)

Fagan appears as a major general in a portrait made probably in Texas or Arkansas during the last year of the war. (Western Reserve Historical Society, Cleveland, Oh.)

✴ *James Fleming Fagan* ✴

James Fleming Fagan was born on March 1, 1828, in Clark County, Kentucky. His family moved west in 1838, settling in Arkansas two years after it gained statehood. He was a 2d lieutenant in Colonel Archibald Yell's regiment during the Mexican War, and afterwards served one term in the state legislature as a Whig. When the war began, he was a farmer, and his first wife was the sister of General W. N. R. Beall. Fagan raised the 1st Arkansas Infantry on May 6, 1861, and on May 27 nine hundred men under him were mustered into the Confederate service at Lynchburg.

In the battle of Shiloh, the 1st Arkansas formed part of the initial advance. During the confused fighting on April 6, Fagan had informed another Confederate unit: "For God's sake to cease firing; that we were killing his men and he was killing ours." Fagan also fought at Farmington, Mississippi, on May 9, and at Corinth. But in May he apparently fell into disfavor with Braxton Bragg; after he reported sighting the enemy—whom Bragg believed was not there—Bragg complained: "I shall suspend Colonel Fagan, who, unfortunately, commands a brigade." Instead, Fagan was transferred to the Trans-Mississippi Department and was appointed a brigadier general on October 2, to rank from September 12, 1862. In October Lieutenant General Theophilus H. Holmes, commanding the department, told Major General Thomas C. Hindman that Fagan had been made a brigadier and "must be put in command of an Arkansas brigade" since Holmes was ordered to brigade the troops by states. Fagan commanded the 1st Arkansas Cavalry (also known as the 6th Arkansas—there were three regiments known as the 1st Arkansas), and fought at Cane Hill on November 28, 1862, and at Prairie Grove, Arkansas, on December 7.

At Prairie Grove Hindman planned an attack upon the troops under James G. Blunt, and at a meeting on the evening of December 6 called his officers together. Fagan, along with John S. Marmaduke, encouraged Hindman to attack immediately, but Daniel Frost and Francis A. Shoup were undecided. Although the attack came off as planned, Blunt was reinforced by Francis J. Herron, and the Confederates were forced to retreat. On July 4, 1863, Fagan took part in the attack upon Union-held Helena, Arkansas, on the Mississippi River. Holmes had planned to capture the hills outside the town and from that position attack the main Federal force. Although Sterling Price reached his objective, the troops under Fagan and Marmaduke were turned back, and Holmes was forced to withdraw. Holmes intimated that Price was to blame for not reinforcing Fagan during the battle. Frustrated and exhausted, Holmes fell ill soon after the battle and transferred command of the District of Arkansas to Price. While Holmes took to his bed to recover, Fagan temporarily replaced Price; on July 23, 1863, Fagan was informed of the situation, and the next day assumed command of Price's division (Fagan's, Parson's, and McRae's brigades of infantry) with headquarters at Searcy. When Price recognized that the Federals planned to advance upon Little Rock, he ordered Fagan to withdraw his forces from Searcy and Des Arc, and to take position upon Bayou Meto, about twelve miles northeast of Little Rock. Fagan remained in command of the division until August 17, when Daniel Frost replaced him and Fagan returned to his brigade.

Probably at the same sitting, Fagan stood for this less-formal pose. (Museum of the Confederacy, Richmond, Va.)

Fagan took part in the defense of Little Rock, but the Federal army captured the town in September 1863. In the spring of 1864 Fagan participated in the Camden Expedition, the Arkansas part of the Red River Campaign. General E. Kirby Smith ordered Fagan to destroy the communications of Frederick Steele's army between Camden and the supply base at Pine Bluff. On April 24 Fagan learned that 240 supply wagons, with an escort of 1,440 men under Lieutenant Colonel Francis M. Drake, had left Camden for Pine Bluff. The attack on the supply train at Marks' Mill lasted less than two hours; Fagan had hit the train first, with Joseph Shelby's assault on the rear completing the triumph. The Confederates won an important victory, wiped out a large relief train, and took over one thousand prisoners. Fagan lost only 150 men. The disaster at Marks' Mills was one of the deciding factors that forced Steele to abandon Camden and retreat toward Little Rock, where the needs of his starving army could be met. As a result of his performance in the Camden campaign, Fagan was promoted to major general on June 13, ranking from April 25, 1864.

In September Fagan headed a cavalry division that accompanied Price on his final invasion of Missouri. On September 19 Price and the Army of Missouri entered the state from three different points; Fagan took the center route through Martinsburg, Reeves' Station, and Greenville while Marmaduke was on his right and Shelby on his left. They were to meet at Fredericktown. On September 27 the Confederates reached Pilot Knob, and Shelby's and Fagan's troops surrounded the stronghold that protected the town, Fort Davidson. The Federals abandoned the position, and the Confederates easily took the empty fortification. From September 28 until October 19 the Confederates moved through Missouri. But on the morning of October 19 the Confederates encountered part of Samuel Curtis' Army of the Border southeast of Lexington. On October 21 and 22 the Union cavalry under Alfred Pleasonton routed Price's rear guard under Fagan on the Little Blue. At Westport Fagan and Shelby were hit again. The Confederates scattered, and Fagan's division dissolved. Nevertheless, the Confederates managed to rally after the defeat and headed south.

From February 1 until the spring of 1865 Fagan commanded the cavalry in the District of Arkansas. In April he was the only major general on active duty in Arkansas and was placed in charge of the district. He was paroled on June 20, 1865, and returned to farming in Arkansas. He became a United States marshal in 1875, receiver for the Land Office in 1877. In 1890 he was defeated in a bid for state railroad commissioner. Fagan died at Little Rock on September 1, 1893, and is buried in Mount Holy Cemetery.

Anne Bailey

Kerby, Robert, *Kirby Smith's Confederacy* (New York, 1972).

This portrait is sometimes identified as being Fagan. If so, it probably shows him early in the war as colonel of the 1st Arkansas. (University of Arkansas, Little Rock)

Featherston appears as colonel of the 17th Mississippi in this 1861 or early 1862 image. (Museum of the Confederacy, Richmond, Va.)

⋆ *Winfield Scott Featherston* ⋆

The youngest of seven children, Winfield Scott Featherston was born on August 8, 1820, near Murfreesboro, Tennessee. His parents, Charles and Lucy Pitts Featherston, had recently relocated to Rutherford County from Virginia. Young Featherston was educated in the local schools, and was attending a Columbus, Georgia, school in 1836, when at age seventeen he dropped out to enlist for service in the Creek War. After being mustered out, he took up the study of law, and was admitted to the bar in 1840 at Houston, Mississippi. He was elected as a Democrat in 1846 to represent the Second Mississippi District in the 30th Congress, in which Abraham Lincoln also sat. Featherston was reelected in 1848 but defeated in 1850, when the states rights candidates were repudiated by the Mississippi electorate. He moved to Holly Springs in 1857, where he continued his law practice.

In mid-December 1860, following the election of Abraham Lincoln, Featherston traveled to Kentucky to discuss the crisis with states rights men and to seek their support. When Mississippi left the Union on January 9, 1861, Featherston organized and captained the Mississippi Guards, which were mustered into Confederate service at Corinth on June 7 as Company G, 17th Mississippi Infantry. He had been elected colonel on the 4th. Featherston and his people left Corinth on June 11 for Virginia, and detrained at Manassas Junction six days later. He first came under artillery fire at Blackburn's Ford on July 18. At First Manassas, Featherston and his regiment crossed Bull Run at Mclean's Ford late in the afternoon and battled the Federals near Rocky Run. He was ordered to the Leesburg area in mid-August. Featherston first distinguished himself in combat at Ball's Bluff on October 21. Upon the death of Colonel E. R. Burt of the 18th Mississippi, he took command of the 17th and 18th Mississippi and attacked the Federals to his front, "capturing two cannon and driving the enemy over the bluff and into the Potomac River." More than five hundred prisoners were captured by the Mississippians.

Known as "Old Swet" by his troops, Featherston was promoted brigadier general on March 6, to rank from March 4, 1862, and in early April placed in charge of a brigade in D. H. Hill's division that included the 27th and 28th Georgia, 4th North Carolina, and 49th Virginia. He led his brigade on the march from the Rapidan to the Yorktown-Warwick line, on the retreat up the Peninsula, where they engaged the enemy at Williamsburg on May 5. Illness prevented his participation in the savage fight at Seven Pines.

On June 12 a second Mississippi brigade, to include the 12th and 19th regiments and the 2d battalion, was organized in the army that since the first of the month had been commanded by Robert E. Lee. The brigade was led by Featherston and assigned to James Longstreet's Division. Featherston and his Mississippians participated in the Seven Days' battles, fighting at Gaines' Mill and Glendale. At the latter battle he was shot in the shoulder and seriously wounded and was commended by Longstreet for his "gallantry and skill."

Featherston returned to duty in the fourth week of August, rejoining his brigade on the march into northern Virginia. The army had been reorganized into two corps, and Featherston's brigade had been assigned to Richard Anderson's Division of Longstreet's corps. As senior officer, he commanded two brigades in Longstreet's August 30 Second Manassas onslaught. Longstreet was not pleased with Featherston's work, and he failed to commend the Mississippian in his report. Featherston missed the Maryland Campaign and returned to duty and command of his brigade in early November. At Fredericksburg, on December 13, Featherston held the rifle-pits west of the Orange Plank Road, where his troops came under heavy artillery fire.

On January 19, 1863, the six-foot, two-inch tall Featherston was detached from the Army of Northern Virginia and ordered to Mississippi, where in early February he assumed command of a Mississippi brigade—the 3d, 22d, 31st, and 33d infantry regiments

119

and 1st Sharpshooter Battalion—assigned to William W. Loring's Division. Featherston's first combat assignment in Mississippi came in late March, when he engaged and helped turn back the Union amphibious expedition that had ascended Steele's Bayou. Featherston's people were lightly engaged at Champion's Hill on May 16, and in the ensuing debacle participated in Loring's retreat to Jackson and joined the army Joseph E. Johnston was gathering to relieve Vicksburg. Johnston's efforts failed, and following the siege of Jackson July 9–16, Featherston and his brigade retreated to Morton.

Two of Johnston's four infantry divisions—Loring's and French's—remained in Mississippi when the others were rushed to northwest Georgia to reinforce the Army of Tennessee and fight at Chickamauga. Featherston and his troops from camps near Brandon and Canton supported Confederate cavalry watching the crossing of the Big Black. Featherston took the field to oppose Union columns that, between February 3 and March 6, 1864, cut a swath of destruction across Mississippi from Vicksburg to Meridian and back.

In May Leonidas Polk and his Army of Mississippi were rushed from western Alabama to reinforce General Johnston's Army of Tennessee as it engaged William T. Sherman in the northern Georgia mountains. Featherston's brigade, reinforced by the 40th Mississippi, reached Resaca on the 12th and participated in the fighting there during the next seventy-two hours. Featherston, during Johnston's retrograde, clashed with the foe at Cassville, on the 19th. Along the New Hope Church line on May 31, Featherston's skirmishers were mauled when they came up against the enemy posted behind breastworks. Upon the death of General Polk at Pine Mountain on June 14, Loring took command of the corps and Featherston of the division. On June 27 at Kennesaw Mountain his troops occupied rifle-pits between the mountain and Bell's Ferry road and more than held their own when attacked. Featherston rejoined his brigade on July 7 when A. P. Stewart assumed command of the corps and Loring resumed leadership of the division.

Featherston and his Mississippians saw desperate fighting at Peachtree Creek on July 20, when almost one-half of those engaged were casualties, and earned a merited commendation from General Loring. At Ezra Church on July 28 Loring was wounded, and Featherston again led the division into battle and continued in command as the soldiers grimly held the Atlanta rifle-pits that guarded the city until Loring's mid-September return to duty. The Confederates, meanwhile, had evacuated Atlanta on the night of September 1 and retreated to Palmetto Station.

In late September Featherston and his brigade crossed the Chattahoochee at Pumpkin Town, along with the other unit of Stewart's Corps, to begin the campaign that carried the Army of Tennessee to the gates of Nashville. Featherston struck the Western and Atlantic Railroad on October 3 and captured Big Shanty. He led his brigade in the desperate fight at Franklin on November 30, where they pressed ahead with dauntless courage but were repulsed with terrible losses, including three battle flags. Featherston and his Mississippians again met the enemy at Nashville and, along with the Army of Tennessee, suffered crushing defeat. On December 20 at Columbia Featherston's was one of six brigades assigned to E. C. Walthall's command and charged with shielding the Confederate retreat. At Anthony's Hill on the 25th and at Sugar Creek the next day, Featherston turned and savaged the oncoming Union cavalry. On the 28th Featherston crossed the Tennessee River and the Yankees abandoned the pursuit.

In February 1865 Featherston and the remnant of Loring's Division were transferred from Tupelo, Mississippi, to North Carolina. He next fought at Kinston on March 10 and at Bentonville March 19–20. He was surrendered by General Johnston on April 26 and paroled at Greensboro on May 1, 1865.

Featherston returned to Holly Springs, resumed his law practice, and had an important role in the mid-1870s' struggle to oust the carpetbag administrations headed by Governor Adelbert Ames. He led the attack on Ames by introducing the impeachment resolution in the Mississippi House of Representatives, and acted as chairman of the committee that prepared the articles and conducted the prosecution. Featherston served two terms in the lower house of the Mississippi legislature (1876–78 and 1880–82). In 1882 he became judge of the second judicial district, and was a member of the state constitutional convention of 1890. He died in his Holly Springs home on May 28, 1891, and is buried in that city.

Edwin C. Bearss

Hooker, Charles E., *Mississippi*, Vol. IX in Evans, *Confederate Military History*.

Memphis, *Commercial Appeal* (May 30, 1891).

Rowland, Dunbar, *Mississippi Statistical Register* (Nashville, 1908).

✶ *Samuel Wragg Ferguson* ✶

No wartime photo of Ferguson showing him in a genuine uniform has surfaced. This was made at West Point when Cadet Ferguson was no more than 23, and probably in 1857. (U.S. Military Academy Archives, West Point, N.Y.)

The son of a politician and planter, Ferguson was born on November 3, 1834, in Charleston, South Carolina. After attending a private school in that city, he received an appointment to the United States Military Academy at West Point. Ferguson graduated nineteenth in a class of thirty-eight in 1857 and became a 2d lieutenant in the United States Dragoons. Ferguson participated in the Mormon expedition under Albert Sidney Johnston from 1857 to 1858 and served at Fort Walla Walla, Washington, from 1859 to 1860. He resigned his commission on March 1, 1861.

Ferguson became a captain of South Carolina regulars shortly after his resignation. Brigadier General Pierre G. T. Beauregard named Ferguson as an aide-de-camp when he assumed command at Charleston Harbor on March 6. Shortly afterwards Ferguson received a commission as a lieutenant in the Confederate cavalry but continued on Beauregard's staff through the bombardment of Fort Sumter and during the First Battle ofManassas, when his horse was killed by an enemy artillery shell. He helped take the captured Federal flags to the War Department in Richmond after the battle, then went west with Beauregard, and by the time of the Battle of Shiloh he had become a lieutenant colonel. Early during the second day of fighting at Shiloh, Ferguson briefly commanded a brigade of the II Corps.

By June 1862 Ferguson had gone to Mississippi, where Major General Earl Van Dorn assigned him to cavalry to guard both flanks of the army at Vicksburg. Ferguson later moved to the upper Yazoo River delta, where he soon led a mixed force of infantry, cavalry, and artillery detailed to protect the corn and cotton crops in that region. During February, March, and April 1863 Ferguson and his men opposed several Union incursions in their area. They were particularly active in the Steele's Bayou and Deer Creek expeditions and played a prominent role in turning back the Federals. Following the Steele's Bayou Expedition, Major General Dabney H. Maury expressed the gratitude felt by troops near Vicksburg. "We owe our escape to Ferguson's gallantry, energy, and good service."

On May 7 Ferguson received a temporary assignment as colonel of cavalry. He was promoted to brigadier general on July 28, to date from July 23, 1863, and from the late summer through the early winter of 1863 led a cavalry brigade composed of Alabama, Mississippi, and Tennessee troopers in northern Mississippi. His men skirmished occasionally with Union troops conducting raids in the area. On October 26 his men attacked and virtually destroyed the 1st Alabama (Union) Cavalry at Vincent's Crossroads, near Bay Springs, Mississippi. Ferguson's brigade was assigned to a division commanded by Brigadier General James R. Chalmers during part of this time period. At other times Ferguson exercised command of all troops in northeastern Mississippi. He led his brigade toward Jackson in late January 1864 and participated in the Meridian Campaign, February 3–March 6. The brigade formed a part of Brigadier General William H. Jackson's division for much of the campaign. Ferguson's men rode north to assist Major General Nathan Bedford Forrest in fighting the raid of Brigadier General William Sooy Smith but arrived after Forrest's defeat of Smith at West Point.

Ferguson held division command (his own and Brigadier General Wirt Adams' brigades) during a few days in late February. In April 1864, in response to Federal movements in northern Alabama, Ferguson received orders to take his brigade to Tuscaloosa. His men chased deserters and stragglers in the area after the Union threat dissipated. When Lieutenant General Leonidas Polk took troops from this Department of Alabama, Mississippi, and East Louisiana to reinforce the Army of Tennessee in northern Georgia in May, Ferguson's brigade moved to Resaca. The brigade again formed a part of "Red" Jackson's division. Ferguson and his men operated mainly on the flanks of the army during the Atlanta Campaign. Portions of the brigade served under Major General Joseph Wheeler when he contested the Union advance at Peachtree Creek on July 17 and 18. Wheeler then took the men to the right of the army to oppose Major General James B. McPherson's flanking movement. Federal attacks on July 20 and 21 against Ferguson's position on Bald Hill drove his men back in confusion.

Ferguson accompanied the army into northern Georgia after the fall of Atlanta and skirmished with the enemy on several occasions. When Jackson's division rode north with the army toward Tennessee, Ferguson's brigade was attached to Wheeler's cavalry corps. The troops offered what opposition they could to Sherman's March to the Sea from October to December. In late November Beauregard recommended Ferguson for a temporary appointment as a major general. Wheeler opposed this promotion in January 1865 when he learned about it. He wrote that Ferguson "was not competent" and complained about the high desertion rate in Ferguson's brigade. In several letters, Wheeler outlined various charges against Ferguson. He said that Jackson had found Ferguson "very inefficient" and "had him tried before a court-martial for neglect of duty." Wheeler claimed that a promotion "would be rewarding bad conduct and unsoldierly spirit," adding that Brigadier General Robert H. Anderson, "who is a friend of General Ferguson...says General Ferguson was insubordinate as a cadet, insubordinate as a lieutenant in the U.S. Army, and insubordinate as a brigadier under General Jackson."

Ferguson's brigade remained in the vicinity of Augusta, Georgia, as a part of Major General Pierce M. B. Young's division during most of Sherman's campaign into the Carolinas. In early April 1865 Ferguson received orders to take his brigade toward Danville, Virginia, to oppose the raid by Major General George Stoneman's Union cavalry into that area. When he reached Greensboro, North Carolina, Ferguson was halted, and his brigade became part of the escort for President Jefferson Davis as he fled toward Georgia. Ferguson and his men parted from the escort at Washington, Georgia, on May 5 under orders from Secretary of War John C. Breckenridge. They were paroled on May 10 at Forsyth, Georgia. Ferguson lived in Greenville, Mississippi, after the war and practiced law there. He served on the Mississippi State Levee Commission in 1876 and in 1885 received an appointment by President Chester A. Arthur to the United States Mississippi River Commission. Ferguson returned to Charleston in 1894, to become a civil engineer, and volunteered for duty in the Spanish-American War. He died in Jackson, Mississippi, on February 3, 1917, and was buried there.

Arthur W. Bergeron, Jr.

Capers, Ellison, *South Carolina*, Vol. VI in Evans, *Confederate Military History*.

☆ Charles William Field ☆

One of the more able brigade and division commanders with the Army of Northern Virginia, Field was a Kentuckian, born April 6, 1828, at the family home, "Airy Mount," in Woodford County. He attended the U.S. Military Academy at West Point and graduated in the class of 1849, too late to see action in the Mexican War. He spent the next twelve years in uniform, but when Virginia and other border states seceded after the opening of the war at Fort Sumter, he resigned his commission in the Old Army and entered Confederate service.

When the 6th Virginia Cavalry was organized, Field gained its colonelcy but saw no action during the months of "phoney war" that followed First Manassas. With more and more Virginia brigades being formed as Joseph E. Johnston built his army that winter of 1861–62, brigadiers were much needed, and on March 14, 1862, President Davis appointed Field a brigadier, to date from March 9. Immediately the Kentuckian took command of a Virginia brigade that Johnston soon attached to the division commanded by General A. P. Hill, though they missed the fighting at Fair Oaks. Field saw his first real action at Beaver Dam Creek on June 26, in the opening of the Seven Days' Campaign.

Field was well liked in the Army of Northern Virginia. Large, burly, and good-humored, he had an easy and affable manner that endeared him to Hill in particular. So did his performance in battle. He led his two-thousand-man brigade into the center of the Confederate line facing FitzJohn Porter and held his position under heavy fire during the ensuing wait for "Stonewall" Jackson to arrive on the field. The subsequent failure of the attack owed nothing to him or his brigade.

Thereafter Field led his brigade with Hill throughout the campaign, and at Glendale on June 30 his men captured Yankee General George A. McCall, and the prisoner himself later paid tribute to the fury of Field's assault, carrying everything before it. Nevertheless, the brigadier and his men suffered considerably during their first days in battle, attracting the attention and admiration of Lee.

Subsequently, Field led his brigade under Jackson at Cedar Mountain, then went on to take a distinguished part at Second Manassas before a very serious wound nearly killed him. Recuperation took months, removing Field entirely from active duty, and then later only allowing him to perform desk duty superintending Richmond's Bureau of Conscription. Only as the spring of 1864 approached was he ready to resume active duty, and in recognition of Lee's confidence in him Davis appointed the Kentuckian a major general on February 12, 1864, to take rank immediately. Since the Confederate senate was then in session, his promotion was confirmed immediately.

With Longstreet due to return to Virginia from his Tennessee adventure, Field was assigned to command Hood's Division while that general recovered from the loss of a leg at Chickamauga. The association with Hood's Division lasted for the remainder of the war.

Field first took his division into combat in the Wilderness. Along with fellow division commander Joseph B. Kershaw, he rushed to the battlefield, arriving on the second day of the fighting just in time to

Quite possibly from the same sitting, this image shows Field late in the war. (James Longstreet, *From Manassas to Appomattox*)

support Hill on the right and deliver a telling counter-punch against Hancock's II Corps. Field narrowly missed being hit in the volley that accidentally killed General Micah Jenkins and wounded Longstreet. Longstreet himself told Field, the senior division commander, to take command of the corps and continue the attack, but Lee called it off.

In subsequent operations throughout Spotsylvania and beyond, Field retained temporary command until Richard H. Anderson was promoted and put in charge of the I Corps. Field led his division on through the Siege of Petersburg and the subsequent retreat to Appomattox, fighting heroically in the army's last days. He gave his parole along with the rest of the survivors of the army and retired once more to private life.

General Field lived exactly twenty-seven years to the day after Lee's surrender, dying on April 9, 1892, in Washington, D.C., and buried in Loudon Park Cemetery in Baltimore. During those years he practiced a succession of professions. In the late 1860s he became an official of the Piedmont and Arlington Life Insurance Company of Virginia and was influential in persuading other distinguished former Confederates to head its various state branches. After the company failed in 1873, he joined several other former generals, like William W. Loring, in taking service in the army of Ishmael Pasha, the khedive of Egypt. Following that service, he moved to Washington, secured a position as doorkeeper of the House of Representatives, became a civil engineer, and for a time managed the Indian reservation at Hot Springs, Arkansas. Prior to his death, he was revered throughout as one of the most dependable and capable division commanders at Lee's command.

General Charles Field, shown here as a major general in 1864 or 1865. (U.S. Army Military History Institute, Carlisle, Pa.)

William C. Davis

Dowdey, Clifford, *The Seven Days* (Boston, 1961).
Steere, Edward, *The Wilderness Campaign* (Harrisburg, 1960).

⭐ *Joseph Finegan* ⭐

"Finegan, me bye, ye know ye are yur mither's darlin'." Thus is recorded just one example of the colorful dialect of this native Irishman, born November 17, at Clones, Ireland. Like thousands of other sons of Eire, he immigrated to the United States in the 1830s, settling in Florida near Jacksonville, where he quickly became a prominent member of the community, operating first a small plantation and later a sawmill. A few years later he removed to Fernandina and began a long and useful association with the influential politician David Yulee, later senator from Florida. Together they commenced construction of a railroad, and Finegan's own importance rose in tandem with Yulee's.

Thus when the state secession crisis loomed, Finegan served as a member of the 1861 state convention that on January 10 voted to withdraw from the Union. For reasons that are unclear, given Finegan's complete lack of military training or experience, Governor John Milton put him in charge of the state's efforts to get onto a war footing. This, plus the political necessities of appointing a sufficient number of brigadiers from Florida, induced President Davis to tender Finegan a commission on April 5, 1862, to take rank immediately. The Senate confirmed the appointment the same day, and Finegan himself accepted it on April 17, thereby becoming one of the senior officers to be appointed from his state.

On April 8, 1862, Finegan took command of the Department of Middle and Eastern Florida, which he held for the next two years. It was a backwater command, largely of importance only for protecting the long coastline, and raising troops, often for service elsewhere. Soon after Finegan took command, R. E.

Lee complimented him on his zeal and productivity at organizing Floridians into companies. Lee was also encouraged by Finegan's very realistic—and all-too-unusual—attitude that only as many state troops as necessary should be kept in Florida, while the majority should go to the main army in Virginia. Finegan's suggestion may have been prompted by a desire that he himself should be reassigned to the main theater of operations, but Lee believed that he could not be spared from Florida.

Finegan would start to see action in his own front later in 1862, as Federal incursions into Florida brought the war to him. While keeping his headquarters at Tallahassee, he oversaw the defense of Tampa in the summer and in September took and occupied Saint John's Bluff. In March 1863 he captured Jacksonville and held it briefly. His great moment, however, came at the Battle of Olustee, when Federals under Truman Seymour made a landing at Jacksonville and moved inland. Finegan assembled hastily the troops of his department and on February 20, 1864, delivered a telling attack that halted the enemy advance and sent Seymour back in retreat.

It was possibly the success at Olustee, combined with the confidence that Lee had expressed earlier in Finegan, that led the Virginia chieftain on May 16 to ask the War Department to have a brigade made up of available Florida troops and sent to him, with the Irishman in command. Gathering forces from all points to resist Grant's advance, Lee needed the man from Florida.

Finegan wears the collar insignia of a colonel, though he was directly commissioned a brigadier. (Museum of the Confederacy, Richmond, Va.)

"Marse Robert" was not to be disappointed. Finegan arrived in time to hold a critical point in the line at Cold Harbor on June 3. When the Federals briefly broke through, Finegan's brigade rushed into the gap, and quickly plugged it once more, winning compliments from many quarters. Thereafter he remained with the Army of Northern Virginia, his brigade soon being reassigned to Mahone's Division of the III Corps. Throughout the remainder of 1864 Finegan led the 2d, 5th, 8th, 9th, 10th, and 11th Florida in the trenches around Petersburg.

In January 1865 prominent Floridians petitioned the government to have him returned to their state. Finegan himself, weary after almost four years of continual service without a rest, also asked that he be reassigned, though as always he revealed a spirit of cooperation when he did not request that his brigade be sent with him, knowing that Lee needed it more. On March 20, 1865, he was reassigned to command in Florida. There in May he rendered his final services to the Confederacy when he assisted Secretary of War John C. Breckinridge and Secretary of State Judah P. Benjamin in successfully escaping through Florida to Cuba and the Bahamas, respectively.

Following the war, General Finegan lived in Jacksonville for a time, then removed to Rutledge, working for a time as a cotton broker, as well as practicing law. He served a term in the state senate, 1865–66, and finally died on October 29, 1885, at Rutledge, and was buried in the Old City Cemetery at Jacksonville. He had shown himself to be one of that class of men who led by raw native good sense. His potential may never have been truly challenged in the Florida command or in his limited field experience in battle, but wherever he served he won the approval of those above and below him.

William C. Davis

Dickison, J. J., *Florida*, Vol. XI in Evans, *Confederate Military History*.

Hanna, A. J., *Flight Into Oblivion* (Richmond, 1938).

One of the war's mystery photos is this, variously identified as Brigadier General T.B. Chaffee or as Captain Fred B. Schaffer. There was no General Chaffee in the Confederate service, nor even a colonel by that or a similar name. And no mere captain would be wearing a uniform with the buttons and sleeve braid of a brigadier. The similarities to Finegan are so strong as to be practically undeniable, however. (Western Reserve Historical Society, Cleveland, Ohio)

This handsome, previously unpublished image of Finley shows him as colonel of the 6th Florida Infantry sometime in late 1862 or 1863. (Museum of the Confederacy, Richmond, Va.)

⭑ *Jesse Johnson Finley* ⭑

The son of a wealthy planter, Finley was born in Wilson County, Tennessee, on November 18, 1812. He was educated at an academy in Lebanon before he read law in Nashville. After being admitted to the bar, he opened a law office in Lebanon. During the Seminole War of 1836, Finley organized a company of mounted volunteers and was appointed captain. He served in Florida for two years, returning to Tennessee in 1838.

Moving often over the next few years, Finley continued to practice law and became very active in politics. In 1841 he was elected state senator from Mississippi County, Arkansas, but resigned his seat in 1842 and moved to Memphis, Tennessee. There he was elected mayor in 1845, but in 1846 moved again to Marianna, Florida. Finley was elected a Florida state senator in 1850 and in 1852 served as a Whig presidential elector. From 1853 to 1861 he served as a judge for Florida's western circuit.

After Florida seceded in 1861, Finley became a Confederate district judge but resigned that post in March 1862 to enlist as a private in the 6th Florida Infantry. Probably because of his political prominence, Finley quickly rose to captain and then to colonel of the regiment. Attached to Col. W. G. M. Davis' Florida brigade in eastern Tennessee, the regiment invaded Kentucky with E. Kirby Smith's column during the late summer of 1862. Following the invasion, Finley oversaw the department's court-martial at Knoxville, Tennessee.

Finley's first real combat experience came at Chickamauga, where his regiment was in Colonel Robert C. Trigg's brigade. On the afternoon of September 19, 1863, the brigade was ordered to support an attack by John Bell Hood. The order to advance somehow miscarried, and Finley soon found himself several hundred yards ahead of the rest of the brigade. Nonetheless, the 6th Florida broke through one Union line and captured a battery of artillery. However, being unsupported, Finley was forced to withdraw after suffering the loss of 165 men. Trigg

wrote of Finley's command, "The fortune of war threw the Sixth Florida Regiment into the post of danger and upon them the heaviest loss, and proved them veterans in their first fight." On the next day Finley again drew praise when he led the 6th Florida and 54th Virginia in a charge against a Union position and captured five hundred prisoners.

On November 8, 1863, Finley was promoted to brigadier general, to rank from November 16, and given command of all the Florida infantry in the Army of Tennessee. He apparently was taken aback by the promotion and wrote Jefferson Davis to assure the president he did not seek the rank. Davis wrote Finley on December 16, "The fact that you did not seek the appointment conferred upon you, and your diffidence in assuming its responsibilities, is to me additional evidence of your fitness to command. I shall but the more confidently rely on one who, ready to serve, does not aspire to command."

Finley's new brigade was placed in line with Braxton Bragg's army near Chattanooga. When the Federals broke through the Confederate line at Missionary Ridge on November 25, 1863, Finley's Florida brigade performed admirably in rear guard action while the army escaped. Bragg said, "I cannot, in justice to the generous and brave, consistently close this without expressing my thanks to Brigadier-General Finley for his gallant bearing and prompt assistance in every emergency."

The winter was a severe hardship for Finley's men. In February 1864 the officers of the Florida brigade forwarded a petition to Finley to be sent to Congress. The officers attached a list showing the outrageous prices they were forced to pay for food and clothing and declared they could not survive on the meager pay allotted them. Finley supported his officers, endorsed the petition, and forwarded it to his superiors, but apparently no action was taken on it by Congress.

During the Atlanta Campaign, Finley's brigade was still in Bate's Division of William Hardee's Corps.

Finley saw heavy fighting in the campaign, but there is little official documentation of it. At Resaca he was badly wounded and put out of action until the army reached Atlanta. Then at Jonesborough shell fragments killed his horse and severely wounded him again, but he refused to be evacuated to Atlanta until all of his wounded men had been removed. Because of this sense of duty, he missed the last evacuation train, and was finally slipped through roving bands of Yankees and back to the hospital in a wagon.

Finley was separated from his brigade for the rest of the war. He tried to rejoin his unit in North Carolina after recovering from the second wound, but Federal troops blocked his way. He therefore reported for duty to Howell Cobb at Columbus, Georgia, and surrendered there with Cobb in April 1865.

Finley settled in Lake City, Florida, after the war and resumed his law practice. He later moved to Jacksonville in the 1870s. Finley reentered politics and served in Congress from 1875 to 1879 before losing his seat in 1879 in a contested election. In 1887 he was appointed to the United States Senate to fill a vacancy but was refused the seat because of a technicality. Returning to the legal profession, Finley served as a Florida circuit court judge from 1887 to 1903. He died in Lake City on November 6, 1904, and is buried in Gainesville.

Terry L. Jones

Dickison, J. J., *Florida*, Vol. XI in Evans, *Confederate Military History*.

Finley appears older and heavier in this later war image which shows stars of rank affixed to what is otherwise a simple broadcloth suit. Though signs of retouching are not apparent, it is faintly possible that the stars are an artist's addition. (Museum of the Confederacy, Richmond, Va.)

⭐ *John Buchanan Floyd* ⭐

This fascinating image of General John Floyd, previously unpublished, is the only genuine portrait known to exist showing him in uniform. The buttons are arranged as for a brigadier, and like Elzey he wears a stripe on his shoulders that is clearly non-regulation. The beard, unknown in any of his prewar portraits, is distinctly a wartime affectation. (William A. Turner Collection)

Floyd was born at "Smithfield," his maternal grandparents' home, in Montgomery County, Virginia, on June 1, 1806. His father, John Floyd, served in the U.S. Congress and as governor of Virginia. Floyd spent his childhood in a frontier area of Virginia, where the outdoors made him muscular and athletic. The remoteness of his home forced his intellectually oriented mother, Letitia Preston Floyd, to educate her son with the aid of her husband's superb library. In 1829 he graduated in the top of his class from South Carolina College and the following year he married his cousin, Sally Buchanan Preston.

Floyd briefly practiced law in Wytheville but soon relocated to Arkansas, where he supplemented his earnings as a lawyer by becoming a cotton planter. In 1837 a malignant fever killed forty of his slaves and shattered his own health. Nearly bankrupt, he returned to Virginia and practiced law in Abingdon. His rapid success enabled him to pay off his substantial outstanding debts from the Arkansas fiasco.

Elected to represent his county in the general assembly in 1847, he won reelection the following year. His advocation of state-funded internal improvements, especially railroads, won him the governorship in 1848, when he used his new office to promote industrialization. In the constitutional convention of 1850 he successfully lobbied for universal suffrage, a popular issue among his western constituents.

He retired from politics in 1852 and returned to his law practice in Abingdon. A states rights Democrat, Floyd did serve as a delegate to the Democratic convention later that year. When the Know-Nothing Party seemed on the verge of carrying the state in 1855, Floyd returned to politics and ran for the general assembly. His successful campaign carried several other Democratic candidates on his coattails, thereby enabling the Democrats to retain control of the state.

His contribution in this, the fiercest political struggle in Virginia prior to the secessionist crisis, was recognized by the national leadership of the party.

In 1857 President James Buchanan appointed Floyd secretary of war. Though he was successful in that position until 1860, three incidents that year would haunt him for the rest of his life. First, he successfully urged Buchanan to appoint Joseph E. Johnston quartermaster general in opposition to then Mississippi Senator Jefferson Davis' request that Albert Sidney Johnston fill the position. Later that year Floyd was accused of transferring excessive amounts of weapons to Southern arsenals. It is probable that these transfers were merely to make room in Northern arsenals for modern percussion rifles already on order by transferring outdated, converted flint-locks. Floyd resigned his position on December 29 because he opposed Buchanan's approval of Major Robert Anderson's continued occupation of Fort Sumter. Regardless of his opinions, following the secession of South Carolina on the 20th, many still believed his character irreproachable. The chairman of the House Committee on Military Affairs, Benjamin Stanton of Ohio, reportedly stated in early 1861 that the accusations made against Floyd were based on "rumor, speculation and misapprehension."

Although Buchanan showed his continued support of Floyd by accepting his offer to continue as secretary of war until replaced, another controversy further tainted his position. In February 1861 a congressional investigation found Floyd guilty of at least "reckless imprudence" regarding the fraudulent expenditures of $870,000 of Indian trust bonds held by the Department of the Interior, although it appears certain that Floyd did not personally profit from the illicit transactions.

Prior to leaving his cabinet post, Floyd adamantly opposed secession. His attitude changed before the firing on Fort Sumter, however, and after the secession of Virginia he raised a brigade of volunteers. Appointed major general of the Virginia State Line by the general assembly on May 17, 1862, Floyd received a brigadier's commission in the Confederate Army six days later, to rank immediately. Floyd led his brigade under General Robert E. Lee in western Virginia, and on August 11 assumed command of the Army of Kanawha. His performance at Cross Lanes on August 26 and at Carnifix Ferry on September 10 earned him congratulations from both President Jefferson Davis and Secretary of War Judah P. Benjamin. Floyd conducted offensive operations in the Kanawha and New River region between October 19 and November 16, engaging in substantial skirmishes at Gauley Bridge, November 1–3.

Floyd was transferred along with his brigade to Bowling Green, Kentucky, in December 1861, where General Albert Sidney Johnston ordered him to take his Virginians to Fort Donelson, Tennessee, where Floyd found himself the ranking officer. Shortly after his arrival at Fort Donelson, he found his garrison trapped against the Cumberland River by Brigadier General Ulysses S. Grant's Union Army. After bungling an attack designed to extricate his troops, the dithering Floyd agreed with his subordinate, Brigadier General Simon Bolivar Buckner, that the only remaining course of action was to surrender. Fearful of the treatment he would receive if captured because of the accusations made against him while secretary of war, Floyd left Buckner to arrange the capitulation while he and most of his Virginia brigade escaped by steamboat. Floyd withdrew to Nashville which, after an abortive attempt to remove supplies, he abandoned.

Floyd's failure to request reinforcements for Fort Donelson or to evacuate the site sooner, coupled with his desertion of the garrison, resulted in his removal from command by President Davis on March 11, 1862. Davis even denied Floyd a court of inquiry.

Despite his tarnished reputation, Floyd remained active in the war effort. Commissioned a major general of militia by the Virginia General Assembly, Floyd used his influence in southwestern Virginia to raise partisans. His troops not only suppressed residents sympathetic to the Union but hampered Confederate officials who attempted to recruit soldiers for the regular army in that vicinity. Exposure from the constant campaigning along the Big Sandy River quickly took its toll and weakened Floyd, who died near Abingdon, in the country estate of his adopted daughter, on August 26, 1863. He is buried in Abingdon.

The talent and determination demonstrated by Floyd during his prewar career, despite the controversies of 1860, gave every indication that he would be an asset to the Confederates. Instead, his credibility and initially successful military career ended with Fort Donelson, before the war had even entered its second year.

Lawrence L. Hewitt

Hotchkiss, Jedediah, *Virginia*, Vol. III in Evans, *Confederate Military History*.

⋆ John Horace Forney ⋆

An outstanding, previously unpublished portrait of General John Forney, the only genuine image known showing him in uniform. It has the often-seen anomalies of brigadier's buttons and sleeve braid, with a colonel's collar insignia. (Alabama Department of Archives and History, Montgomery, Al.)

Forney was born on August 12, 1829, at Lincolnton, North Carolina. His older brother, William Henry Forney, also served as a general officer in the Confederate Army. In 1835 his parents moved to Calhoun County, Alabama, where he received his early education at the hands of private tutors. Forney attended West Point and graduated twenty-second out of forty-three in the class of 1852. He received a commission as a brevet 2d lieutenant in the 7th United States Infantry and by 1855 had become a 1st lieutenant in the 10th Infantry. Forney saw garrison duty in Kentucky, served on frontier duty in the Indian Territory, and participated in the Utah Expedition of Albert Sidney Johnston. In 1860 he became an instructor in infantry tactics at West Point.

Forney resigned his commission, the resignation being accepted on January 23, 1861, and on January 22 Governor A. B. Moore of Alabama appointed him colonel of the 1st Regiment of Artillery and special aide with orders to go to Pensacola, Florida. There he would drill the Alabama troops stationed near the town and assist in its defense. For a time Forney exercised command of Fort Barrancas and Barrancas Barracks. Major General Braxton Bragg appointed him as an acting inspector general in March, and Forney organized a harbor police force to prevent contact between Pensacola and Fort Pickens on Santa Rosa Island. Forney also assisted in supervising the construction of earthworks and the mounting of artillery. On March 16 he was appointed a captain in the Confederate artillery corps. Forney became colonel of the 10th Alabama Infantry when it was organized on June 4 and went with his unit to Virginia, where the

10th Alabama became a part of the Army of the Shenandoah. On July 21 Forney assumed command of the 5th Brigade of that army at Piedmont, Virginia. The brigade soon joined the army of General Joseph E. Johnston at Manassas. Forney led his regiment in an engagement at Dranesville, Virginia, on December 20 and received a severe wound while leading a charge. Brigadier General James E. B. Stuart said that Forney's "conspicuous bravery…was the admiration of all." In January 1862 General Johnston recommended Forney as a brigadier, saying he was "as fit for promotion as any colonel in the service of the Confederate States." Forney received his promotion on March 14, to date from March 10, and on April 2 was ordered to report for duty at Mobile, Alabama.

The War Department intended that he replace Major General Samuel Jones so that the latter could join the Army of Mississippi at Corinth. Forney reached Mobile on April 11, but since he was in poor health and still suffering from his wound, he received a brief leave to recuperate. When he returned to duty on April 28, he assumed command of the Department of Alabama and West Florida, which had responsibility primarily for the defense of Mobile and Pensacola. He began construction of a line of earthwork forts and redoubts around the city designed to protect it from a land attack. Creation of Department No. 2, or the Western Department, on July 2 resulted in Forney's command being redesignated the District of the Gulf. When General Braxton Bragg took his army through Mobile toward Chattanooga later that month, he planned to leave Sam Jones in Mobile and take Forney with him so the latter could have an active command in the field, possibly taking over Jones' division. Jefferson Davis urged Bragg to reconsider his purpose, so Bragg allowed Forney to retain his position in the Gulf city. On October 27, 1862, Forney received promotion to the rank of major general. His health began to fail about that same time, and his personal physician informed Bragg that Forney was "not in condition for such an important command, & ought to be relieved from command until his health is restored." Bragg relieved him of command on December 8, and Forney relinquished his position to Brigadier General William W. Mackall.

Forney had returned to duty by late March 1863 and commanded a division of two brigades near Vicksburg, Mississippi. On April 17 he assumed direction of a division recently led by Major General Dabney H. Maury. Forney took his men into the trenches at Vicksburg upon the approach of Grant's Union Army. They held the left center of the line and saw heavy fighting during the ensuing siege. After the surrender of the Vicksburg garrison Forney commanded camps of paroled prisoners at Enterprise, Mississippi, and Demopolis, Alabama, into early 1864. He requested assignment to field duty in late February. The War Department responded, "Your gallantry and efficiency are highly estimated," but it had no vacancy available for him.

Finally, on May 6, Forney received orders to report to General Edmund Kirby Smith in the Trans-Mississippi Department. Smith planned to have him replace Major General John G. Walker in command of a Texas infantry division. At first the Texans openly rebelled against Forney's assignment, and Smith considered cancelling his orders, but Forney finally assumed command of the division on September 3. He did not endear himself to the Texans because of his insistence on strict military discipline. His division formed a part of the District of Arkansas for some weeks, occupying camps at several places in the southern part of that state. The division then did garrison duty in northwestern Louisiana for three months before receiving orders to march to Hempstead, Texas. Since Forney outranked Walker, the commander of the District of Texas, Smith ordered Major General John B. Magruder from Arkansas to Texas so that Forney would not claim command of the district. Forney's men disbanded there May 19–20, 1865, after learning of the impending surrender of Confederate forces in the Trans-Mississippi Department.

Forney returned to Alabama at the end of the war and became a planter in Marengo and Calhoun counties. He also worked as a civil engineer for a time. Forney died in Jacksonville, Alabama, on September 13, 1902, and was buried there.

Arthur W. Bergeron, Jr.

Daugette, Annie Forney, "The Life of Major General John H. Forney, Written by His Daughter," *Alabama Historical Quarterly*, IX (1947), pp. 361-83.

Owens, Thomas McA., *History of Alabama and Dictionary of Alabama Biography* (Spartanburg, 1978).

✶ *William Henry Forney* ✶

No uniformed image of William Forney has been unearthed. This postwar portrait probably dates from the 1880s. (Museum of the Confederacy, Richmond, Va.)

Born in Lincolnton, North Carolina, on November 9, 1823, Forney moved to Alabama in 1835, where he was educated, practiced law, served in the state legislature, and went to the Mexican War as a 1st lieutenant in the Alabama Infantry Regiment.

With the outbreak of the Civil War, four Forney brothers entered the Confederate Army. William joined in May 1861, and on June 4 was elected captain of the "Pope Walker Guards," which became Company G of the 10th Alabama Infantry, commanded by his younger brother, Colonel (later major general) John H. Forney.

The regiment moved to Virginia in July. As part of the 5th Brigade of General Joseph E. Johnston's army, the 10th Alabama reached Manassas Junction from the Shenandoah Valley too late to fight at First Bull Run. William Forney's initial combat came at Dranesville on December 20, where he was shot in the shin—his first wound, but not his last. On January 28, while still convalescing, he was promoted to major, ranking from December 20. Then, as the regiment reorganized at Yorktown on May 3, its lieutenant colonelcy was accorded to him, dating from March 14. Before he could be mustered at that grade, however, the Butternuts began retreating up the Peninsula. He went into the ensuing Battle of Williamsburg still serving as major and acting lieutenant colonel of the 10th.

He emerged from that combat a wounded hero and a prisoner of war. The 10th formed the right of Cadmus Wilcox's Brigade in successfully attacking the Union III Corps. The brigadier reported that Forney "fell severely wounded while encouraging his men in the thickest of the fight, stricken down with a painful wound while leading his regiment, displaying both coolness and skill." That shoulder wound, which broke his right arm, proved so serious that he had to be left at William and Mary College and thus fell into Federal hands on May 6. He was paroled on July 29 and was exchanged on August 31.

Meantime, his brother's successor, John J. Woodward, had been killed at Gaines' Mill. To replace him, William Forney was promoted colonel of the 10th Alabama as of June 27, 1862. On into mid-April 1863, however, his nagging wound still confined him to courts and boards of James Longstreet's Corps.

He did command his outfit in the Chancellorsville Campaign and was heavily engaged at Salem Church. Although the 10th temporarily broke and fled at a key stage of that combat, he rallied it to resume fighting. Wilcox included Forney in the praise awarded all his regimental commanders: "intelligent, energetic, and gallant in commanding, directing, and leading their men." In this engagement, the junior officer was again wounded, this time slightly in the leg.

He remained with his regiment as it marched to Gettysburg. First fighting on July 2 embroiled him with Berdan's Sharpshooters and the 3d Maine Infantry in Pitzer's Woods. "In this affair so creditable to the 10th Alabama and its gallant colonel," reported Wilcox, "this regiment lost 10 killed and 28 wounded." Despite recent allegations that Forney was shot to pieces there, he actually survived that combat unscathed and participated in the main attack on Daniel Sickles' line later that day. Twice wounded in the fighting along the Emmitsburg Road, he took a third bullet that rebroke his right arm. Still he pressed on until his left heel was shot away in the "swale."

As at Williamsburg, his wounds proved so severe that he had to remain behind when the Southerners retreated. The Yankees captured him in the abandoned Confederate hospitals on July 5. Not until April 23, 1864, was he released from medical care. He was then imprisoned at Fort McHenry and was transferred to Fort Delaware on June 15.

Also in mid-June, potentially dangerous events in South Carolina affected Forney and other senior officers at Fort Delaware. The secessionists placed fifty captured officers, among them five generals, in Charleston, potentially under artillery fire. While the opposing chieftains argued matters of morality, Federal commander John G. Foster requested five captured Confederate generals and forty-five field officers to confine on Morris Island under Southern fire. Generals Edward Johnson, Franklin Gardner, James Archer, George Steuart, and Merriwether Thompson, seventeen majors, fourteen lieutenant colonels, and fourteen colonels (including Forney) were sent to Hilton Head on June 26. They were confined there on the brig *Dragoon*, guarded by the *Wabash*, but were not actually placed at the front under Butternut shelling. Both sides withdrew from extremes of retaliation, and some Confederate officers recalled that their stay at Hilton Head was relatively pleasant. The hostages were exchanged on August 3, first with a shipboard fete and then with celebration in Charleston.

The released secessionists received leaves of absence. Forney's lasted until November, when he returned to his unit at Petersburg. As senior colonel, he assumed command of Wilcox's old brigade, consisting of the 8th, 9th, 10th, 11th, and 14th Alabama infantry regiments. The 13th Alabama transferred to the brigade on January 9.

On the 18th the brigade's officers petitioned for Forney's promotion to permanent command. As early as August 1863, R. E. Lee had considered him for that position. "An excellent officer and worthy of promotion," the army commander called him then; "the person best entitled and best qualified...is Colonel Forney...an officer of intelligence, energy and bravery and of long and faithful service." Yet Lee realized that Forney was a prisoner in 1863. Two other able generals went to their deaths leading that brigade in 1864; it had been without a general since August 21. But now Forney was finally available. He was appointed brigadier general on February 23, ranking from February 15. As colonel, he led the brigade at Hicksford and Second Hatcher's Run. As general, he commanded it at Bermuda Hundred and Cumberland Church. At Appomattox his brigade mustered nine hundred fifty men, the fourth largest in Lee's army.

Postwar, Forney practiced law and served in Congress from 1875 to 1893. He was buried in Jacksonville, Alabama, following his death on January 16, 1894.

A brave, heroic regimental battle commander who earned his superiors' praise from brigade level to army level, Forney gave promise of being an able brigadier. Parole and promotion, however, came too late for him to be fairly tested at that higher rank.

Richard J. Sommers

Freeman, Douglas Southall, ed., *Lee's Dispatches: Unpublished Letters of General Robert E. Lee, C.S.A., to Jefferson Davis and the War Department of the Confederate States of America, 1862–65* (New York, 1957).

Wheeler, Joseph, *Alabama*, Vol. VII in Evans, *Confederate Military History*.

One of the finest portraits ever made of Nathan Bedford Forrest shows him as a major general or lieutenant general, and was taken in 1864 or 1865. (Alabama Department of Archives and History, Montgomery, Al.)

⭐ Nathan Bedford Forrest ⭐

The first of six sons, Forrest was born on July 13, 1821, at Chapel Hill, which was then in Bedford (presently Marshall) County, Tennessee. He was a fraternal twin, but his sister did not live to maturity. His father, William, was a frontier blacksmith and his mother, Marian Beck Forrest, was a formidable figure of backcountry Scots-Irish parentage. When Bedford, as he was called, was thirteen, the family relocated to Tippah County in northern Mississippi, settling near Salem. His father died in 1837, and the eldest son, not yet sixteen, became the man of the house.

In 1842 Forrest moved to Hernando, Mississippi, where he joined his uncle in a livestock and livery stable business. Three years later his uncle died in a shoot-out on the town's public square, and Bedford killed his first man, his uncle's murderer. The same year he married Mary Ann Montgomery. In 1851 the couple and their growing family relocated to Memphis, where Forrest traded in cotton, real estate, and slaves. A successful businessman, he soon accumulated sufficient capital to become a planter, purchasing two north Mississippi cotton plantations. In 1858 he was elected a Memphis alderman, but the next year shut down his slave trading and real estate enterprises, resigned as alderman, and settled on his Coahoma County plantation in Mississippi.

On June 14, 1861, six days after the voters had ratified Tennessee's secession, Forrest enlisted as a pri-

vate in Captain J. S. White's company of Tennessee Mounted Rifles. Private Forrest stood six feet, two inches tall, was lithe and powerful of frame, and had blue-gray eyes, iron-gray hair, and a short black beard. Forrest did not remain a private long. In early July he was discharged by action of Governor Isham G. Harris and authorized to recruit a battalion of mounted rangers for Confederate service. By the second week of October, he had raised and equipped, at his own expense, an eight-company battalion of which he was elected lieutenant colonel. Forrest and his unit took quickly to the field, joining Confederate forces in southwestern Kentucky headquartered at Hopkinsville.

Forrest's leadership and military skill first came to the attention of his superiors and the public at Fort Donelson in mid-February 1862. On the 12th he clashed with the Union columns closing in on the Confederate defenses, and on the 15th he and his "critter cavalry" were in the forefront as the Confederates rolled back the right wing of U. S. Grant's investing army, only to see their gains thrown away by irresolute and faint-hearted generals. Opposed to the decision by the generals to surrender, he, with their permission, escaped from Fort Donelson

Believed to be a previously unpublished image of Forrest as colonel of the 3d Tennessee Cavalry, probably in the spring of 1862. (North Carolina Division of Archives and History, Raleigh, N.C.)

Brigadier General Forrest, taken in 1862 or 1863. (Barker Texas History Center, University of Texas, Austin, Tx.)

with his battalion and a number of resolute soldiers by crossing ice-fringed Lick Creek, through water saddle-skirt deep.

On March 16 the battalion, having been reinforced, was reorganized as the 3d Tennessee Cavalry and on April 2 Forrest was elected colonel. Forrest was at Shiloh, and on April 8, while screening the Confederate retreat, he clashed with a pursuing Union column led by William T. Sherman. Charging the bluecoats, Forrest found himself nearly surrounded; seriously wounded when shot through the body, he seized an enemy soldier and employing him as a shield, rode off.

In June Forrest assumed command of a mounted brigade numbering fourteen hundred strong. On July 13 his aggressive tactics, along with a threat to "have every man put to the sword," bluffed the enemy commander at Murfreesboro, Tennessee, into surrendering his twelve-hundred-man garrison and $250,000 in Union property. On July 21 he was promoted to brigadier general, effective immediately, and participated in Braxton Bragg's Kentucky Campaign from August 18 through September 25. Relieved of command of his brigade, he then returned to middle Tennessee to recruit and organize raw levies into what years later grizzled veterans proudly referred to as Forrest's "Old Brigade."

During the six months between mid-December 1862 and mid-June 1863, Forrest turned the Old Brigade into a mobile force of mounted infantry. The efficacy of this mode of warfare was dramatically proved by the West Tennessee Raid, December 11–January 2, in which Forrest overwhelmed Union garrisons, inflicted more than fifteen hundred casualties on the foe, wreaked destruction on the Mobile & Ohio Railroad and closed it to traffic until March 7, and outdistanced and fought off all pursuers. A sharp and decisive repulse at Dover on February 3 led to hot words tainted with insubordination from Forrest to his immediate superior, Brigadier General Joseph Wheeler. The destruction of a twenty-eight-thousand-man Union task force at Thompson's Station on March 5 was followed by a clash with the equally high-strung Earl Van Dorn, in which both generals drew their sabers. Between April 28 and May 3, Forrest's hard-driving pursuit through the north Alabama mountains led to the capture of Abel D. Streight's seventeen-hundred-man mule-mounted column at Straight-Neck Precinct, Alabama, and prevented the destruction of bridges and trestles on the Western & Atlantic Railroad, General Bragg's lifeline.

On June 14 Forrest nearly lost his life in a confrontation with one of his officers, Lieutenant A. Willis Gould. Shot through the body at point-blank range by Gould, he used his knife to disembowel the lieutenant. Before Gould died of his wound, he and his general were reconciled, Forrest weeping as he clasped the young officer's hand. Within two weeks he had recovered sufficiently to leave his bed to take command of the deceased Van Dorn's cavalry troops.

Commanding Van Dorn's two mounted divisions, Forrest was an active participant in the Tullahoma Campaign, June 23–July 3, and in events leading up to and during the Battle of Chickamauga, August 16–September 20. Disenchanted by General Bragg's failure to follow up on the victory and enraged by orders from Bragg to turn over his command to General Wheeler, Forrest confronted his general, denounced him, and said, "You have played the part of a damned scoundrel, and if you were any part of a man I would slap your jaws and force you to resent it.... If you ever again try to interfere with me or cross my path it will be at the peril of your life."

Forrest was promoted to major general on December 4, 1863, to rank immediately. Accompanied by his shock troops—his escort company, Woodward's Battalion, and one company of artillery—he was sent to north Mississippi and west Tennessee to command, reorganize, and make more effective the mounted and artillery units that had harassed the march of Union reinforcements eastward from Memphis to the relief of Chattanooga. Once again Forrest met this challenge as a superior administrator and inspired leader, knowing that war means fighting and fighting means killing.

Forrest forged a formidable fighting force of mounted infantry out of what had heretofore been heterogeneous and lackluster units. He did this, as one Union officer wrote, by conscripting "anything that looked like a man," and turning them into soldiers who, until their dying day, proudly exclaimed, "I rode and fought with Old Bedford."

Forrest's military maturity was underscored in 1864 when he showed his military genius. As an independent battlefield commander in late February at Okolona, he challenged, battered, and turned back a Union cavalry column of sixty-six hundred that W. Sooy Smith had proclaimed the best-outfitted cavalry in the world. On a raid that carried him as far north as

A retouched but still genuine image of Forrest as a major general, taken probably early in 1864. (Tulane University, New Orleans, La.)

The best-known of Forrest's several wartime portraits, and probably made in mid- or late 1864. (U.S. Army Military History Institute, Carlisle, Pa.)

Paducah on the Ohio River, he bolstered his Kentucky brigade with recruits and deserters.

Next came the controversial Fort Pillow Massacre on April 12, and two campaigns undertaken by Samuel Sturgis under orders from William T. Sherman to rout Forrest and keep him from attacking the Union army group's railroad lifelines. On the first occasion, in early May, Forrest and his people avoided Sturgis, and on the second, at Brice's Cross Roads on June 10, they drubbed the eighty-one hundred Yanks and sent survivors of the battle stampeding back to Memphis.

On July 13, and at the Battle of Tupelo the next day, Forrest was not at his best, underscoring his limitations as a team player, as the Confederates commanded by S. D. Lee were first outmaneuvered and then suffered frightful losses in piecemeal suicidal frontal attacks on infantry posted behind breastworks. At Oldtown Creek on the 15th Forrest was wounded again, this time in the foot, but continued to command from a buggy until able to remount.

On August 21 Forrest used the indirect approach to frustrate a powerful Union force closing in on Oxford by dashing into Memphis. This caused General Stephen Hurlbut to exclaim, "They removed me from command because I couldn't keep Forrest out of West Tennessee, and now [Major General C. C.] Washburn [the Memphis commander] can't keep him out of his own bedroom!"

It was September 21, three weeks after Sherman's capture of Atlanta, and by then too late to have any immediate effect on the north Georgia campaigns, that Forrest and his corps crossed the Tennessee River. After savaging the Tennessee & Alabama Railroad north to Pulaski and capturing a number of garrisons numbering more than 2,360 officers and men, Forrest returned to west Tennessee. In late October and early November he raided as far north as Fort Heiman, Kentucky; attacked Union shipping plying the Tennessee River; captured and manned with horse marines several gunboats; and compelled panic-stricken Yankees on November 4 to destroy $2,200,000 in public property and evacuate their huge Johnsonville depot.

Forrest spearheaded John B. Hood's Army of Tennessee as it crossed into Middle Tennessee on November 21. At first Forrest had the "bulge," as he outmaneuvered and battered Union cavalry led by James H. Wilson. Beginning at Franklin on the 30th, the tide began to turn as Wilson's troopers more than held their own against Forrest. Near Murfreesboro, on December 7 Forrest was bested by Union infantry in the

A very slight variant of the previous image, and one of the few images in which the intimidating general does not look directly into the lens. (William A. Turner Collection)

Battle of the Cedars, when Confederate foot soldiers panicked. Forrest again stood tall as he shielded Hood's broken columns on the terrible retreat from Nashville.

On March 2 he was promoted lieutenant general, to rank from February 28, 1865. With his outnumbered corps he opposed Wilson's powerful columns, the most formidable mounted force fielded during the Civil War, as they thrust deep into the Confederate heartland. At Selma on April 2 Wilson's bluecoats whipped Forrest and his command. On May 4 the Confederate forces in General Richard Taylor's department surrendered, and on the 9th at Gainesville Forrest made his farewell address to his troops, and his "critter cavalry" scattered to their homes.

The war—a conflict that saw Forrest advance in rank from private to lieutenant general—was over. He had had twenty-nine horses shot from under him, killed or seriously maimed at least thirty enemy soldiers in hand-to-hand combat, and himself suffered four wounds.

Forrest returned to his Coahoma County cotton plantation. In April 1867 he was elected Grand Wizard of the Ku Klux Klan, organized the previous year at Pulaski, Tennessee, and held this position until he ordered its dissolution in 1869. Meanwhile, in 1867, he had returned to Memphis to become president of the Planters' Insurance Company, but his economic situation was bleak, and on February 5, 1868, he filed for bankruptcy. That summer his rights as a U.S. citizen were restored to him by President Andrew Johnson. On December 31, 1868, he became president of the newly formed Selma, Marion & Memphis Railroad, which he had promoted, with the goal of building and operating a through line from Memphis to Selma. In 1874 Forrest resigned as president of the debt-ridden company.

Plagued by ill health and debts, Forrest died of diabetes in Memphis on October 29, 1877, and was buried in the city's Elmwood Cemetery. In 1905 Forrest's remains, along with those of his wife, were reinterred beneath an equestrian statue in Memphis' Forrest Park, an area dedicated to his memory.

Edwin C. Bearss

Bearss, Edwin C., *Forrest at Brice's Cross Roads* (Dayton, 1979).

Henry, Robert, *"First With the Most" Forrest* (Jackson, 1944).

Wyeth, John A., *Life of Gen. Nathan Bedford Forrest* (New York, 1899).

An outstanding portrait of the seasoned general whom many regard as the greatest cavalryman America has produced. (Museum of the Confederacy, Richmond, Va.)

⋆ *John Wesley Frazer* ⋆

Though showing obvious signs of artistic retouching, this portrait still appears to be a genuine uniformed view of John Frazer, the only one to come to light. (Duke University Library, Durham, N.C.)

Frazer was born on January 6, 1827, in Hardin County, Tennessee. He received an appointment to the United States Military Academy from Mississippi and graduated thirty-fourth of forty-three in the class of 1849. Frazer's army career consisted primarily of garrison duty in New York, California, and Virginia. He saw some service as a recruiter in the late 1850s and was a captain in the 9th United States Infantry, stationed in Washington State, when he resigned his commission on March 15, 1861. The next day he was commissioned a captain in the Confederate infantry.

Frazer soon received an appointment from the War Department as lieutenant colonel of the 8th Alabama Infantry. Organized at Montgomery in May 1861, it was the first regiment from that state to enlist "for the war." The 8th Alabama went to Virginia and was assigned to duty on the Peninsula below Richmond. Frazer seems to have exercised temporary command of the regiment while its colonel acted as post commander at Yorktown, but Frazer resigned to become colonel of the 28th Alabama Infantry, which was organized on March 29, 1862, at Shelby Springs, Alabama. The regiment joined the Army of Mississippi at Corinth after the Battle of Shiloh and was assigned to the brigade of Colonel Arthur M. Manigault.

The men saw some skirmishing with the enemy during the operations around Corinth in May, then Frazer and his regiment accompanied the army on its Kentucky Campaign. They were present but not engaged in the fighting at Munfordville on September 14–17, 1862, and the regiment was engaged in a skirmish at Little Rock Castle Creek (or River) on October 19, during the retreat from Kentucky. Frazer and his men acted as the rear guard that day in relief of Colonel Joseph Wheeler's cavalry, which had become exhausted. The 28th Alabama succeeded in holding the enemy in check all day without support.

Frazer resigned in late 1862 prior to the Battle of Murfreesboro but received an appointment as brigadier general on May 19, 1863, though records of his commission have disappeared. He assumed command of the 5th Brigade, Army of East Tennessee, which comprised three or four regiments from Georgia and North Carolina, on June 8. His brigade helped oppose a raid of fifteen hundred Union cavalrymen under Colonel William P. Sanders from Mt. Vernon, Kentucky, into eastern Tennessee, June 14–24, 1863. During July and August his regiments split up to guard various mountain passes in the area of Cumberland Gap. Frazer reported numerous desertions by North Carolina troops, whom he said were too near their homes and families.

On August 3 Major General Simon B. Buckner assigned Frazer to replace Brigadier General Archibald Gracie as commander at Cumberland Gap. Union troops from Major General Ambrose E. Burnside's army began moving into East Tennessee in late August. Frazer received conflicting orders concerning holding or evacuating Cumberland Gap over the next week or so but determined not to give up the important post. By September 7, Federal troops under Brigadier General John M. Shackleford and Colonel John F. DeCourcy had surrounded the gap from the south and north, respectively. Both Union commanders demanded that Frazer surrender, but he refused those demands until September 9. On that day, he surrendered unconditionally his garrison of about seventeen hundred men and twelve field pieces.

This action led to criticism from Jefferson Davis and others and undoubtedly caused the Confederate Senate to vote unanimously on February 16, 1864, against confirming his nomination as a brigadier. From prison at Fort Warren, New York, Frazer wrote a lengthy reply to the criticism. He complained that all of his regiments were poorly disciplined and drilled. He stated, "The character, confidence, and condition of the troops hastily collected to defend the gap were such as to justify no hope of a successful defense against an equal number of the enemy, much less such an overwhelming force as threatened the position in front and rear....I saw it would be a mad and wicked attempt to defend the post."

One source says that "when all the facts were made known," Frazer was exonerated. Nevertheless, he remained in prison until the end of the war, apparently without the Confederate government making an attempt to obtain his exchange. He and fourteen other generals signed a letter addressed to Lieutenant General Ulysses S. Grant in which they expressed regret over the assassination of Abraham Lincoln.

After his eventual release, Frazer lived in Arkansas, where he owned a plantation. He moved to New York City and entered business. Frazer died on March 31, 1906, in that city, and his body was taken to Clifton Springs for burial.

Arthur W. Bergeron, Jr.

Porter, James D., *Tennessee*, Vol. X in Evans, *Confederate Military History*.

✶ *Samuel Gibbs French* ✶

A splendid, previously unpublished portrait of Major General Samuel French, taken quite possibly in Mobile, Alabama, sometime in 1863. (Alabama Department of Archives and History, Montgomery, Al.)

New Jersey contributed more than one general to the Confederates, among them this native of Gloucester County, born November 22, 1818. French attended the Military Academy at West Point, graduating with the class of 1843, just in time to go to Mexico as a 2d lieutenant. His service with Zachary Taylor's army won his two brevet promotions to 1st lieutenant, then captain, but his serious wound at Buena Vista early in 1847 put him out for the rest of the war. It served him well in one way, however, for in the field hospital after the battle he formed an acquaintance with the man on the next litter, Colonel Jefferson Davis. The friendship thus started continued when French bought a plantation in Mississippi and later resigned from the military in 1856 to become a planter.

When Mississippi seceded, and Davis was briefly major general in command of state troops, French was appointed his chief of ordnance by Governor John Pettus. However, now-President Davis later appointed his old friend a brigadier in the Confederate service on October 23, 1861, to rank from that same date, and French formally accepted the promotion on November 6.

His first active service came in the Department of North Carolina overseen by Daniel H. Hill in 1862–63, encompassing Richmond, southern Virginia, and North Carolina. French commanded the troops in and around the department headquarters at Petersburg, and during the summer of 1862 he oversaw the beginning and eventual substantial completion of the lines of earthwork defenses that were used two years later in the siege. Though Hill left to join Lee for the

Antietam and Fredericksburg campaigns, French stayed behind and thus missed the summer and fall campaigns in Virginia, but his services in fortifying the capitol area were recognized when Davis appointed him major general on October 22, 1862, to rank from August 31.

On January 27, 1863, Davis put French in charge of Confederate troops in North Carolina temporarily, relieving G. W. Smith, but within a few days D. H. Hill arrived to take over once more. On April 1 he assumed command of the Department of Southern Virginia, having previously contributed yet again to the later defense of a vital Confederate bastion by encouraging the work of building Fort Fisher to guard Wilmington, North Carolina.

French did not remain long in Virginia. With Vicksburg threatened, he was ordered out of Mississippi to join with the relief army being gathered by Joseph E. Johnston. French joined Johnston in Jackson, too late to help Vicksburg. Thereafter he remained in Mississippi, first under Johnston, and later under Leonidas Polk, until the concentration in north Georgia preparatory to the Atlanta Campaign. French led his small, two-thousand-, five-hundred-man division first to Rome, Georgia, and then to Johnston's main army near Resaca. French was with the army during much of the ensuing campaign, and retained command of his division after Hood superseded Johnston in July. His division consisted of the brigades of William H. Young, Claudius Sears, and Francis M. Cockrell, and was merged into the corps commanded by A. P. Stewart.

However, French saw increasingly limited service with the Army of Tennessee as 1864 wore on, in part because of a nagging eye infection that at times left him all but blind. Still, he led his command in the October 1864 attack on the Union garrison at Allatoona, where on October 5 he demanded its surrender and received a defiant reply from General John M. Corse even though French had him practically surrounded. Sherman had told Corse to "hold the fort," and hold it he did, despite French's spirited and costly attack. In the end, French himself had to retire to avoid being caught in the rear by reinforcements sent by Sherman.

In Federal ranks, where French's attack was a recorded grudging admiration, it was rumored that Hood relieved French from his command as punishment for failing to take Allatoona. However, French remained at the head of his division during the invasion of Tennessee, and led it at Franklin on November 30. However, his eye problem flared up once more soon thereafter, and on December 15, just before the commencement of the Battle of Nashville, he left the army on sick leave. Following his recovery, French took an assignment at Mobile, where he served under Dabney H. Maury, even though his own commission predated Maury's and made him the senior officer present. French gave his parole along with the rest of the Mobile defenders when it surrendered in April 1865.

Following the war, French at first returned to his Mississippi plantation but eventually moved to Florida, where he lived until April 29, 1910. He devoted many of his last years to writing his memoirs, *Two Wars*, published in 1901 in Nashville, containing excellent accounts of his service in Mexico and throughout the Civil War, and making it one of a handful of the best memoirs by Confederate major generals.

William C. Davis

Bridges, Hal, *Lee's Maverick General* (New York, 1961).

French, Samuel G., *Two Wars* (Nashville, 1901).

Hay, Thomas R., *Hood's Tennessee Campaign* (New York, 1929).

✶ Daniel Marsh Frost ✶

A magnificent portrait of General Daniel Frost made between March 1862 and the fall of 1863, showing him in the full uniform of a Confederate brigadier. (Missouri Historical Society, St. Louis, Mo.)

Frost was born on August 9, 1823, in Schenectady County, New York. His father, who worked on the Erie Canal, wanted him to become a gentleman and obtained an appointment to West Point for his son, who graduated from the academy in 1844, fourth in a class of twenty-five. While at West Point he made friends with numerous Southerners, and was greatly impressed with the men who came from below the Mason-Dixon line. He imitated Southern mannerisms, and cultivated a carefully practiced Louisiana drawl. During the Mexican War he earned a brevet for gallantry at Cerro Gordo, and afterwards served on the frontier. The army sent him to Europe for one year on "professional duty" before he resigned in 1853. Frost settled in St. Louis, married, and engaged in manufacturing, then served in the state legislature, and became a radical supporter of Southern rights. He also served on the USMA Board of Visitors.

When the secession crisis came to Missouri, Frost, who headed the state militia, suggested establishing a small camp with the intention of using it as a base for operations against the St. Louis arsenal. When General Nathaniel Lyon moved to take Camp Jackson on May 10, 1861, Frost protested that the camp housed state militiamen who had violated no law. But Lyon ordered immediate surrender and, faced with overwhelming odds, Frost had no choice but to yield. Unfortunately, as the captives were marched through the streets of St. Louis, the event turned violent. Frost claimed that the Unionists had opened fire upon his "disarmed and surrounded" troops, "and a number of my men [were] put to death, together with several innocent lookers-on—men, women and children." When the affray ended, many people lay dead, and numerous more were wounded.

After his arrest at Camp Jackson, Frost took the oath of allegiance and was paroled. He remained in St. Louis for several months; rumor said that he was acting as a Southern spymaster.

In 1862 he joined Sterling Price's army camped in the southwest corner of Missouri, and participated in the Battle of Pea Ridge, where he led the 7th and 9th divisions of the Missouri State Guard. After the battle he reported that his men had "behaved in the most admirable manner. The only deficiency observable among them was a want of practical knowledge; but this was more than compensated for by cool, determined courage, exhibited on all occasions and to a degree seldom equaled."

Following Pea Ridge he raised an artillery brigade, and crossed the Mississippi River. On April 15, 1862, Frost was instructed to go to Memphis and report to Sterling Price. During the siege of Corinth he served as Braxton Bragg's inspector general, from May 8 until May 26. Appointed a brigadier general on October 10, 1862, to rank from March 3, Frost was ordered on October 11 to report to Lieutenant General Theophilus H. Holmes in the Trans-Mississippi Department.

He returned to Arkansas in time to participate in the battle at Prairie Grove, where he commanded a division. He had originally discouraged Major General Thomas C. Hindman in his plan to attack the Federal force under Federal General James G. Blunt, and had only reluctantly agreed. But Blunt's force was reinforced, and the Confederates were forced to retreat. On January 30, 1863, when Hindman was relieved from command and ordered to Mississippi, Frost assumed command of the division, then was relieved by Sterling Price on March 30, 1863, and resumed command of his brigade.

When Theophilus H. Holmes, commander of the District of Arkansas, fell ill in July, Price temporarily took command of the district. As soon as Price recognized that the Federal army planned to advance on Little Rock he ordered Frost, commanding the defenses of the lower Arkansas near Pine Bluff, to move at once with his infantry and artillery to Little Rock. Price ordered Frost to move his brigade to the northern side of the Arkansas River, and to assume command of Price's division, which comprised almost all of the infantry near Little Rock. The Confederates, however, were unable to protect the state capital, and it fell on September 10. On September 25 Holmes returned from Shreveport and resumed his duties as district commander. Price resumed command of his division, and Frost returned to his brigade.

Frost soon heard that his wife had been banished from their home near St. Louis, and he headed for Canada, where he joined his family. Failing to go through the formalities that should accompany an official resignation, he was dropped from the Confederate army rolls on December 9, 1863—the only general ever removed for such a reason. After the war ended, Frost came back to the area around St. Louis, where he farmed until his death on October 29, 1900. He is buried in St. Louis in Calvary Cemetery.

Anne Bailey

Castel, Albert, *General Sterling Price and the Civil War in the West* (Baton Rouge, 1967).

Moore, John C., *Missouri*, Vol. IX in Evans, *Confederate Military History*.

This earlier portrait of Frost shows him as a brigadier general of the Missouri state militia in 1861 sometime prior to the surrender of Camp Jackson. (Museum of the Confederacy, Richmond, Va.)

⋆ *Birkett Davenport Fry* ⋆

Despite his extensive service, Fry seems not to have left behind a uniformed portrait. This is almost certainly a post-war view from the 1870s. (Museum of the Confederacy, Richmond, Va.)

Born in Kanawha County, (West) Virginia, on June 24, 1822, Fry attended the Virginia Military Institute and West Point one year each without graduating from either. He was a lieutenant of the Voltigeur Regiment 1847–1848, and a general under William Walker in Nicaragua.

A cotton manufacturer in Tallassee, Alabama, Fry raised the 13th Alabama Infantry Regiment and became its colonel on July 19, 1861. His unarmed out-fit was ordered to Virginia on July 22. The main Confederate commander there, Joseph E. Johnston, formerly Fry's Voltigeur colonel, requested the 17th from Richmond, but it went instead to Norfolk and Yorktown, where it eventually joined the brigade of Gabriel J. Rains (later Alfred H. Colquitt).

Fry helped defend besieged Yorktown and served in reserve at Williamsburg. A severe wound in the right hand at Seven Pines on May 31 incapacitated him for six weeks, but he returned to duty for South Mountain and Antietam. His conduct on September 17 caused his division commander, D. H. Hill, to call him "heroic."

A bone-shattering wound that day nearly cost Fry his left arm and his life, but, rejecting amputation, he saved both life and limb. Not until March 1863 could he resume command. By then, per orders of January 19, his regiment had joined James J. Archer's Brigade. Fry was heavily engaged at Chancellorsville on May 3. The following day, when Archer commanded the Light Division, Fry temporarily succeeded him as brigadier, only to be slightly wounded.

That same month Johnston, now commanding in Mississippi, requested his erstwhile adjutant be pro-moted brigadier general to command the late Edward Tracy's Alabama Brigade. Events in the East, however, kept the colonel there for the Pennsylvania Campaign. The capture of Archer early on July 1 at Gettysburg caused brigade command to devolve on Fry. He regrouped the stricken outfit—consisting of his own regiment, the 5th Alabama Infantry Battalion, and the 1st (Provisional Army), 7th, and 14th Tennessee infantry regiments—and used it to guard his divi-sion's right flank against threatened cavalry attack during the onslaught that afternoon. Two days later he participated in the grand assault. Although wounded in the right shoulder during preliminary shelling, he went forward with his men. The connecting unit between Johnston Pettigrew's and George Pickett's divisions, his brigade became the guide for the entire attack force.

Shot in the leg after crossing the Emmitsburg, Fry was left behind on the slope and fell into Northern hands. With his thigh bone fractured, he was hospitalized at Gettysburg until July 12, when he was transferred to Fort McHenry and thence to Johnson's Island on September 28. Unlike most officers there, he benefited from a special release. Paroled on March 29, 1864, he was exchanged at City Point on April 5.

Fry's West Point classmate Pickett readily considered him to command the disappointing Seth Barton's Virginia infantry brigade. However, the colonel, probably still recuperating from captivity, remained in Richmond until the Bermuda Hundred Campaign. With the capital imperiled, he was ordered to organize convalescents, attendants, and guards from Richmond hospitals on May 9. When division commander Robert Ransom removed Barton on May 10, General-in-Chief Braxton Bragg tapped Fry to fill the vacancy. The Alabaman took over Barton's brigade, containing the 9th, 14th, 38th, 53d, and 57th Virginia infantry regiments, on May 11. After helping defend Richmond, he fought at Second Drewry's Bluff, reportedly not to Ransom's entire satisfaction.

Fry left Bermuda Hundred on May 18 and reached R. E. Lee's Army on May 21. Attached temporarily to the III Corps, his brigade served in the North Anna operations. On May 24 he was promoted brigadier general to rank immediately and reassigned to his old brigade in Henry Heth's Division. Although it was not formally announced until June 9, he immediately assumed command of the wounded Henry H. Walker's brigade. That outfit included Archer's former brigade (minus the 5th Alabama Battalion) and also the 40th, 47th, and 55th regiments and 22d Battalion of Virginia Infantry. The 2d Maryland Infantry Battalion joined him on June 7.

The new brigadier fought at Totopotomoy Creek, Bethesda Church, Second Cold Harbor, and Second Riddell's Shop. Early in the Siege of Petersburg, he served on the Swift Creek sector. He did not remain there long. Unwell since May, probably from rigors of imprisonment, he went on prolonged sick leave on June 28. Fry never returned to the Army of Northern Virginia.

On September 14 he was assigned to command Augusta, Georgia, and arrived there on the 18th. This critical railroad crossing and ordnance facility was potentially endangered by the fall of Atlanta. William T. Sherman did demonstrate toward Augusta during the March through Georgia and the Carolinas Campaign but did not attack. During both crises, more senior officers with reinforcements—Bragg in November, D. H. Hill in February—exercised overall command. As the threat receded, those generals and their troops moved elsewhere, and Fry resumed charge. He briefly headed the District of Georgia in March but usually commanded just the post.

In the Confederate collapse, the gold train entered Augusta in April, and the presidential party in May used a pontoon bridge Fry had previously constructed higher up on the Savannah River. The general, however, thought further resistance useless. Spared attack from Federal cavalry at Macon by the Sherman-Johnston truce of April 19, he—remarkably—paroled twenty-two hundred of his own men that month without any Yankee officers present. When Emory Upton's Iowans reached Augusta on May 1, few Butternuts remained except the Georgia Military School cadets, whom Fry had retained to preserve order. The brigadier himself apparently did not await Upton but escaped to Cuba.

In 1868 he returned to Alabama. After residing in Florida and Virginia, he died in Richmond on January 21, 1891, and is buried in Montgomery, Alabama.

Bragg called Fry "a man of gunpowder reputation," but a friend described him as being "of slight physique and medium height, and of mien so modest and gentle that a stranger would never have suspected that a form so frail held the lion spirit of so redoubtable a warrior. He was a man of fine intellectual gifts and attainments, and a critical observer." This brave and able regimental commander might well have become a good combat brigadier, but illness, injury, and imprisonment left too little time to test him at higher rank.

Richard J. Sommers

Brock, Robert A., "General Birkett Davenport Fry," *Southern Historical Society Papers*, Vol. XVIII: 286–288, 1890.

Cook, Roy Bird, "The Last Time I Saw General Lee," *Confederate Veteran*, Vol. XXXV: 287, 1927.

Fry, Birkett D., "Pettigrew's Charge at Gettysburg," *Southern Historical Society Papers*, Vol. VII: 91–83, 1879.

Wheeler, Joseph, *Alabama*, Vol. VII in Evans, *Confederate Military History*.

⋆ Richard Montgomery Gano ⋆

Gano was born on June 17, 1830, in Bourbon County, Kentucky, the son of John Allen Gano, who raised thoroughbred horses and was an early minister of the Disciples of Christ Church. The young Gano attended country schools, had one year at Bacon College, Harrodsburg, Kentucky, and then completed his academic studies at Bethany College in Virginia. After graduation from college he attended the Louisville University Medical School, and became a physician in Bourbon County for eight years. In 1859 Gano moved by covered wagon to Texas, where he raised fine horses and cattle on a ranch in Grapevine Prairie in Tarrant County, and also gained experience fighting Indians in the frontier region west of Fort Worth. In 1860 and 1861 he served as a member of the Texas legislature, representing Tarrant County.

When the Civil War began, he organized two companies of Texas cavalry at Albert Sidney Johnston's request for service in Kentucky as scouts, a force known as Gano's Texas Cavalry Battalion, the Gano Guards, or Gano's Squadron. Gano reached Shiloh several days after Johnston's death, and P. G. T. Beauregard ordered him to report to Chattanooga for service with John Hunt Morgan's cavalry. When Gano arrived, he had almost as many Union prisoners, captured along the Mississippi River, as he had Confederate cavalrymen.

Gano's Squadron became the nucleus of the 7th Kentucky Cavalry in Morgan's brigade, and after Morgan's first Kentucky raid, Morgan spoke of the "small body of men commanded by Maj. [R. M.] Gano, of whom I cannot speak too highly, as they have distinguished themselves ever since they joined my command not only by their bravery, but their

good, soldier-like conduct." Gano also served with Morgan in the Tullahoma Campaign, but in June 1863 illness forced him temporarily out of action.

He returned home, and in July 1863 was placed in command of all the cavalry of the Texas state troops called out under Governor F. R. Lubbock. On September 1, 1863, Gano was ordered to report to Bonham, Texas, to join the eighteen hundred troops and minute men assembling there, the authorities hoping he could "put these troops upon an efficient footing." On October 10, 1862, Gano arrived at the Bonham headquarters where Brigadier General Henry McCulloch met him. McCulloch wrote: "I am highly pleased with him, and will put him in command of the State troops at once, and with his help hope soon to make them efficient." But McCulloch was having serious problems with a brigade of Texas cavalry under Smith P. Bankhead, and instead of taking command of the state troops, Gano was instructed to assume command of this rebellious force of over two thousand, most of whom came from the same region of Texas as himself.

Although the Texans preferred Gano to their previous commander, many of the men remained unarmed, and shortages of food, clothing, and blankets continued to fuel discontent. In spite of this, on October 24, 1863, Gano was ordered to report with his cavalry to Brigadier General William Steele in the Indian Territory. But Steele noted in November: "The Texas troops, suffering for want of proper clothing for the season, were commencing to desert." Steele reported by late November that Gano's brigade numbered little

A late wartime view of Gano, apparently still a colonel. (Museum of the Confederacy, Richmond, Va.)

over one thousand. Gano, however, moved his men to a position in the eastern Indian Territory, where he was instructed to prepare "a vigorous resistance to the invasion of Texas." In December Samuel B. Maxey wrote: "The only forces that could be safely counted on for a fight are Gano's brigade and the Indian brigade." In December Gano became ill while out on a reconnaissance and was out of action for over a month.

He recovered, however, in time to accompany Maxey from the District of the Indian Territory to Arkansas, where he fought in the Camden Campaign against Union General Frederick Steele. Because of desertions, by the time Gano arrived in Arkansas in April 1864, his brigade numbered only between three hundred and five hundred men. Sterling Price reported after the campaign: "I regret the country was deprived, temporarily, of the services of Brigadier-General Gano (of Maxey's division) by a severe and painful wound received in a skirmish near Munn's Mill, at a period when that bold and experienced officer would have added fresh laurels to those already gained on many hard-fought fields."

On April 28 General Maxey was relieved from duty in the Army of Arkansas and returned, along with Gano, to the Indian Territory. Gano commanded the Confederate cavalry in the action at Hays Station (near Fort Gibson) on September 16, and at Cabin Creek and Pryor's Creek on September 19. After the engagement at Cabin Creek, Douglas Cooper praised Gano, saying that the "gallant bearing, energy, and promptness which has characterized that officer in the execution of every order and instruction from his brilliant dash at Diamond Grove to the splendid achievement at Cabin Creek." Gano had cooperated with the Indians under Stand Watie at Cabin Creek, and although he was Watie's senior, he deferred command and acted "in perfect harmony and concert for the common good." Maxey said that Gano's "patriotism," "delicacy," and sense of "justice" were exemplary. Robert Kerby wrote that Gano "played an important part in allowing Watie, the only nonwhite [general] officer in either Civil War army, to prove that he had the capacity to conduct 'one of the most brilliant and skillfully managed cavalry raids of the war.'"

Finally Gano was promoted to brigadier general on March 18, to rank from March 17, 1865. After the war he returned to Kentucky and tried to farm and raise stock, but in 1866 he returned to Texas and became a minister in the First Christian Church, serving for more than forty-five years. He was active in the United Confederate Veterans, and died March 27, 1913, in Dallas, Texas.

Anne Bailey

Kerby, Robert, *Kirby Smith's Confederacy* (New York, 1972).

Major General Franklin Gardner, possibly in 1863 prior to the surrender of Port Hudson. (Louisiana and Lower Mississippi Valley Collection, Louisiana State University, Baton Rouge, La.)

✳ *Franklin Gardner* ✳

Franklin Gardner was born in New York City on January 29, 1823. His father was a career army officer stationed in Iowa when he secured his son an appointment to West Point from that state in 1839, and he ranked seventeenth out of the thirty-nine cadets who graduated in 1843; Ulysses S. Grant finished twenty-first. Initially a brevet 2d lieutenant in the 7th Infantry, Gardner served at Pensacola, Florida, and on the frontier. He attained the rank of 2d lieutenant on September 12, 1845.

During the Mexican War, his heroism earned him a brevet 1st lieutenancy at Monterrey on September 23, 1846, and a brevet captaincy at Cerro Gordo on April 18, 1847. He also fought at Vera Cruz, Contreras, Churubusco, and Molino del Rey. His promotion to full 1st lieutenant came on September 13, 1847. He served as regimental adjutant from July 14, 1847, until November 16, 1853. Between 1847 and 1855, Gardner fought Seminoles in Florida, served in Louisiana, and patrolled the Indian Territory from a post in Arkansas. He became a captain upon his transfer to the 10th Infantry on March 3, 1855, and he led his company on the Utah Expedition against the Mormons in 1857. He remained in the Utah Territory, headquartered at Fort Bridger, until the secession of Louisiana.

Both Gardner and his sister, Anne Emma, had married into the Mouton family of Louisiana. Anne Emma became the second wife of Alfred Mouton in 1842, the same year her U.S. senator husband was elected governor of Louisiana. Franklin married a daughter of his brother-in-laws by his first wife. This unusual relationship made Franklin both the brother-in-law and the step-uncle of Confederate Brigadier General Jean Jacques Alfred Alexander Mouton.

Undoubtedly because of his wife, Gardner disregarded the pleas of his Unionist father and did not even bother to resign his commission before joining the Confederate Army. He was dropped from the U.S. Army's rolls on May 7, 1861, for "leaving…and abandoning his command." Commissioned a lieutenant colonel of infantry in the Regular Confederate Army on March 16, 1861, Gardner rose rapidly in spite of his limited combat experience and his having been arrested at least once for public drunkenness during his early days in the Southern army.

Assigned to Major General Braxton Bragg's command on the Gulf Coast, Gardner soon found himself under arrest for having appeared on the streets of Mobile in a state of intoxication. Apparently nothing came of the charges, and in the spring of 1862 he exercised command of a cavalry brigade in Mississippi and Tennessee. Although part of the advance from Corinth in early April, Gardner's command guarded the flanks of the army and consequently saw no action at Shiloh.

Although Gardner was not engaged in the battle, General P. G. T. Beauregard thanked him for his participation in the campaign: "The general commanding avails himself of this occasion to return his thanks to General Gardner for his services in the reorganization in the cavalry of this army." The compliment was followed with a promotion to brigadier general on April 9, to rank from April 11.

Quite possibly taken at the same sitting as the previous portrait, this image shows much of the relaxed nature for which Gardner was known. (Museum of the Confederacy, Richmond, Va.)

An older Gardner, with thinning hair, appears in this image, very likely made after his release and exchange in August 1864. (Confederate Museum, New Orleans, La.)

Probably made at the same time as the standing view previous, this vignette of Gardner also should date from the late war period. (U.S. Army Military History Institute, Carlisle, Pa.)

Gardner led an infantry brigade in General Bragg's invasion of Kentucky that fall. Appointed but not confirmed a major general on December 20, to date from December 13, Gardner was transferred to the Department of Mississippi and East Louisiana by the authorities in Richmond, who disregarded Bragg's request that Gardner be assigned a division in his Army of Tennessee, which was on the eve of the Battle of Murfreesboro.

Assigned to command the southernmost district of the department, Gardner established his headquarters at Port Hudson, Louisiana, before the end of the year. During the early months of 1863, Gardner endeavored to do all in his power to strengthen Vicksburg's counterpart on the Mississippi River. The new major general readily perceived the importance of his command, for his assignment constituted the Confederacy's southern anchor on the Mississippi. On March 14, Gardner's cannons arrayed along a high bluff rained destruction down upon the hapless fleet of Rear Admiral David Glasgow Farragut when he attempted to run past the Port Hudson batteries with seven vessels. Only two succeeded in gaining a position on the Mississippi between the two Confederate bastions, and the *U.S.S. Mississippi* was destroyed.

When Farragut's naval blockade of the Red River failed to force Gardner to abandon Port Hudson, Union Major General Nathaniel P. Banks finally moved against Gardner in May 1863. Gardner received orders from theater commander General Joseph E. Johnston to evacuate, but Johnston's subordinate and Gardner's departmental commander, Lieutenant General John C. Pemberton, told Gardner that President Jefferson Davis insisted that Port Hudson be held. Gardner chose to follow Pemberton's instructions. Although most of the twenty-three thousand troops stationed at Port Hudson in March had already been transferred to the Vicksburg area, Gardner gathered what forces he could—less than seven thousand men fit for duty when Banks' army of nearly thirty thousand surrounded the garrison on May 22.

During the siege that ensued, Gardner would demonstrate that the authorities in Richmond had selected well. His troops would endure almost constant bombardment for forty-nine days and repulse two major assaults, on May 27 and June 14. Gardner smoked dried magnolia leaves and dined on fresh rats. When the garrison ran out of beef, he set the example by eating the first mule steak. Although most of his men had less combat experience than he had, Gardner managed to instill in them his determination to withstand anything. Only on July 7, after he learned of the surrender of Vicksburg, did he contemplate surrender. Terms were negotiated on the 8th, and on the morning of July 9 less than three thousand Confederates had the strength to stand during the official surrender ceremony. Gardner and his men had endured the longest true siege in American military history.

He was prisoner until August 1864, and following his exchange Gardner was assigned to command a district in Lieutenant General Richard Taylor's Department of Alabama, Mississippi, and East Louisiana. His commission as major general had been finally confirmed on June 10, 1864. Apparently Gardner was included in Taylor's surrender in May 1865.

After the war, Gardner lived quietly on his plantation in Vermillionville, now Lafayette, Louisiana. He died on April 29, 1873, and is buried in Lafayette.

Lawrence L. Hewitt

Dimitry, John, *Louisiana*, Vol. XIII of Evans, *Confederate Military History*.

Heitman, Francis B., *Historical Register and Dictionary of the United States Army* (New York, 1986).

Hewitt, Lawrence Lee, *Port Hudson: Confederate Bastion on the Mississippi* (Baton Rouge, 1987).

A retouched but still genuine image of Gardner, of war vintage
but uncertain date. (Courtesy of Jack Maguire)

✵ *William Montgomery Gardner* ✵

A civilian portrait of General Gardner made probably before the war, no uniformed portrait having come to light. (Museum of the Confederacy, Richmond, Va.)

Like many another future general, Gardner did not turn in an exemplary performance at West Point. Born in Augusta, Georgia, June 8, 1824, he secured an appointment to the U.S. Military Academy in 1842, finishing an unimpressive fifty-fifth in a class of fifty-nine. With the war in Mexico just breaking out, the War Department immediately commissioned Gardner a brevet 2d lieutenant in the 1st Infantry and sent him across the border. He fought at Vera Cruz, Contreras, and Churubusco, and was badly wounded in the last battle, receiving a brevet for his performance. Thereafter he spent much of his remaining thirteen years in the Old Army on the frontier, both at garrisons and on scouting duty, eventually rising by the slow process of seniority to captain.

Gardner heeded the call of his native state when secession erupted, and on January 19, 1861, resigned his commission and offered his services to the Confederacy. Almost immediately Georgia gave him a lieutenant-colonelcy in the 8th Georgia Infantry, and with the regiment he went to First Manassas, his immediate commander being the immensely popular Francis Bartow. When Bartow fell early in the battle, Gardner took over the regiment, only to be himself dangerously wounded in the leg and incapacitated for field duty for the rest of the war. General Joseph E. Johnston hailed his performance as "gallant," and Beauregard also complimented him.

Initially it was feared that Gardner's wound was mortal, and reports did go out that he had died. However, he slowly recovered. On November 14, 1861, the president appointed him a brigadier, effective immediately, and the Senate confirmed the appointment on December 13. Gardner himself accepted his new wreath for his stars on November 29, but the secretary of war still reported him as too confined by his wound to assume command of the brigade awaiting him. Late in the winter he returned to Augusta to continue his convalescence, and while he was there, the citizens petitioned that he be put in charge of maintaining order in the city. As late as June he was reported as "a cripple," and even as late as February 1863 President Davis was asking, "Is there anything known of General Gardner?"

That same month the War Department ordered the invalid general to sit on the court looking into the fall of New Orleans, and it does not appear that he was actually able to exercise any sort of command again until the fall. In October he was commanding a Georgia brigade in Stevenson's Division of the Army of Tennessee, when on October 6 Richmond assigned him to command the Department of West Florida. He assumed his new command on the 30th, with headquarters at Quincy.

It was a small command, with a motley brace of brigades of Floridians and Georgians, no more than twenty-four hundred of all arms. Gardner went to work immediately reorganizing and implementing efficiencies, to be able to defend his own territory as well as to cooperate with other forces in Florida and even South Carolina to meet threats. The major threat came in February 1864, when Truman Seymour marched his small Yankee command inland toward Olustee. Gardner arrived too late for the battle, but assumed command immediately afterward and stopped the pursuit of the retreating Federals, which caused some unhappiness with his superior, General P. G. T. Beauregard. Soon afterward Patton Anderson superseded Gardner, who was to command a division under him, but wound up back in command of his subdistrict instead.

In May 1864 the War Department summoned Gardner to Richmond to sit on Seth Barton's court of inquiry, and the next month directed that he report to General Robert Ransom for duty with the Richmond defense forces. Gardner spent most of the rest of the war in the Confederate capital. In July he was assigned command of all military prisons east of the Mississippi excepting those in Georgia and Alabama, having previously spent a brief month in command of the post of Richmond. Thereafter these duties seemed to have overlapped, for at times Gardner was once again in charge of the post of Richmond, while also being assigned temporarily as commissary general of prisoners.

Finally on March 3, 1865, he was relieved of his command of the post, and his prisoner duty, and ordered to report to Georgia once more. However, he got only as far as North Carolina, where he took command of about three thousand infantry and fourteen field pieces—the artillery commanded by now-lieutenant colonel John C. Pemberton—defending the town of Salisbury. There, on April 12, 1865, he fought one of the last small engagements of the war in the East when he tried to resist the advance of General George Stoneman. In a single overwhelming charge, the Federals captured all of the artillery and nearly half of Gardner's force, putting the rest to flight.

With the war over, Gardner returned to Augusta, and then relocated to Rome, Georgia. He lived almost forty years from the day that a bullet shattered his leg at Manassas, and spent his last years in Memphis, living with his son. There he died on June 16, 1901, and there he was buried in Elmwood Cemetery.

William C. Davis

Derry, Joseph T., *Georgia*, Vol. VI in Evans, *Confederate Military History*.

An excellent image of Samuel Garland, probably as colonel of the 11th Virginia, for he has a colonel's sleeve braid and collar stars, despite his brigadier's buttons. (William A. Turner Collection)

⭐ *Samuel Garland, Jr.* ⭐

Born on December 16, 1830, in Lynchburg, Virginia, and a collateral descendant of President James Madison, Garland graduated from the Virginia Military Institute in 1849. Two years later he received a law degree from the University of Virginia and opened an office in Lynchburg. In 1859 he organized a militia company, the Lynchburg Home Guard, and was named its captain.

When Virginia seceded after the firing on Fort Sumter in April 1861, Garland was commissioned colonel of the 11th Virginia. The regiment was assigned to the brigade of James Longstreet and, on July 18, fought in its initial engagement at Blackburn's Ford along Bull Run. Longstreet reported later that Garland "displayed more coolness and energy than is usual amongst veterans of the old service" during the combat. The regiment held a reserve position during the First Battle of Manassas three days later.

Garland's next opportunity to demonstrate his combat prowess came months later, on December 20, at the Battle of Dranesville. He led his regiment in a spirited attack, and although it was repulsed, his conduct elicited praise. A restless, studious officer who could be trusted with the command of men, Garland seemed destined for higher command.

On May 5, 1862, in the Battle of Williamsburg on the Virginia Peninsula, Garland once again led his regiment in an attack and fell wounded. In the words of his brigade commander, A. P. Hill: "Colonel Garland, though wounded early in the action, refused to leave the field, and continued to lead his regiment until the battle was over, and his example had a most happy effect in showing his men how to win the battle."

Promotion to brigadier general followed swiftly after Williamsburg, on May 23, to rank immediately. He assumed command of a brigade composed of the 2d Florida, 2d Mississippi Battalion, 5th and 23d North Carolina, and 24th and 38th Virginia in the division of D. H. Hill. A week later, his brigade spearheaded Hill's assault at Seven Pines on May 31. Garland had two horses shot from under him in the combat, and his brigade suffered 740 casualties, over one-third of its numbers.

In the weeks after the Battle of Seven Pines, the Confederate Army was reorganized under Robert E. Lee. Garland remained under D. H. Hill's command, but his brigade now consisted of five North Carolina regiments—the 5th, 12th, 13th, 20th, and 23d. It was these regiments he led during the Seven Days' Campaign. Hill praised Garland for "boldness" in the brigade's attack at Gaines' Mill on June 17. Garland's losses during the week of battle amounted to over eight hundred.

Hill's division remained in Richmond during most of July and August, missing the Second Battle of Manassas. It rejoined Lee's army for the invasion of Maryland in September. On the 14th, Hill's command guarded Fox's and Turner's gaps on the crest of South Mountain, protecting the rear of Lee's scattered units. That morning Federal units, in overwhelming numbers, advanced to the attack.

Garland's thousand-man brigade held Hill's right at Fox's Gap. As Eliakim Scammon's Union brigade of three Ohio regiments, supported by a battery, drove up the mountainside against the North Carolinians, Garland rode to his threatened left flank. There he met Colonel Thomas Ruffin of the 13th North Carolina. Ruffin said, "General, why do you stay here? You are in great danger."

"I may as well be here as yourself," replied Garland.

Ruffin then reminded the brigadier that his place was with his regiment and Garland's was in the rear of the brigade.

Ruffin had barely spoken when he fell with a bullet in the hip. Moments later Garland tumbled to the ground with a mortal wound, dying on the field.

Garland was subsequently buried in Lynchburg, beside his wife and son, who had both died after the war began.

A Confederate artilleryman who knew Garland described him as "a man of that mould and with those advantages of nature and accident that no position was higher than his legitimate hopes." Lee called him "that brave and accomplished officer."

D. H. Hill, an officer noted for his own bravery, once claimed that Garland was "the most fearless man I ever knew." After the brigadier's death, Hill wrote: "Had he lived his talents, pluck, energy and purity of character must have put him in the front rank of his profession, whether in civil or military life." One of the army's most promising generals died on South Mountain.

Jeffry D. Wert

Freeman, Douglas Southall, *Lee's Lieutenants: A Study in Command* (1942–1944).

Hotchkiss, Jedediah, *Virginia*, Vol. III in Evans, *Confederate Military History*.

Sears, Stephen W., *Landscape Turned Red: The Battle of Antietam* (Boston, 1983).

Garland as captain of the Lynchburg Home Guard at the beginning of the war. (Museum of the Confederacy, Richmond, Va.)

✶ *Richard Brooke Garnett* ✶

Probably the only genuine war vintage photo of Garnett in uniform, this one shows him in his old U.S. Army uniform with his initial rank as major in the Confederate service indicated by the star on his collar. *If* the star is not an artist's addition, that is, for the uniform shows signs of retouching. If genuine, it would date the image to the summer or early fall of 1861. (William A. Turner Collection)

Often confused with his cousin, General Robert S. Garnett, with whom he grew up in Essex County, Virginia, Richard Garnett was born at the family home, "Rose Hill," on November 21, 1817. Both he and his cousin attended the U.S. Military Academy at the same time, graduating in the class of 1841, after which he took his commission as a brevet 2d lieutenant of infantry and went almost immediately to active service in Florida against the Seminoles. Garnett remained in the Army for almost twenty years, though his service was confined to garrison and frontier duty, and he missed the action in the Mexican War, where his cousin won acclaim and promotion.

When Virginia seceded, Richard Garnett resigned his commission in May 1861 and accepted a commission as a major in the Confederate Regular Army. The early months of the war were quiet ones for him as he missed the fight at First Manassas, but on November 14, 1861, President Davis appointed him a brigadier general, to rank from the same date, and assigned him to the Shenandoah Valley command of General Thomas J. Jackson, who was assembling a small army to defend the valley. By the following spring, Garnett was commanding Jackson's own old Stonewall Brigade, and led it into the fabled Valley Campaign.

At Kernstown in March 1862 Garnett pulled his brigade out of the fight at a critical juncture, contributing in part to a defeat that Jackson would most likely have suffered in any case due to the larger-than-expected force facing him. Nevertheless, he put Garnett under arrest immediately and subsequently filed against him a general charge of neglect of duty supported by a number of specific allegations. The campaigning of the next several months prevented a court-martial from meeting to try the case, and meanwhile Garnett languished without a command. By August a court had met to consider a few of the charges, but then adjourned when the principals were called into the field for the Second Manassas Campaign. Garnett was at last released from arrest and sent back into the field, though only against the strenuous objections of Jackson, who declared that he believed Garnett "so incompetent an officer" that he would turn any good brigade into a bad one.

Upon careful study, the whole affair shows Jackson in a very uncomplimentary light. Kernstown was one of his very few tactical failures, and he may have sought a scapegoat in Garnett. Certainly he made attempts to get people who spoke well of Garnett in their reports to change their accounts, and asked others who would testify in the court-martial to alter their testimony. He kept Garnett under arrest for several weeks without filing charges and may only have done so when the War Department insisted. The trial, in fact, would never come to a conclusion, for campaigning postponed it repeatedly, and then Jackson's death in May 1863 ended the matter. It is difficult not to conclude that Jackson was pursuing a personal issue with Garnett, as he had with A. P. Hill, and that the affair illustrated Jackson's occasional tendency to be blinded by his single-minded nature.

Garnett meanwhile took command of Pickett's old brigade, now a part of D. R. Jones' Division of Longstreet's Corps. Garnett led the 8th, 18th, 19th, 28th, and 56th Virginia infantries at Antietam, where he was not engaged until late in the day on the Confederate right, where Longstreet had posted Jones' tiny division to cover Sharpsburg and all the ground south of the town. Garnett helped to meet and repulse Burnside's repeated attempts to push across the Rohrback Bridge and drive to the Harpers Ferry Road, and Lee's rear, holding out until Hill's timely arrival saved the day.

Following Fredericksburg, where Garnett was not engaged, he was assigned to North Carolina in March 1863, under the command of D. H. Hill. Inadequate transportation prevented him from engaging in Hill's March 13–15 attack on New Berne, but did participate in the siege of Washington, North Carolina, commencing on March 30. Before it could be completed, however, Longstreet ordered Garnett away to join in his Suffolk Campaign, in part because of Garnett's own

expressed pessimism that Washington could be taken. When the siege was abandoned, Garnett was ordered back to Longstreet, who was himself soon on his way back to join Lee in Virginia.

Garnett's war would end in Pennsylvania. On July 3, having seen little activity during the first two days of Gettysburg, Garnett and the rest of Pickett's Division were to participate in the great assault. Constituting the center of the massive attacking wave, Garnett's brigade marched out, their brigadier riding with them. Several generals, including Armistead and Alexander, rode along with Garnett part of the way to wish him good luck. Once the firing started as the Confederates came in range of Union guns, Garnett could still be seen astride his horse, and heard shouting his orders over the din. A kick from that same horse a few days earlier had made it impossible for him to walk, and thus Garnett may have been the only Confederate in the charge to stay mounted throughout. But then, when the assaulting column was within twenty yards of the Cemetery Hill position, and almost immediately in front of the famed "copse of trees" at which the attack was aimed, he disappeared. Amid the smoke and confusion, no one saw him fall. Indeed, no one ever saw him again, only his bloodied horse running to the rear. Some of his effects, including his sword, turned up years later in Baltimore, probably taken from his corpse by a Federal. With no other indications of his rank presumably about him, and perhaps too disfigured by his death wound for identification, he almost certainly went into one of the common trenches in which hundreds of Confederate dead were buried. He may lie there still, or his remains, along with others, may have been removed after the war to one of several mass graves in the South.

William C. Davis

Bridges, Hal, *Lee's Maverick General* (New York, 1961).

Coddington, Edwin B., *The Gettysburg Campaign* (New York, 1968).

⋆ *Robert Selden Garnett* ⋆

Robert Selden Garnett held the unfortunate distinction of being the first general to die on the battlefield during the Civil War. Born at "Champlain," Essex County, Virginia, on December 16, 1819, he inherited a name long prominent in the intellectual and political life of his state. He also was heir to a military tradition through his maternal grandfather, the French general Jean Pierre DeGouges. Garnett entered West Point in September 1837, joining his cousin Richard Brooke Garnett, who had preceded him at the academy by fourteen months.

Graduating twenty-ninth in the class of 1841 (two places ahead of his cousin), he was commissioned brevet 2d lieutenant in the 4th Artillery on July 1 of that year. After a tour of duty along the Canadian border, during which he was promoted to 2d lieutenant on January 31, 1842, Garnett served as an assistant instructor in infantry tactics at West Point from July 1843 to October 1844. He spent the next five years as a staff officer, first with General John E. Wool and later with General Zachary Taylor.

Garnett compiled an excellent record as one of Taylor's aides during the war with Mexico, participating in all the major battles fought on the northern frontier. Perhaps his greatest opportunity came at Buena Vista, where at a critical moment he manned a cannon that helped repulse a Mexican assault. Garnett's actions in Mexico earned him promotion to 1st lieutenant on August 18, 1846, as well as the brevet ranks of captain (for the battles around Monterrey) and major (for Buena Vista).

Transferred to the 7th Infantry on August 31, 1848, Garnett received his captaincy on March 9, 1851. While stationed in Texas during 1852, he refused a direct order to seize property from American citizens alleged to be direct supporters of a Mexican insurgent. A resulting court-martial brought acquittal, after which Garnett returned to West Point for a two-year stint as commandant of cadets and instructor in infantry tactics. He quickly acquired a reputation among the cadets as a fair, if exacting, officer. One young Georgian, who spent his plebe year under Garnett, observed that the commandant's "whole aspect was to me military discipline idealized and personified."

Assigned to the 1st Cavalry as a captain on March 3, 1855, Garnett was promoted to major of the newly organized 9th Infantry on the 27th of that month and sent to Fort Stellacoom in the Pacific Northwest. He campaigned against the Yakima Indians in 1856 and subsequently conducted operations along the Yakima River from Fort Simcoe. While at Fort Simcoe he lost his wife, the former Mary Neilson of New York City, whom he had married in 1857, and their only child. Mary Boykin Chesnut later commented about Garnett's prewar reputation as "proud, reserved, and morose...But for his wife and child, he was a different creature. He adored them and cared for nothing else." Their deaths, stated Chesnut, "left him more frozen and stern and isolated than ever—that was all."

Garnett took a long leave following this tragedy, spending a year in Europe. War clouds lay heavy on the horizon by the time he sailed for the United States in 1861. William Howard Russell of *The Times* of London, who traveled on the same vessel, left a memorable

The only known genuine uniformed photo of Robert Garnett shows him as a major in the old U.S. service before the war. Since he lived less than three months after joining the Confederacy, he probably never had time to get a new uniform or a photo. (Museum of the Confederacy, Richmond, Va.)

description of his fellow passenger: "He was an officer of the Regular Army of the United States, who had served with distinction in Mexico; an accomplished, well-read man; reserved, and rather gloomy; full of the doctrine of States' Rights, and animated with a considerable feeling of contempt for the New Englanders, and with the strongest prejudices in favour of the institution of slavery." Garnett arrived in the country while the Virginia State Convention deliberated secession; shortly after that body voted to leave the Union, he submitted his resignation, which was accepted on April 30, 1861.

Five days before his official separation from the United States Army, Garnett had accepted the position of adjutant general of Virginia's volunteer troops with the rank of colonel. He thus joined the staff of R. E. Lee, who commanded all the state's military forces and under whose superintendency Garnett had served at West Point 1852–54. On April 26 Garnett commenced the arduous task of drafting orders, answering correspondence, and overseeing myriad bureaucratic details necessary to mobilize Virginia's manpower. He labored at these tasks in Richmond until appointed brigadier general in the Confederate Army on June 6, 1861, to take effect immediately, and directed to assume command of the forces defending northwestern Virginia. One witness related that the night before leaving to take up his new command, Garnett stated quietly, "They have not given me an adequate force. I can do nothing. They have sent me to my death."

A difficult task did in fact confront him. Federals had pushed defending Confederates southward from Grafton through Philippi toward Beverly, a vital crossroads Garnett had to protect if he hoped to reclaim the northwestern portion of Virginia. He had collected a force of about six thousand men by the first week in July and fortified Buckhannon Pass, where the Staunton–Parkersburg turnpike crossed Cheat Mountain due east of Beverly, and the gap between Cheat Mountain and Laurel Hill, which lay north of Beverly and carried the Grafton–Beverly road. The bulk of the Confederate strength was at Laurel Hill under Garnett's immediate command; a smaller contingent under Colonel John Pegram guarded Cheat Mountain.

George B. McClellan advanced against Garnett with about fifteen thousand men during the first week in July. On July 11 the Federals drove Pegram off of Cheat Mountain, threatening Garnett's left rear. Fearful lest he be cut off entirely, Garnett abandoned Laurel on July 12 and withdrew in a confused march to the northeast. The Federals caught his weary column the next day at Carrick's Ford on the Cheat River. Most of his command had crossed the river when Garnett learned of the approaching enemy. Hastening to the ford, he had just instructed an aide not to duck enemy bullets when a ball struck him, inflicting a mortal wound. Garnett's body was recovered by the Federals and placed on ice in Grafton until sent to his family for ultimate burial in Greenwood Cemetery, Brooklyn, New York.

Brief controversy followed the Confederate disasters in northwest Virginia, and Garnett received some blame for mounting an inept defense. In truth, Federal numbers and McClellan's careful planning and execution largely decided the campaign. Soon Garnett was forgotten, a figure of high promise denied an opportunity to justify his reputation. McClellan spoke of "the unhappy fate of Genl Garnett, who fell while acting the part of a gallant soldier." The perceptive Edward Porter Alexander wrote after the war of "Poor old Gen. Bob [Garnett]...who left no family & whose name is now never mentioned, but who had he lived I am sure would have won a reputation no whit behind Stonewall Jackson's." No one captured the tragedy of Garnett's life better than Mary Chesnut, who summed up his personal and military fortunes in a single sentence: "He has been an unlucky man clear through."

Gary W. Gallagher

Heitman, Francis B., *Historical Register and Dictionary of the United States Military* (Washington, 1902).

Russell, William Howard, *My Diary North and South*, ed. by Fletcher Pratt (New York, 1954).

☆ *Isham Warren Garrott* ☆

The only known image of General Garrott shows him as colonel of the 20th Alabama. (Cook Collection, Valentine Museum, Richmond, Va.)

Isham Garrott, a native of North Carolina, was born in either Wake or Anson County in 1816. He matriculated at the University of North Carolina in Chapel Hill and, after graduating, read law and was admitted to the bar. In 1840 Garrott headed west and settled briefly in Greenville, Alabama.

The next year, he relocated to Marion, and entered into a law partnership with James Phelan, who was destined to represent Mississippi in the Confederate Senate. Keenly interested in public affairs, Garrott, having moved to Perry County, was elected to the Alabama legislature in 1845. He was reelected in 1847. In politics, he was a spokesman for the states rights wing of the Democratic party, and in the 1860 presidential election served as a John C. Breckinridge elector. In the weeks following the January 11, 1861, secession of Alabama, Garrott was sent by Governor Andrew B. Moore as a commissioner to North Carolina to lobby the latter state's legislators and to build public support in the Old North State for severing its ties to the Union and joining the Confederacy.

Garrott in the late summer of 1861, responding to a call for volunteers to serve for three years, played a leading role in raising companies of infantry from five Black Prairie counties that on September 16 were organized and mustered into Confederate service at Montgomery as the 20th Alabama Volunteer Infantry. Robert T. Jones of Perry County was elected colonel and Garrott lieutenant colonel of the unit, but Garrott was promoted colonel on October 8 following Jones' reassignment to the 12th Alabama. Garrott and his unit spent four weeks at the Auburn camp of instruction before being sent to Camp Goode, near Mobile, where he reported to Brigadier General Jones M. Withers.

On February 18, 1862, four weeks after the Rebel rout at Mill Springs, Kentucky, and forty-eight hours after the surrender of Fort Donelson, Garrott and his regiment departed Mobile en route to Knoxville to bolster Confederate strength in East Tennessee, a hotbed of Unionism. Garrott and the 20th Alabama, upon reporting for duty, were assigned to Seth M. Barton's brigade posted at Clinton.

In mid-June, Union troops led by General George W. Morgan outflanked the Confederates and compelled Barton's brigade to evacuate Cumberland Gap, the rugged portal on the principal road between Knoxville and the Kentucky Bluegrass country. Edmund Kirby Smith, with East Tennessee threatened by Morgan's column as well as by Union troops advancing across North Alabama toward Chattanooga, called for reinforcements and reorganized the troops in his District of East Tennessee. On July 3, Garrott and his regiment were assigned to the brigade led by Colonel Alexander W. Reynolds in Major General Carter L. Stevenson's division. Smith in mid-August boldly seized the initiative, and with three divisions crossed the Cumberland Mountains at Rogers' Gap, seventeen miles southwest of the Union Cumberland Gap stronghold, and occupied Barbourville on the Kentucky road. Garrott and his regiment, along with Stevenson's Division, crossed Powell River and closed in on Cumberland Gap from the Tennessee side. On the night of September 17 General Morgan, with Confederates to his front and Kirby Smith's army deep into the Bluegrass country, evacuated Cumberland Gap. The ten thousand Federals headed north on a 219-mile retreat through the mountains and hollows of eastern Kentucky that took them back across the Ohio River. Garrott and his Alabamans hounded the retreat as far as Manchester before pushing on to Versailles, where they rendezvoused with Smith's army.

Miscalculations and errors by senior Confederate officers that climaxed at the Battle of Perryville on October 8 doomed this great offensive. Garrott, along with thousands of other Confederates, had returned to Tennessee by the end of the month, camping at Lenoir, and again passing through Cumberland Gap. In early November, Garrott's 20th Alabama was brigaded with two Alabama infantry regiments—the 23d and 46th—and the 43d Georgia and Waddell's Alabama Artillery commanded by Edward D. Tracy of Huntsville. Mid-December found Garrott and the brigade camped at Readyville, ten miles east of Murfreesboro, satisfied that the year's campaigning was over and that they would soon be in winter quarters.

On December 18, Stevenson's three-brigade division, reinforced by A. W. Reynolds' brigade then posted near Knoxville, was ordered to Mississippi. Garrott and the 20th Alabama, traveling by rail, passed through Atlanta and Mobile. New Year's Day was spent at Meridian, Mississippi. Garrott reached Vicksburg on January 2, 1863, too late to participate in the defeat of William T. Sherman's army at Chickasaw Bayou. Before leaving for Mississippi, the 30th and 31st Alabama had been assigned to Tracy's brigade and the 43d Georgia detached.

Garrott and his regiment camped in and around Vicksburg until 7 P.M. on April 29, when the brigade made a forty-mile forced march to Port Gibson. Tracy was killed at an early hour in the battle west of Port Gibson on May 1, and Garrott assumed command of the Alabama brigade until relieved by General S. D. Lee on May 5. Garrott led his regiment at Champion's Hill on May 16, and his conduct was commended by General Lee.

At the Vicksburg siege, the 20th Alabama was posted in Square Fort and in the rifle-pits to the right and left of this strong point. Garrott "cheerfully bore the privations and perils of the siege, and set his men an example of the courage and spirit with which a true soldier endures every trial." He spent an inordinate amount of time in the rifle-pits encouraging his troops, and this proved to be his undoing. On June 17 Garrott took one of his men's rifle-muskets and stepped onto one of Square Fort's firing steps to carry on a vendetta with Yankee snipers then harassing his regiment. But before Garrott squeezed off a round, a Union soldier perched in a tree took aim, shooting the colonel through the heart. Garrott had been advanced to the rank of brigadier general on May 29, to rank from the day before, but that news had not yet reached beleaguered Vicksburg. The Confederates promptly redesignated Square Fort as Fort Garrott in honor of their dead leader.

He was buried by his troops in the garden of the Finney House in Vicksburg. His remains and gravesite were destroyed when Finney Street was opened in the 1890s.

Edwin C. Bearss

Manuscript Records, 20th Alabama Infantry, Files Vicksburg National Military Park.

Wheeler, Joseph, *Alabama*, Vol. VIII in Evans, *Confederate Military History*.

✳ *Lucius Jeremiah Gartrell* ✳

No uniformed portrait of Gartrell has surfaced. This one is postwar. (Museum of the Confederacy, Richmond, Va.)

The son of a rich planter and merchant, Lucius Jeremiah Gartrell was born on January 7, 1821, in Wilkes County, Georgia. From 1838 to 1841 he attended Randolph-Macon College in Virginia and studied for a year at Franklin College in Georgia. Following his formal education, Gartrell read law under Robert Toombs in Washington, Georgia, and was admitted to the bar in 1842. Gartrell then opened his own law office in Washington and became involved in state politics. He was elected solicitor general of the northern judicial district and served in that capacity 1843–47. In 1847 and 1849 he was elected to the state legislature, first on the Whig ticket, then as a Democrat. In the legislature, Gartrell was a strong pro-slavery advocate and opposed compromising on the issue. After moving to Atlanta in 1854, he served as a presidential elector for James Buchanan in 1856 and was elected to Congress in 1857. In Congress Gartrell continued to speak out for the pro-slavery faction and introduced a strong "States Rights Resolution." He later became a staunch secessionist.

Gartrell resigned from Congress in January 1861 and returned to Georgia, where he organized the 7th Georgia Infantry and was elected its colonel. At the First Battle of Manassas, Gartrell fought in Francis Bartow's brigade. He was at Bartow's side when he was killed and caught Bartow as he fell from his horse. Gartrell's sixteen-year-old son was also killed in the battle. In his report of the fight, Joseph E. Johnston mentioned Gartrell in a list of colonels "who deserve distinction."

In November 1861, Gartrell was elected to the Confederate Congress and resigned his commission in

January 1862. During his tenure Gartrell was a strong supporter of Jefferson Davis and served as chairman of the House Committee on the Judiciary. He supported legislation to make Confederate money legal tender, end all military exemptions, strengthen the army, set price limits on certain goods, and suspend habeas corpus whenever Davis deemed it necessary.

By 1864 Gartrell wanted to reenter the military, so he refused to seek reelection.

In February 1864 he applied to Davis for a commission as brigadier general to command a part of the Georgia reserves. After Congress adjourned, Gartrell began organizing companies of reserves and by March reported to Secretary of War James Seddon that he had twenty companies ready for service. Thus on August 23 he was appointed brigadier general, to rank from the day before, and later was given command of the four regiments comprising the 2d Brigade of Georgia Reserves.

The appointment was not without controversy, however. Brigadier General John Winder, under whom Gartrell would serve, bitterly complained of having another brigadier serving as his second in command. It would be, he wrote, "embarrassing in a command like this." Winder's superior, General Howell Cobb, dismissed his objections and implied Winder was simply a whiner. The general claimed Winder would complain of the arrangement even if Gartrell "had been the equal in every respect to General R. E. Lee."

The only major action Gartrell saw with his brigade was a four-day battle near Coosawhatchie, South Carolina, in early December 1864. A force of Union infantry landed near Gartrell on the Coosawhatchie River in an attempt to cut off William Hardee's retreat from Savannah. On December 6 Gartrell made the mistake of sending only 150 of his sixteen hundred men to try and check the advance of several thousand Yankees. His men were pushed back and when Gartrell brought up his entire brigade, it too was overwhelmed. Gartrell blamed the reversal on his green troops, who were demoralized and would not fight. On December 7 Gartrell was to make a demonstration at Coosawhatchie while General Samuel Jones attacked the enemy. Jones, who criticized Gartrell's handling of his men on the first day, characterized Gartrell's demonstration as feeble. The attack failed, but fighting continued until December 9, when Gartrell was wounded by a shell fragment. Although Gartrell was criticized for his role in the battle, the action around Coosawhatchie kept the enemy at bay and allowed Hardee to escape.

Gartrell was transferred to his home in Augusta, Georgia, to recover from his wound and was out of action until the war ended. After the war he resumed his law practice and became known as Georgia's best criminal lawyer. During Reconstruction he defended Georgia's Republican governor, Rufus Brown, when criminal charges were brought against him. In 1877 he served as a leader of the state's constitutional convention, and in 1882 lost the Democratic gubernatorial nomination to Alexander Stephens. Gartrell died in Atlanta on April 7, 1891, and is buried in Oakland Cemetery. He was married three times and had eleven children.

Terry L. Jones

Derry, Joseph T., *Georgia*, Vol. VI in Evans, *Confederate Military History*.

An unusual and previously unpublished photo of Gary as colonel of the Hampton Legion. (Museum of the Confederacy, Richmond, Va.)

✴ *Martin Witherspoon Gary* ✴

Born in Cokesbury, South Carolina, March 25, 1831, Gary became a prominent secessionist state legislator. As a colonel in the 2d South Carolina Militia Cavalry Regiment, he was made aide to General Richard Dunovant on Sullivan's Island, April 16, 1861. Gary, however, declined the appointment and raised Company B, the "Watson Guards" for the Infantry Battalion of the Hampton Legion. As its captain, he entered Confederate service June 12, 1861.

The battalion reached Manassas July 21, just in time to fight. He captured Ricketts' battery and by that afternoon was leading the legion. Another captain declared, "Some companies have especially distinguished themselves, and ... Gary's ranks among the first." Resuming company command, he fought at Eltham's Landing and Seven Pines.

When the legion reorganized, he was elected its lieutenant colonel June 16, 1862. With Wade Hampton leading a brigade, Gary commanded the infantry battalion. Within John B. Hood's Brigade, the legion fought at Gaines' Mill, Malvern Hill, Freeman's Ford, Thoroughfare Gap, Second Manassas, South Mountain, and Sharpsburg. Gary's men captured the 22d New York Infantry Regiment's flag August 29. He himself carried the legion's colors after four flagmen fell September 17. During its service with Hood, recalled the brigade historian, Gary's battalion displayed "a grit, a staying quality, and a dash that was admirable."

In the ensuing army reorganization, the legion became a regiment and transferred to Micah Jenkins' Brigade November 18, 1862. Gary became its colonel December 12, ranking from August 25. His unit saw little action at Fredericksburg and Suffolk and missed Gettysburg and Chickamauga. His next big battles were Wauhatchie, Campbell's Station, Knoxville, and Bean's Station.

The Hampton Legion was ordered to Greenville, South Carolina, March 17, 1864, to be mounted for service at Richmond. Gary's men received twenty-day furloughs to find horses. They were still in South Carolina when the spring campaign erupted. Ordered to Virginia May 5, they had not departed by May 12 but arrived May 19.

As senior colonel, Gary commanded the Cavalry Brigade, Department of Richmond, containing his own regiment, the 7th South Carolina, and the 42d Virginia Cavalry Battalion (redesignated the 24th Virginia Cavalry Regiment June 8). The 1st Virginia Local Defense Cavalry Battalion frequently served with him, and the 7th Georgia Cavalry Regiment joined his brigade November 6.

As early as July 8, 1863, and again December 30, 1863, Jenkins had recommended Gary for cavalry brigadier. "His Regt.," wrote the general, "he has by untiring energy & organization made one of the most efficient in the service ... Gary's dashing qualities as a fighter as well as his disciplinary powers peculiarly fit him for such a position." Hampton too praised Gary's "skill & gallantry." Influential War Department staff officer Samuel W. Melton hailed Gary as "a thoroughbred fighter, cool and deliberate, with great good sense, and that rare quality which enables him to make his men confident and firm under him." The major's March 14 recommendation caused Gary's transfer from Tennessee to Richmond. Melton's June 7 suggestion comparably gave Gary his brigadier generalcy. He was promoted June 14, ranking from May 19, and accepted July 3.

He proved worthy of such promotion. Although repulsed by overwhelming force at Mattadequin Creek (where his horse was killed), he fought successfully at Second Riddell's Shop, St. Mary's Church, First and Second Deep Bottom, Chaffin's Bluff, First and Second Darbytown Road, and Second Fair Oaks. His troopers were the only mounted Confederates protecting Richmond September to December. Particularly valuable was his delay of the Union drive for the capital September 29, and his formulation and implementation of the attack against the Yankee right October 7.

The return of Fitzhugh Lee's Cavalry Division in January 1865 brought Gary under its operational control. That connection ended March 7, resumed temporarily in mid-month, and terminated with Lee's transfer to Petersburg March 28.

Gary remained on the Peninsula and led the rearguard from Richmond early April 3. During the ensuing retreat, he fought at Jetersville, Painesville (where he personally sabered three Bluecoat raiders), Farmville, Cumberland Church, and Appomattox Station. His soldiers conducted some of the final fighting at Appomattox Court House even after the truce. Incredulous at the disaster, Gary declared, "We are South Carolinians and don't surrender." Although most of his brigade did capitulate (833 men, the largest cavalry component to yield), the general escaped with sixty troopers. Unlike other units which also rode away but soon disbanded or surrendered, Gary's contingent continued to North Carolina. Now numbering two hundred men, they helped escort Jefferson Davis. Gary accommodated the presidential party overnight, May 1-2, in his mother's home near Cokesbury.

When Davis proceeded into Georgia, the general stayed at Cokesbury. Gary remained unparoled. A leader in redeeming South Carolina from Carpetbaggers in 1876, he died April 9, 1881, and is buried in Cokesbury.

Nicknamed "the Bald Eagle of Edgefield," Gary was later described as "an old bachelor ... bald as a billiard ball .... looks like a man of eighty and acts like one of twenty. He is fiery, fearless, and ... fascinating." He neither drank nor smoked (unlike his brother-in-law Nathan G. Evans), but he admired fellow swearers. Gary's voice, recalled a veteran, "was very peculiar and shrill when raised and could be distinguished above almost any confusion." His sister acknowledged that "a certain recklessness of manner and speech made an impression on strangers of a wild and thoughtless man, but this did not affect his intrepid spirit." His ordnance officer later summarized: "...Gary was very popular with the men of his command ... Gary was not ... a "red tape" disciplinarian, he had no faith in the "pomp" of War, and his study was not to make a cheap reputation by the imposition of unnecessary restrictions, but to alleviate the hard lot of his soldiers ... No man however laid greater stress upon the essentials of real discipline ... He rested his authority not so much on his rank as on his conscious ability and fitness for command. No general officer was more familiar with or accessible to his men. He recognized the high character of the Confederate private, and respected his rights and feelings."

A natural leader in both war and peace, Gary ranks with Rufus Barringer and James Dearing as the best cavalry brigadiers to emerge in Virginia in the war's final year.

Richard J. Sommers

Boyd, Robert W., "Gary as a Soldier in the Civil War, 1861-65," in Louella Pauline Gary, *Biography of General Martin Witherspoon Gary*, manuscript, Virginia Historical Society.

Boykin, Edward M., *The Falling Flag* (New York, 1874).

Gary, Martin W., "Reunion of Hampton's Legion," *Confederate Veteran*, vol. XXVI, 1918, 298-299.

Brigadier General Martin Gary, photographed during the last year of the war. (Cook Collection, Valentine Museum, Richmond, Va.)

☆ *Richard Caswell Gatlin* ☆

The stars on the collar in this postwar photo of General Gatlin are a clumsy artist's addition, to make up for the absence of any wartime uniformed portrait. (Museum of the Confederacy, Richmond, Va.)

A native of North Carolina, born January 18, 1809, in Lenoir County, Gatlin first attended the University of North Carolina and then obtained an appointment to the U.S. Military Academy in 1828. He finished in 1832, graduating thirty-fifth in a class of forty-five. He received his brevet lieutenancy in the 7th Infantry and spent nearly thirty years in the Old Army, first on frontier duty in the old Indian Territory, then in the Black Hawk War, and on to the Seminole fighting in Florida 1839–1842. When war with Mexico erupted, he went to the land of the Montezumas. He fought at Fort Brown in May 1846, participated in the storming of Monterrey a year later, and received a wound and a brevet promotion for his efforts. When his home state raised a volunteer regiment to send to the war, it offered him the colonelcy of the 1st North Carolina, but he declined to give up his Regular commission.

Following the Mexican War, Gatlin, now a captain, went on the expedition to subdue the Mormons in Utah, fought the Seminoles again, and saw extended frontier duty on the Plains. In February 1861 he was finally promoted major of the 5th Infantry, and was on duty at Fort Craig, New Mexico Territory, when secession erupted. He paid a visit to Fort Smith, Arkansas, in April 1861, and there on April 23 new Confederate forces of the recently seceded state took him prisoner. Almost immediately they released him on his parole, and a few days later, in May, he resigned his commission and followed newly seceded North Carolina into the rebellion.

His native state made him adjutant general of state forces, with a militia commission as major general, and at the same time President Davis commissioned him a colonel in the Confederate forces. Within a few months, Davis appointed him a brigadier, on August 15, effective July 8. The Senate confirmed the commission on the very day of the appointment, and Gatlin accepted his new rank on August 25. Davis put him in charge of the Department of North Carolina on August 19, with headquarters at Goldsborough, and Gatlin assumed his duties the next day.

Less than a week later Gatlin learned that a Yankee fleet was steaming toward the coastline of his department, and soon it became apparent that their goal was Hatteras Inlet and the forts guarding it. Gatlin himself reached Goldsborough, staging area for the defense, on August 29, only to learn that Hatteras had already surrendered earlier that day.

Thereafter Gatlin devoted his energies to erecting defenses to hinder any further penetration of the state's rivers and harbors by the Federals, and to organizing the scanty troops and means in his department. Then in January 1862 came Burnside's expedition, and the subsequent fall of New Berne and Roanoke Island. Gatlin himself fell ill just before he intended to go to New Berne to supervise its defense in March, and thus was not there when the Federals attacked.

This last made him especially unpopular with many in North Carolina, not least Governor Henry Clark. There were complaints that he never left his headquarters, made only one inspection trip around his command, and even accusations that he was a drunkard. Undoubtedly as a result—especially given the nationwide outcry over the loss of Roanoke Island—Secretary of War Judah P. Benjamin relieved him of his command on March 15, ostensibly due to ill health. In fact, Benjamin needed a scapegoat for his own culpability for ignoring Gatlin's and others' repeated pleas for reinforcements and support in North Carolina. Gatlin seems to have anticipated almost every potential danger and asked for help in meeting it, and got from Benjamin nothing in return. He vehemently denied the charges of drinking, to which his physician was quite willing to offer favorable testimony. "These failures do not by right rest with me," he protested in a later report of his activities, and in large part he seems to have been justified in his claim.

Gatlin was fifty-three by this time, and definitely not in good health. Languishing without assignment through the spring and summer of 1862, and no doubt angered by the blame falling on him, he finally resigned his Confederate commission on September 8, though he remained in the service of North Carolina as adjutant and inspector general, right until the end of the war. In 1865, as Sherman was marching through North Carolina, authorities continued to refer to him as General Gatlin, and he provided some advice to Joseph E. Johnston on the final futile efforts to resist Yankee advance.

Following the war, Gatlin left North Carolina and returned to the frontier where his best years had been spent. He settled in Sebastian County, Arkansas, as a farmer, then moved to Fort Smith, where his Confederate career had begun, in 1881. There he lived to nearly ninety, dying at Mount Nebo on September 8, 1896, the thirty-fourth anniversary of his resignation of his generalcy. He is buried in the National Cemetery at Fort Smith, along with veterans from the Old Army service he loved, and men who fought both for blue and gray.

William C. Davis

Hill, D. H., Jr., *North Carolina*, Vol. VI in Evans, *Confederate Military History*.

✶ *Samuel Jameson Gholson* ✶

Gholson was born on May 19, 1808, in Madison County, Kentucky. His father died while he was still a child, and he moved in 1817 with his father's family to northern Alabama. After some education in common schools there, Gholson studied law in Russelville and was admitted to the Alabama bar in 1829. The next year he moved to Mississippi and began a practice at Athens, in Monroe County. He served in the state legislature 1835–1836, and again in 1839. Gholson served in the United States House of Representatives 1836–1838. During his term he became involved in a heated debate with Henry A. Wise of Virginia, and it is said that only the intervention of John C. Calhoun and others prevented the two from fighting a duel. Gholson was appointed judge of the United States district court of Mississippi in 1838 and held that position until he resigned in 1861. He presided over the Democratic state convention in 1860 and served as a member of the Mississippi secession convention, where he strongly supported severing ties with the Union.

Gholson resigned his judgeship shortly after the convention passed an ordinance of secession. The author of a book on Mississippi's early legal history expressed surprise that Jefferson Davis did not appoint Gholson as judge of the Confederate district court in that state, saying, "He had been a lifelong friend of Mr. Davis, personally, politically, and officially." He enlisted as a private in Company I, 14th

Mississippi Infantry, but was soon elected captain of his company. Before the end of 1861, Gholson had been promoted to colonel and later brigadier general in the Mississippi militia.

He took a command to Kentucky to reinforce General Albert Sidney Johnston's army and was assigned to Fort Donelson, where Gholson received a wound in his right lung during the siege of the latter's garrison and became a prisoner of war when the post surrendered.

After his exchange, Gholson returned to the field. He led troops in the battles of Iuka and Corinth and received a severe wound in his left leg during the latter engagement. Governor John J. Pettus appointed him as a major general in the Mississippi state militia on April 18, 1863, and sent him into the northeastern part of the state to organize state troops recently raised there. Gholson made his headquarters at Okolona and Tupelo at various times, and led about two hundred state troops in helping oppose a Union cavalry raid from LaGrange, Tennessee, toward Okolona April 29–May 5. He often received criticism from regular Confederate officers in the area for interfering with their efforts to recruit men and to gather supplies, but General Joseph E. Johnston authorized him on June 2

Samuel Gholson left behind no uniformed portrait that has been found, and this postwar image probably dates from the 1880s. (Museum of the Confederacy, Richmond, Va.)

to raise and organize as many cavalry units as he could for temporary service in the Confederate Army.

By October 1863, Gholson was again commanding state troops in northeast Mississippi, Governor Pettus wanting troops there to protect that part of the state while the legislature was in session. Gholson's men cooperated with regular Confederate troops in harassing raids on the Memphis & Charleston Railroad during the first week in November, and during Brigadier General William Sooy Smith's raid into northern Mississippi in February 1864, Gholson commanded about four hundred state troops cooperating with the forces of Major General Nathan Bedford Forrest. The Federals routed Gholson's men in a skirmish near Houston on February 19. Nevertheless, he led the pursuit of Smith's raiders after Forrest defeated them at Okolona on February 22. In March Forrest promised to recommend Gholson for appointment as a brigadier general in the Confederate army as soon as a brigade of state troops Gholson was organizing was transferred to Confederate service. Governor Charles Clark added his support to Gholson's appointment in a letter to Jefferson Davis. The president replied, "I have long recognized the patriotic service of General Gholson, and it would give me pleasure to nominate him for the brigade."

This transfer occurred on May 1, and Gholson received his commission as brigadier on June 28, dated June 1 and ranking from May 6. Major General Stephen D. Lee, commanding cavalry forces in Mississippi, ordered the brigade to assist in watching the Federal garrison at Vicksburg. Gholson's brigade was assigned to Brigadier General Wirt Adams' Division in June, and Adams soon found the brigade unreliable, and recommended that the men be dismounted and placed in other units. The brigade helped oppose a Union expedition from Vicksburg to Pearl River, July 2–10, and in a skirmish at Jackson on July 7, Gholson received another severe wound.

Gholson's brigade was then ordered to Georgia to reinforce the Army of Tennessee, but he appears not to have accompanied his men. He returned to duty in the fall of 1864 and in late December was stationed at Corinth. Gholson and his brigade fought in an engagement against Union cavalry raiders at Egypt, Mississippi, on December 28, where after a "gallant defense," the Confederates retreated. Gholson was seriously wounded in the left arm and captured, the wound resulting in the amputation of the arm, and Gholson saw no further active service.

In February 1865 the regiments of Gholson's brigade were consolidated and placed in other commands. Brigadier General James R. Chalmers informed Gholson that Forrest, then commanding all cavalry in northern Mississippi, had "a high appreciation of your gallantry and capacity as a soldier and an officer." According to Chalmers, Forrest would try to find a command for Gholson if he were "ever again...fit for active duty."

Gholson was elected to the Mississippi legislature in 1865, serving as speaker of the house, but was ousted from office after the passage of the Reconstruction Act of 1867. He resumed his law practice in Aberdeen and worked to overthrow the Republican government of the state. Gholson was again elected to the legislature in 1878. He died on October 16, 1883, in Aberdeen and is buried there in Odd Fellows Cemetery.

Arthur W. Bergeron, Jr.

Hooker, Charles E., *Mississippi*, Vol. IX in Evans, *Confederate Military History*.

Rowland, Dunbar, ed., *Mississippi* (Atlanta, 1907).

Colonel Randall Gibson, 13th Louisiana, probably in 1862. (Albert Shaw Collection, Courtesy of Mr. and Mrs. Bruce English, U.S. Army Military History Institute, Carlisle, Pa.)

⋆ *Randall Lee Gibson* ⋆

Gibson was born on September 10, 1832, at "Spring Hill" Plantation near Versailles, Kentucky, while his parents were visiting his mother's family. A private tutor gave him his early education on his father's plantation near Houma in Terrebonne Parish, Louisiana, then he later attended schools in his home parish and at Lexington, Kentucky. Gibson graduated from Yale College in 1853 and from the Law Department of the University of Louisiana in 1855. He traveled to and studied in Europe and served for six months as an attache to the American embassy in Madrid, Spain. When Gibson returned to the United States in 1858, he became a planter in Lafourche Parish, Louisiana.

At the outbreak of the Civil War, Gibson became an aide-de-camp to Governor Thomas O. Moore. He received an appointment as captain of Company D, 1st Louisiana Heavy Artillery Regiment, on May 8, 1861, but resigned his commission on September 6 to become colonel of the 13th Louisiana Infantry, which was organized five days later and ordered to Columbus, Kentucky. After the evacuation of the latter post, Gibson took his regiment to Corinth, Mississippi, where he was commanding a small brigade by late March 1862.

At the Battle of Shiloh April 6–7, Gibson led a brigade in Brigadier General Daniel Ruggles' division of the II Corps. His men made four bloody attacks on the Hornets' Nest and were repulsed each time. In the second day of fighting, Gibson's brigade attacked the enemy and captured an artillery battery. Major

General Braxton Bragg somehow gained the impression that Gibson had not done his full duty in the attacks on the Hornets' Nest and made a mild rebuke of Gibson in his official report of the battle. In a letter to his wife Bragg called Gibson "an arrant coward," and he continued to hold Gibson in low esteem from that point onward. Gibson learned of the "censure" in Bragg's report about a year later and asked for a court of inquiry, but the War Department did not think such a proceeding was necessary.

The 13th Louisiana joined Brigadier General Daniel W. Adams' brigade prior to the Kentucky Campaign. Adams praised Gibson for his actions in the Battle of Perryville on October 8 and stated, "I will recommend Colonel Gibson for skill and valor to be brigadier-general." The 13th Louisiana and 20th Louisiana regiments were consolidated on November 30, and Gibson became colonel of the new unit. When Adams was wounded and disabled on December 31 at the Battle of Murfreesboro, Gibson assumed command of the brigade and led it through the rest of the battle. Major General John C. Breckinridge said that in the fighting Gibson "discharged [his] duties throughout with marked courage and skill." Gibson continued in brigade command until Adams returned to duty.

On March 1, 1863, Bragg issued orders sending Gibson on conscript and recruiting duty and replacing

Following his January 1864 promotion to brigadier, Gibson sat again for the camera, seated at left with a friend. (Ted R. Rudder Collection)

Gibson was fond of the camera, and in 1864 posed yet again, probably just prior to the Atlanta Campaign. (William A. Turner Collection)

Later that year he sat again, this time sporting a handsome beard. (Alabama Department of Archives and History, Montgomery, AL.)

Gibson posed for the camera at almost every rank he held. Here he stands as a lieutenant colonel, or perhaps colonel. (Ted R. Rudder Collection)

protested this action to the secretary of war and was restored to command. His regiment participated in the Siege of Jackson, Mississippi, July 9–16, and accompanied Breckinridge's division to Georgia to reinforce Bragg's army in September. Gibson led his regiment in the Battle of Chickamauga on September 20 and again succeeded to brigade command when Adams was wounded and captured. Late that afternoon, Gibson's brigade attacked the Union left flank and drove the enemy back until darkness halted the fighting. Breckinridge again praised Gibson for his "courage and skill" in the battle.

Gibson's brigade saw only light fighting at the Battle of Missionary Ridge on November 25, but on February 1, 1864, he received promotion to brigadier general to rank from January 1.

His brigade was in reserve during Union demonstrations against the Confederate positions at Dalton, Georgia, February 22–27, 1864, and again was only slightly involved in the action, but Gibson and his men distinguished themselves in the various engagements of the Atlanta Campaign, particularly at Resaca and New Hope Church. The brigade lost heavily in attacks on the enemy in the battles of Ezra Church, July 28, and Jonesborough, August 31. During the latter battle, Gibson seized the flag of one of his regiments and led his men up to the Federal works. Major General Henry D. Clayton, Gibson's division commander, reported that this brave conduct "created the greatest enthusiasm throughout his command."

The brigade accompanied the army on its campaign against the Union supply line in northern Georgia, and on October 29 Gibson's men captured Florence, Alabama, and secured a safe crossing of the Tennessee River for the army. Clayton's Division demonstrated in front of Federal forces at Columbia, Tennessee, while General John B. Hood led the army around to the enemy's rear at Spring Hill. As a result, the division did not reach the field of the Battle of Franklin until the fighting had ended on November 30. In the first day's fighting at the Battle of Nashville on December 15, Gibson's brigade was ordered to support the army's left flank as it began to give way, and his men helped stop the Union advance. The next day the brigade repulsed all attacks on its front and fell back only after the Federals crushed the army's left flank. Gibson's brigade formed part of the army's rear guard during the retreat from Nashville, and the men several times blunted enemy pursuit.

In February 1865, Gibson's brigade was detached from the Army of Tennessee and ordered to Mobile, Alabama. Gibson commanded the garrison at Spanish Fort east of Mobile during the Union siege of that place, March 27–April 8. Lieutenant General Richard Taylor wrote, "Gibson's stubborn defense and skillful retreat make this one of the best achievements of the war." Major General Dabney H. Maury, commander at Mobile, echoed this assessment: "It is not too much to say that no position was ever held by Confederate troops with greater hardihood and tenacity, nor evacuated more skillfully after hope of further defense was gone." Gibson and his brigade surrendered with Taylor's army at Cuba Station, Alabama, on May 8, 1865.

Following the war, Gibson practiced law in New Orleans. He was elected to Congress in 1872 but denied his seat. He was elected again in 1875 and served in the House of Representatives until 1882. Gibson then was a United States senator from Louisiana 1883—1892. He persuaded the Federal government to transfer the barracks at Baton Rouge to become the home of Louisiana State University, and he helped to found Tulane University, of which he was president of the Board of Administrators 1882—1892. Gibson died on December 15, 1892, at Hot Springs, Arkansas, while visiting the health spas there and is buried in Lexington, Kentucky.

Arthur W. Bergeron, Jr.

Dixon, Donald Eugene, "Randall Lee Gibson of Louisiana, 1832–1892," unpublished master's thesis, Louisiana State University, 1973.

McBride, Mary G., "Randall Lee Gibson," *Dictionary of Louisiana Biography*, ed. by Glenn R. Conrad (Lafayette, 1988).

Another outstanding, previously unpublished portrait of Gibson, this probably from late in the war. (Southeastern Louisiana University, Hammond, La.)

✯ Jeremy Francis Gilmer ✯

This son of an army officer was born in Guilford County, North Carolina, on February 23, 1818, received an appointment to West Point, and graduated fourth in the class of 1839. Because of his high ranking, Gilmer was able to choose service in the engineers. After teaching engineering at the academy for a year, Gilmer began a distinguished career as an army engineer. From 1840 to 1844 he was assistant engineer for the construction of Fort Schuyler, New York, then he was transferred to Washington, D.C., as its assistant chief of engineers, and was promoted to 1st lieutenant in 1845. During the Mexican War Gilmer was chief engineer for the army in New Mexico and built Fort Marcy at Santa Fe. From the end of the Mexican War until the Civil War, Gilmer worked to improve various harbors, bays, and fortifications. His assignments included Fort Jackson, Louisiana; Fort Pulaski, Georgia; and the Savannah River system. By 1861 he was a captain in charge of building the defenses for San Francisco.

On June 29, 1861, Gilmer resigned his commission. The Confederacy, for whom Gilmer's brother served as congressman, quickly gave him a captain's commission in the engineers.

In the autumn of 1861 he was assigned to Albert S. Johnston in Tennessee. Johnston had Gilmer inspect the lower Cumberland River for the best defensive site to protect Nashville from a river attack, and Gilmer recommended Fort Donelson as the river's best defensive position and helped prepare it and Fort Henry for action. Gilmer happened to be at Fort

Henry when Union gunboats attacked it in early February 1862.

The fall of Fort Henry impressed upon Gilmer the power of the Union fleet. At Fort Donelson he insisted that the greatest threat was from the navy, not from U. S. Grant's approaching army. "I feel much confidence," he wrote, "that we can make a successful resistance against a land attack." When Fort Donelson's defenses crumbled a few days later, Gilmer accepted Gideon Pillow's invitation to join him in his escape from the doomed fort.

By March 1862 Gilmer was a lieutenant colonel and head of Johnston's engineering department. At Shiloh his actions are undocumented, but one of Johnston's aides said the general "was actively and efficiently assisted by Colonel Gilmer." In his official report, P. G. T. Beauregard wrote that "after having performed the important and various duties of his place with distinction…[Gilmer] was wounded late on Monday. I trust, however, I shall not too long be deprived of his essential duties." The circumstances of Gilmer's wounding were never mentioned.

On July 12, 1862, Gilmer was ordered to take command of Robert E. Lee's engineering corps. That summer he worked on completing the Richmond defenses and by October was chief of the Bureau of Engineers. As head of the Confederacy's engineers, Gilmer was

This previously unpublished portrait of Major General Jeremy F. Gilmer was made during the last two years of the war, and is the only uniformed view known to have survived. (Museum of the Confederacy, Richmond, Va.)

closely involved in all major defense projects. His telegrams and correspondence reveal a meticulous eye for detail and an in-depth knowledge of many technical subjects. He dealt with personnel problems, river obstructions, gunboat construction, torpedoes, fortifications, railroads, and more. His recommendations and orders were clearly written, often being enumerated in order to be perfectly clear. He was opinionated and acted with conviction, and nearly all of his recommendations were accepted.

On August 25, 1863, Gilmer was promoted from colonel to major general and was quickly made second in command of Beauregard's Department of South Carolina, Georgia, and Florida. Moving to Charleston, Gilmer's primary duty was overseeing the city's defense. On at least two occasions he inspected Fort Sumter while under a Yankee bombardment and was able to discern better ways to protect the fort. In September he was at Morris Island and was present when it was abandoned to the enemy. Beauregard wrote that although Gilmer was on the island for only a few days, "he was, nevertheless, active, zealous, and of assistance to me in holding the island to the last moment." In addition to his duties at Charleston, Gilmer also found time to advise on Mobile's defenses and make an inspection of Columbus, Georgia.

Gilmer's service was impressive and caught the eye of his superiors. In December Lee speculated to Jefferson Davis that if Beauregard was ever transferred, Gilmer might replace him at Charleston. Later that month Gilmer was given temporary command of the District of Georgia and the Third District of South Carolina, while remaining second in command in Beauregard's department. From January to May 1864 he was often in Savannah trying to fend off the Union attack there, and in February and March he was inspecting Mobile.

Finally, on April 2, 1864, Gilmer was relieved of his duties in the Department of South Carolina, Georgia, and Florida and resumed his post as chief of the Bureau of Engineers at Richmond. For the remainder of the war, he worked tirelessly. Not only did he oversee his engineers, but he also made another inspection of Mobile, personally supervised repairs to the Danville Railroad, and met Beauregard in North Carolina to advise on ways to slow up the Union advance there. When the collapse of the Confederacy came in April 1865, Gilmer traveled with Secretary of War John C. Breckinridge before finally surrendering.

Gilmer emerged from the Civil War with the reputation of being one of the South's best engineers. After the war he worked briefly as a civil engineer in Savannah and was involved in the railroad industry. In 1867 he became president of the Savannah Gas Light Company and served in that capacity until his death on December 1, 1883. Gilmer is buried in the Laurel Grove Cemetery in Savannah, Georgia.

Terry L. Jones

Hill, D. H., *North Carolina*, Vol. IV in Evans, *Confederate Military History*.

✳ *Victor Jean Baptiste Girardey* ✳

Born in Lauw, France, on June 26, 1837, Girardey came to Augusta, Georgia, five years later. By 1861, he resided in New Orleans.

Even before Louisiana seceded, Girardey, as a subaltern temporarily commanding the Louisiana Guards militia company, helped seize the Baton Rouge arsenal on January 10. Then, when war erupted, the Guards offered their services on April 15, with Girardey their junior second lieutenant. They became Company A of the 1st Louisiana Infantry Battalion on April 16.

By then, they were traveling to Pensacola, where their battalion temporarily served within the 1st Louisiana Regular Infantry Regiment against Fort Pickens. The battalion was ordered to Richmond on May 30, where it was formally organized on June 11. Forwarded to General John B. Magruder at Yorktown, it precipitated one of the war's earliest affrays, Newport News, on July 5, where battalion commander Charles Dreux was slain. Girardey escorted his corpse back home.

Girardey resigned on October 12, 1861, to immediately become staff 1st lieutenant and aide-de-camp to General Albert G. Blanchard, commanding first a district and later the 3d Brigade, Department of Norfolk, guarding Portsmouth. After General Benjamin Huger withdrew on May 9, the brigade served in his division at Seven Pines.

Blanchard left the eastern army on June 18, but his successor, General Ambrose R. Wright, retained Girardey as brigade assistant adjutant general. The junior officer became captain on July 11, ranking from June 21. In the ensuing thirteen months, he distinguished himself in all the brigade's battles. More than a headquarters administrator, Girardey represented his brigadier in reconnoitering, directing movements, and even leading troops in combat.

His bravery and initiative repeatedly earned him praise. Wright hailed his "coolness, courage, and daring intrepidity" at Oak Grove and his "valuable services" at the Seven Days' battles and Chancellorsville. Acting Brigadier Charles H. Andrews reported that at Manassas Gap Girardey's "gallant behavior nerved the weakest soldier to a full discharge of his duty." Division Commander Richard H. Anderson summarized Girardey's service up to August 1863: "He is a most capable, energetic, and indefatigable officer. His great courage, daring and composure under fire have been repeatedly exhibited in battle to the admiration and satisfaction of the officers and soldiers.... He has on all occasions rendered valuable and meritorious service as a staff officer."

Despite such recognition, Girardey resigned on July 19, 1863 for pressing family considerations in Augusta. Richmond would not permit losing that valuable officer,

A clumsy attempt has been made to highlight the collar insignia on this faded image of General Girardey, but the uniform is genuine, apparently. The uniform shows two rows of buttons, which he would not have worn as a captain, and since he was jumped directly from captain to brigadier, this image was therefore probably taken during the two weeks between his promotion and his death in 1864. (Museum of the Confederacy, Richmond, Va.)

but it granted him twenty days leave on August 18. That absence lasted eight months. Starting August 24, Girardey used the time well by raising five companies of unconscriptable youths to help guard the crucial Augusta Arsenal, where his brother, Major Isadore P. Girardey, served as military storekeeper. Those companies and one other became the 27th Georgia Infantry Battalion on April 25, 1864. The officers, however, did not elect Victor Girardey their major. Three days later, on arsenal commander George W. Rains' behalf, Isadore approached Victor about becoming lieutenant-colonel of an expanded battalion. The 27th's officers themselves, including the major, petitioned Victor on May 19 to accept that higher rank.

Although he still welcomed promotion, it was then too late, for the War Department recalled him to Virginia on April 5. Robert E. Lee returned him to Wright's Brigade on April 27. Lamentably, ill feelings over his Georgia "leave" led both Wright and Girardey to protest the assignment. Their superiors, accordingly, reassigned him. Although ordered to Richmond on May 21, the captain actually served at division headquarters under Anderson and later William Mahone. Following the capture of Major Thomas S. Mills on June 22, Girardey became acting assistant adjutant general of Mahone's Division. From the Wilderness to Petersburg, he won new renown.

In seeking a staff lieutenant-colonelcy for Girardey, Mahone on July 6 declared that the captain "by his efficiency and gallantry has well earned promotion. He combines in his superior qualities and capacity as a staff officer a knowledge & familiarity with military matters generally and an aptness for these which make up the useful and accomplished officer. In the Staff Dept., he is at home; upon the field he is competent to conduct a regiment or to handle a brigade. His services during the campaign have been invaluable to me and full of fruit to the country." Lee himself endorsed that "I consider Capt. Girardey one of our boldest & most energetic officers. He has been particularly efficient on the field."

Greater opportunity opened on July 20, when Mahone recommended Girardey to command the brigade of Wright, who was absent on prolonged sick leave. "During the Current Campaign," wrote Mahone, "no one under my observation has better earned such promotion or shown himself more competent for the Command of a Brigade." Corps Commander A. P. Hill concurred: "Capt. Girardey is

eminently qualified for the command of this Brigade because of his own fitness for the position, his association with the brigade, and his acceptability to it…. The Brigade needs it, and the Country needs it."

Adjutant General Samuel Cooper, while recognizing Girardey's "zeal, energy, gallantry, and efficiency," said the staff promotion was illegal. Events overtook such objections. Girardey helped lead Mahone's counterattacks, which recaptured the Crater on July 30. "Capt. Girardey," remembered Mahone in 1892, "like the brilliant officer he was—never failing to do precisely the right thing at the right time—rushed with uplifted sword to the front of the brigade." Their service that day earned both officers promotion. Girardey was made brigadier general on August 3, ranking from July 30, the only Confederate general elevated from captain in one step. He accepted on August 11, but immediately assumed command of Wright's Brigade (containing the 3d, 22d, 48th, and 64th regiments and 2d and 10th battalions of Georgia Infantry) on August 3.

His tenure terminated tragically. In his next battle, Second Deep Bottom, the skirmishers' opening fire at Fussell's Hill on August 16 killed him with a bullet in the forehead. His brigade then fled, leaving his corpse in Northern hands. Returned during the truce on August 17, his body was buried in Augusta.

"Girardey was one of the bravest men in Lee's army," recalled an Alabama captain of Mahone's Division. "Insensible of fear, regardless of life, he was always found where danger was greatest." His brilliant staff service certainly suggests his suitability for generalcy—but, as happened so often in Confederate command, death destroyed a promising career.

Richard J. Sommers

Bergeron, Arthur W., *Guide to Louisiana Confederate Military Units, 1861–1865* (Baton Rouge, 1989).

Bernard, George S., *War Talks of Confederate Veterans* (Petersburg, 1892).

Derry, Joseph T., *Georgia*, Vol. VII in Evans, *Confederate Military History*.

Dimitry, John, *Louisiana*, Vol. X in Evans, *Confederate Military History*.

An unpublished portrait of Gist as brigadier general of the South Carolina militia, probably in early 1861 before he entered formal Confederate service. (Museum of the Confederacy, Richmond, Va.)

⋆ *States Rights Gist* ⋆

Gist was born on September 3, 1831, in Union District, South Carolina, the son of a wealthy planter and future governor of the Palmetto State. After attending neighboring schools, he went to a preparatory school in Winnsboro, South Carolina, then graduated from South Carolina College in 1852 and studied at the Harvard University Law School, from which he graduated in 1854. He practiced law in Union District and entered the state militia. In 1859, Gist received an appointment as brigadier general in the militia, then became the state's adjutant and inspector general with the rank of major general following secession.

He worked actively to prepare for the militia's occupation of Charleston Harbor and for the capture of Fort Sumter. Gist accompanied Brigadier General Barnard E. Bee to northern Virginia as a volunteer aide-de-camp with the rank of colonel. After all of the field officers of the 4th Alabama Infantry Regiment were disabled at First Manassas, General Pierre G. T. Beauregard placed Gist in command of the regiment, calling him "an able and brave commander" whom he "greatly esteemed." Gist quickly gained the confidence of the men and led the unit during the remainder of the battle.

He returned to South Carolina after the fight to organize more units for war service, and on March 20, 1862, was commissioned brigadier general in the Confederate service, to rank from that date, and soon received orders to report to Major General John C. Pemberton, commander of the Department of South Carolina and Georgia. Pemberton assigned Gist to his 2d Military District under Brigadier General Roswell S. Ripley. Ripley placed him in command on James Island. Superseded shortly afterwards by Brigadier General William D. Smith, Gist commanded a portion of the troops on the island. Gist again assumed direction of the forces on the island during Smith's illness but was replaced in mid-October by Ripley. On October 22, Gist received orders to take two thousand men to Pocotaligo to assist in the defense of that area, then threatened by enemy troops. He led five thousand men northward to Wilmington, North Carolina, in mid-December to help defend against an expedition of Union troops moving from New Berne toward Goldsborough.

His force returned to Charleston later that month, but Gist was again ordered to Wilmington on temporary duty in early January 1863. By February, Gist was back in South Carolina, where Ripley assigned him to command of James Island and St. Andrew's Parish. He held this position on April 7 when Union ironclads attacked Fort Sumter and Charleston Harbor. Gist stationed himself in Fort Johnson, but that work was too far away to aid in the defense of Sumter. The garrison only fired two rounds from one of its mortars. On May 3, Gist was relieved from duty in the department and given a brigade under orders to reinforce General Joseph E. Johnston at Jackson, Mississippi. He reached Brandon, east of Jackson, on May 14 and Johnston placed him in charge of collecting troops in that area. Thus, he did not lead the portions of his brigade engaged in the Battle of Jackson that day. Gist joined Johnston's forces at Canton several days later,

An excellent portrait of the most unusually named general in the Confederacy, States Rights Gist. Made probably in late 1862 or 1863, it shows him as a brigadier. (South Caroliniana Library, University of South Carolina, Columbia, S.C.)

General William H. T. Walker. He participated in the remaining marches and engagements of Johnston's army in central Mississippi during the Union siege of Vicksburg.

Gist's men went with Walker's division when it reinforced the Army of Tennessee in northern Georgia in September, but the brigade was on detached service at Rome and did not participate in the first day of fighting in the Battle of Chickamauga on September 19. Gist reached the field early on September 20 and moved to the army's right flank. There Walker, temporarily commanding the Reserve Corps, gave Gist direction of his division of three brigades. The division saw heavy fighting against Union Major General George H. Thomas' corps on Horseshoe Ridge, then Gist resumed command of his brigade after the army reached Chattanooga. Walker went on leave on November 12, and Gist took command of the division, which was stationed at the base of Lookout Mountain. Gist's men assisted Major General Patrick R. Cleburne's Division as the army's rear guard in the retreat after the disastrous Battle of Missionary Ridge on November 25 and helped repulse all pursuit by the enemy.

Gist led his brigade during the long Atlanta Campaign the following spring. Just before the army reached Atlanta, Gist's brigade was increased by three regiments and a battalion from a brigade that had been broken up. In the Battle of Atlanta on July 22, Gist received a wound that kept him out of action for more than a month. Walker's death in this battle led to his division being broken up, and Gist's brigade received assignment to Major General Benjamin F. Cheatham's Division. Gist had returned to duty by late September and accompanied the army in its campaign against Major General William T. Sherman's supply lines in northern Georgia. Gist led his brigade northward into Tennessee and took it into the Battle of Franklin on November 30, 1864. In the first charge against the Union positions that day, Gist's horse was killed, and he continued on foot. Shortly, an enemy bullet struck him in the chest. He fell not far from Brigadier General Otho F. Strahl. Gist was taken to a field hospital, where he died that night. The next day, he was buried at the residence of William White. In later years, Gist's remains were moved to the churchyard of Trinity Episcopal Church in Columbia, South Carolina.

Arthur W. Bergeron, Jr.

Capers, Ellison, *South Carolina*, Vol. VI in Evans, *Confederate Military History*.

Losson, Christopher, *Tennessee's Forgotten Warriors: Frank Cheatham and His Confederate Division* (Knoxville, 1989).

McDonough, James Lee, and Thomas L. Connelly, *Five Tragic Hours: The Battle of Franklin* (Knoxville, 1983).

Probably the last photo made of Gist prior to his November 30, 1864, death in battle at Franklin, Tenn. (U.S. Army Military History Institute, Carlisle, Pa.)

✶ *Adley Hogan Gladden* ✶

Almost certainly, Adley Gladden never had a photo taken in uniform, and certainly not as a general, since he only lived a few months after his commission. (Alabama Department of Archives and History, Montgomery, Al.)

Born in Fairfield District, South Carolina, on October 28, 1810, Adley Hogan Gladden moved to Columbia in 1830 and became a cotton broker. After Gladden's service in the Seminole War, President John Tyler appointed him postmaster of Columbia. In the Mexican War Gladden also served with distinction, being chosen major of the famed Palmetto Regiment. He rose to colonel and command of the unit when the two ranking field officers were killed at Churubusco, and later Gladden himself was badly wounded during the attack on Belen Gate in Mexico City.

Following the Mexican War, Gladden moved to New Orleans. After South Carolina seceded in December 1860, he accepted an appointment as lieutenant colonel of the 1st South Carolina Regiment but soon resigned to become a delegate to Louisiana's secession convention. Once his adopted state seceded, Gladden was appointed colonel of the 1st Louisiana Infantry.

Assigned to Pensacola, Florida, under Braxton Bragg, Gladden was promoted to brigadier general on September 30, 1861, to rank immediately. He apparently was in command of Richard H. Anderson's brigade for a while, for on October 12, 1861, Gladden was ordered to relinquish command of Anderson's brigade and take over Daniel Ruggles' brigade. Anderson was second in command to Bragg, and when an undisclosed "disability" interfered with his duties, Gladden was given temporary command of the Pensacola post on October 22.

On November 22 Union forces at Fort Pickens began bombarding the Confederate positions at Pensacola. Gladden's brigade manned a sand battery at Fort McRee and was hotly engaged. For two days his men were pounded so heavily that fish in the bay were killed by the concussion of the battle. Although the fort suffered heavy damage, Gladden's losses were slight and Bragg praised him for his defense.

Gladden's handling of his brigade impressed Bragg. When Bragg was offered command of Confederate forces in north Mississippi, he considered Gladden an indispensable officer. On January 6, 1862, Bragg wired the secretary of war to discuss the new position. He expressed concern over the lack of discipline among the Confederate troops in Mississippi and asked to take a contingent of three regiments from Pensacola with him. This unit would be used as a role model of discipline around which other troops could be organized. Bragg declared, "I should desire Brigadier-General Gladden to command them."

This plan was not followed up, but Bragg did find another use for Gladden. Disliking the performance of General Leroy P. Walker, who commanded at Mobile, Alabama, Bragg transferred him to Montgomery on February 1 and gave his brigade to Gladden. Of Gladden, Bragg wrote, "From his energy, zeal, great efficiency as a disciplinarian and infantry instincts…I hope for the happiest results." Gladden was in Mobile for only a short time when Bragg reported conditions there had changed much for the better. In early March Gladden's duties were expanded when he was also placed over the garrison at Pensacola. He apparently never exercised this command, however, for by March 9 he was near Purdy, Tennessee, commanding two brigades under Leonidas Polk.

Throughout March Gladden kept an eye on Union movements in his area. By April he was leading a brigade of Alabama infantry in J. M. Withers' Division of Bragg's Corps. In the attack at Shiloh on April 6, 1862, his brigade was posted on the right of William Hardee's Corps. Charging in the first line of battle, Gladden was soon hit by a shell fragment that mangled his arm. His arm was quickly amputated on the field, and Gladden was taken to P. G. T. Beauregard's headquarters near Corinth, Mississippi. There he died on April 12. In his battle report, Bragg noted that Gladden was struck down "while gallantly leading his command in a successful charge. No better soldier ever lived." Gladden is buried in the Magnolia Cemetery at Mobile.

Terry L. Jones

Dimitry, John, *Louisiana*, Vol. X in Evans, *Confederate Military History*.

✶ *Archibald Campbell Godwin* ✶

Research has failed to yield either Godwin's exact date of birth, or the place, though it is assumed to have been in Nansemond County, Virginia, sometime in 1831. He may have been orphaned at an early age, or otherwise put out by his parents to grow up with a grandmother in Portsmouth. Thus was set early a pattern of rootlessness. In 1849 or 1850 he went West while still in his teens to California's gold fields, and achieved success rapidly. First he made a comfortable stake from his "diggings," and then translated that into enhanced fortune at livestock ranching. During the same time he rose to prominence in state politics and in 1860 missed capturing the Democratic gubernatorial nomination by a single vote.

Like several other Californians sympathetic to the South, Godwin made the long trek eastward when Virginia seceded, and immediately gave his allegiance to the new Confederacy. President Jefferson Davis commissioned him a captain and assigned him as assistant provost marshal of Libby Prison in Richmond. Later in 1861, however, Godwin was reassigned to organize and command the Salisbury, North Carolina, prison camp, and he remained there until January 1862, when the War Department ordered him back to Richmond. Promoted to major that spring, he appears nevertheless not to have returned. In July 1862, now with the rank of colonel, he was still in command of the prison as Salisbury, where incarcerated Federals reported him as being a severe jailor.

In fall 1862 he finally escaped his prison duty. Authorized to raise a regiment locally, he had recruited

the 57th North Carolina Infantry that July, and was now ordered to bring it Virginia to join the Army of Northern Virginia.

Godwin and his regiment were initially assigned to Joseph R. Davis' brigade, then forming in Richmond, and it was not until late November that the unit was actually sent forward to Lee. By this time, however, Godwin had been reassigned to Evander Law's Brigade of Hood's Division. With that unit, Godwin saw his first action, at Fredericksburg, where Law paid tribute to his "great skill and coolness" in handling his men in their initial battle, and Hood singled out Godwin for praise in his report. The fury of Godwin's fighting told in the casualty figures, for he attacked a considerably superior number of Yankees in fighting at the railroad cut near Deep Run on the Confederate right center. When it was finished, he had regained the lost ground, and his regiment suffered more in killed and wounded than all the rest of Hood's Division combined.

Godwin and his regiment were in the works at Fredericksburg in May 1863 during the Battle of Chancellorsville, then marched into Pennsylvania to Gettysburg, now with Robert Hoke in command of his brigade. Hoke having been wounded in the May Fighting at Fredericksburg, Colonel Isaac Avery commanded the brigade at Gettysburg, and led it in the first day's fighting with Ewell's Corps, July 1. Godwin

Unfortunately no uniformed photo of the gallant General Godwin has surfaced. This old portrait is prewar. (*Confederate Veteran*, XXVIII, April 1920)

and his regiment were heavily engaged throughout that afternoon and evening, participating in the fighting in the vicinity of the railroad cut and in driving the Federals back into and through the town itself. That evening Godwin took command of the brigade; Avery had been mortally wounded. He and his brigade took position in the streets of Gettysburg and saw little action during the remaining two days of the battle.

That fall Godwin relinquished command of the brigade when Hoke returned to duty, though not before the November 7 engagement at Rappahannock Station, where Godwin won the admiration of the entire army. In a confused affair, his command was cut off and surrounded, with his back to the river. Facing overwhelming numbers, he still led his men time after time in desperate attempts to cut their way out. As one who escaped later described the scene, Godwin "did not for a moment dream of surrendering." Even when his command was reduced to fewer than one hundred, and his own men were intermixed with the enemy who had surrounded them, he fought on. Someone called out that Godwin had ordered his remaining men to surrender. Enraged, the colonel called out for the man who said that, threatening to blow his brains out, "declaring his purpose to fight to the last moment." Within minutes the Federals finally overwhelmed him and took him and his men prisoners. His division commander, Jubal Early, made a special plea to Lee to work for Godwin's exchange.

Godwin spent nearly a year in a Federal prison, finally being exchanged in the summer of 1864. Almost immediately the president appointed him a brigadier general on August 9, to rank from August 5, and gave him permanent command of his old brigade, now a part of Ramseur's Division in Early's army in the Shenandoah. He now commanded the 6th, 21st, 54th, and 57th North Carolina but was not destined to command them for long.

With barely more than eight hundred men, he went into the Battle of Winchester on September 19, and during the fighting that day an exploding Federal shell struck and killed him instantly. When the Confederates were driven out of the town that afternoon, Godwin's body was left behind, and the Yankees probably later saw to its burial in the Stonewall Cemetery, where he still lies.

Godwin was, by any definition, an instinctive fighter, one who got the best for himself and his men. Little by way of personal recollection has been left of him, but his record in action speaks of one who could rightly stand at the front rank of the regimental and brigade commanders of the Lost Cause.

William C. Davis

Clark, Walter, *Histories of the Several Regiments...from North Carolina...*(Raleigh, 1901).

Hill, D. H., Jr., *North Carolina*, Vol. IV in Evans, *Confederate Military History*.

✶ James Monroe Goggin ✶

One of the more dilettantish men to wear stars on his gray, Goggin was born October 23, 1820, in Bedford County, Virginia, and thereafter rarely stayed with anything for long. In 1838 he gained an appointment to the U.S. Military Academy, but dropped out before completing the course. Instead he went west to the new Republic of Texas, where commissions and advancement could come more quickly than in the Old Army. He became a lieutenant in the Texas Army and bought the beginnings of a ranch in Waller County. But a few years later the lure of California took him to the far west in 1848, and he remained there after the boom days following the gold strike. However, instead of panning for gold, he made his fortune by initiating and managing overland stage mail routes.

Even the lures of Eldorado could not hold him for long; in the 1850s he was to be found in the cotton brokerage business at the busy port of Memphis. The outbreak of war afforded Goggin merely another opportunity to move again, and he returned to his native Virginia following her secession to obtain a commission as major in the 32d Virginia Infantry.

By fall 1861 he was serving on the Peninsula, exercising a small command at Bethel Church, including companies of his own regiment and a squadron of dragoons. The old restlessness must have gotten the better of him, however, for by the spring of 1862 Goggin had left the field and taken a staff appointment as adjutant for General Lafayette McLaws. He was with McLaws during the siege of Yorktown, and won special praise for his aid in moving troops at Williamsburg. Indeed, throughout the Seven Days' Campaign that followed, McLaws repeatedly mentioned Goggin in his reports.

Goggin continued to serve McLaws and he earned praise during the Antietam Campaign when his general referred to his "great daring and cool, sound judgment." Goggin actually oversaw the placement of some of McLaws' units during the fight at Antietam on September 17. McLaws, who was never sparing with praise for his staff, also complimented Goggin for his efforts the next year at Fredericksburg, noting that his services were "important and distinguished, as they have always been." At Chancellorsville General Cadmus Wilcox paid tribute to Goggin's aid and his "gallant and valuable services" during the Salem Church fighting.

Not surprisingly, when McLaws' division went west with Longstreet, Goggin went along, by now apparently the general's special confidant. He was with McLaws constantly during the Knoxville Campaign in fall 1863, aiding in moving the troops and showing considerable ability—in McLaws' opinion—in the administration of the noncombat functions of command. "I know of no officer more deserving of promotion to the rank of brigadier than himself," McLaws said in his campaign report, "or who possessed higher qualities to illustrate the position. His experience in military affairs, his calm, cool courage, his strict integrity and impartiality, and straightforward manner would soon give him the confidence of any community or any body of men, and his services entitle him to high preferment." Goggin appeared as a witness at McLaws' court-martial the following winter, and when the general was removed from his command and later reassigned to Savannah,

In spite of distinguished war-long service, General Goggin has not left behind a uniformed photograph that has come to light. This one probably dates from the 1850s. (Warner, *Generals in Gray*)

he tried to have Goggin assigned with him. The War Department, however, chose to have Goggin remain with McLaws' successor, Joseph B. Kershaw, and the Virginian served on his staff through most of 1864.

When General James Connor was badly wounded on October 13, Kershaw assigned Goggin temporarily to command of Connor's brigade, which he subsequently led through the remainder of the Valley Campaign. Goggin commanded it at the Battle of Cedar Creek on October 19. He appears to have managed the command well early in the day, but toward the close of the battle, as the Federals were making their counterattack, his brigade was temporarily disorganized by having to cross a very high fence. Before Goggin could reform them, the first of a stream of fugitives from Sheridan's attack came rushing into them, throwing Goggin's men into confusion, and shortly impelling them to join in the precipitate retreat.

It would appear that the praise of McLaws and others, combined with his own performance, finally gained Goggin that year the brigadier's appointment that he seemed to deserve. Sources are so sketchy that little can be said with certainty, but it appears that in early or mid-December he was appointed to rank from December 4. However, either Goggin declined the commission or the president decided to withdraw it, for at the end of 1864 he is on the records as a major, still as adjutant to Kershaw, and thus he remained until the end of the war, when he and the rest of his division were overwhelmed at Sayler's Creek on April 6, 1865.

Following his parole, Goggin once more left Virginia and returned to his land in Waller County, Texas, and then moved to the capital at Austin, where he died on October 10, 1889, and where he now lies buried in the Oakwood Cemetery.

There are few generals of the Confederacy about whom less is known with certainty. His may have been the shortest service as a general of any of them, other than those killed immediately after their appointments. Nor can much be said of his ability or potential as a brigadier, for his time in command was so brief and in only one—unsuccessful—battle. Certainly he shone in the administration of a division's affairs and earned the confidence of more than one estimable commander. This, in the end, probably speaks best for Goggin, what he was, and what perhaps he might have been, given the opportunity.

William C. Davis